Collins

THE FAMILY
DOG

THE FAMILY DOG

AN OWNER'S GUIDE TO ALL ASPECTS OF CARING FOR YOUR DOG

CONSULTANT EDITOR:

DAVID TAYLOR BVMS, FRCVS, FZS

First published in 2000 by
HarperCollins*Publishers*
77–85 Fulham Palace Road
Hammersmith
London W6 8JB

Collins is a registered trademark of HarperCollins Publishers Limited

The HarperCollins website address is www.fireandwater.com

06 05 04 03 02 01 00
9 8 7 6 5 4 3 2 1

Text, design and illustrations © HarperCollins*Publishers* Ltd, 2000
Photographs © HarperCollins*Publishers*, ARK photography,
Marc Henrie, TRU Photo Agency and Rolando Ugolini (pages 19, 20tr, 23, 28b,
30t, 31b, 36bl, 38, 39, 40, 43, 47t, 49b, 55, 63, 65b, 67t, 82, 94, 95, 134, 137, 140,
166tl, 168, 188bl only)

David Taylor hereby asserts his moral rights to be identified as the author of
his Contribution. Robert Killick hereby asserts his moral rights to be identified
as the author of his Contribution. Nick Henderson hereby asserts his moral
rights to be identified as the author of his Contribution.

A catalogue record of this book is available from the British Library

ISBN 0 00 413402 8

This book was created by
SP Creative Design
EDITOR: **Heather Thomas**
ART DIRECTOR and PRODUCTION: **Rolando Ugolini**
ARTWORK ILLUSTRATIONS: **Rolando Ugolini**

PHOTOGRAPHY
Photography key: t - top, b - bottom, l - left, r - right, c - centre
ARK photography: 186br
Charlie Colmer: 1, 3, 5, 12, 16, 18, 24t, 29, 30b, 31t, 32b, 35tl, 35b, 44b, 46b,
47b, 48t, 49t, 50, 54b, 56tr, 58t, 60, 61, 68b, 70, 71, 74, 75, 76, 77bl, 77t, 78, 79,
86l, 88t, 89, 90tr, 90br, 92tl, 92bl, 92bc, 93tl, 97, 98, 100, 101, 114, 117, 122, 124,
127, 138t, 138bl, 139br, 144, 146, 147t, 148, 152, 160, 161, 163b, 164, 165,
166tr, 166b, 167, 170t, 170bl, 171, 172tr, 172b, 174, 176, 177, 178, 180, 181,
182tl, 183, 184, 187bl.
David Dalton: 14, 15, 22, 26, 27, 28t, 32t, 32r, 33, 34l, 36t, 42, 44t, 45, 52, 56l,
56b, 57b, 62, 64, 67b, 68tr, 72, 73, 77br, 77r, 84b, 85t, 86t, 87, 88b, 90l, 92tr,
92br, 93b, 96, 136, 138b, 139tl, 142bl, 149, 151r, 156, 157t, 157br, 158, 159t,
159br, 162t, 162bl, 169tr, 169b, 175, 185, 186tl, 187tc, 187br, 188tr.
Bruce Tanner: 20tl, 20b, 24b, 35tr, 37br, 46t, 48b, 51tl, 51b, 54t, 58b, 59, 157bl,
159bl, 162br, 188tl, 188bc, 189tl, 189bc.
Marc Henrie: 141, 145, 147b, 150, 151t, 163t, 173, 179.
Rolando Ugolini: 19, 20tr, 21, 23, 28b, 30t, 31b, 34bl, 34br, 36bl, 38, 39, 40, 43,
47t, 49b, 51tr, 55, 63, 65b, 65t, 66, 67t, 68tl, 69, 71tr, 82, 90bl, 93tr, 94, 95, 104,
106, 107, 112, 121, 123, 126, 128, 129, 130, 134, 137, 140, 166tl, 168, 170br,
186tr, 187tr, 188bl 189tc.
TRU Photo Agency: 7, 8, 10, 13, 25, 40, 53, 57t, 80, 83, 85br, 91, 99, 155, 169tl,
172tl, 182b, 182tr, 186bl, 186bc, 187bc, 187tl, 188tc, 189tr, 189bl, 189br.

Colour reproduction by Colourscan, Singapore
Printed and bound by Printing Express Ltd, Hong Kong

Contents

Part One

The right dog for you

CHAPTER ONE – *Robert Killick*
Choosing a dog *12*

CHAPTER TWO – *Robert Killick*
The perfect puppy *24*

Part Two

Good dog behaviour

CHAPTER THREE – *Nick Henderson*
Communicating with your dog *42*

CHAPTER FOUR – *Nick Henderson*
Curing common problems *52*

CHAPTER FIVE – *Nick Henderson*
Training is fun *62*

Part Three

Caring for your dog

CHAPTER SIX – *Robert Killick*
Daily care 82

CHAPTER SEVEN – *David Taylor*
Healthcare 98

Part Four

Advanced dog care

CHAPTER EIGHT – *Robert Killick*
Showing your dog 136

CHAPTER NINE – *Robert Killick*
Breeding 144

Part Five

The most popular dog breeds

CHAPTER TEN – *Robert Killick*
Dog breed guide 154

ACKNOWLEDGEMENTS 190
USEFUL ADDRESSES 190
INDEX 191

Consultant editor

David Taylor BVMS, FRCVS, FZS

David Taylor is a well-known veterinary surgeon and broadcaster and the author of over thirty books, including six volumes of autobiography, some of which formed the basis for three series of the BBC television drama *One by One*.

He has also written the *Small Pets Handbook* and *Collins Family Pet Guides: Rabbit*. The founder of the International Zoo Veterinary Group, he has exotic patients across the world, ranging from crocodiles to killer whales and giant pandas. He lives in Richmond, Surrey, with his wife, four cats and a hamster called 'Fudge'.

Contributors

Robert Killick

Robert Killick is a prominent breeder and exhibitor of Welsh Terriers, winning at the major Championship shows. He has a Judge's Diploma (Credit) and judges all breeds at Open Show level and his own breed at Championship level.

After a lifetime in the theatre as a stage manager, director and actor, he turned to freelance journalism. In 1990, he became a weekly columnist for the UK canine newspaper *Our Dogs*. He also writes monthly columns in *Dogworld USA*, the world's largest circulating dog magazine, and the Swedish magazine *Hundesport*, and is a feature writer for *Dogs Today* in the UK.

In 1994, his poems were published by the American National Library of Poetry for which he received the award of 'Poet of Merit' from the International Society of Poets, and he was nominated for 'Poet of the Year' in 1995.

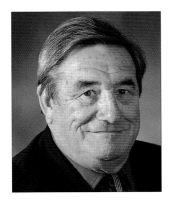

Nick Henderson
BSc (Edinburgh), MRCVS

Nick Henderson qualified as a veterinary surgeon with a degree in veterinary science from Edinburgh University. Since then he has played an active role in the veterinary profession, being a founder member of the British Small Animal Veterinary Association, lifetime President of the Veterinary Marketing Association and author of a number of books, among them several paperbacks on petcare (Corgi), *Cats – an Intelligent Owner's Guide* (Faber and Faber), *Cats and Cat Care* (David & Charles), *Rabies – The Facts you Need to Know* (Barrie and Jenkins), *The Book of Dogs* (Albany Books) and *The Book of Cats* (Albany Books).

Nick Henderson is an experienced broadcaster and has appeared on TV and radio both in the UK and the USA talking about petcare. He is now a professional consultant in both the human and animal healthcare sector.

Foreword

We enter the new millennium with the domestic dog as popular and remarkably useful an animal as ever. Whether as a decorative, loyal, amusing companion, a valued co-worker, be it sniffing for contraband drugs or delectable truffles, guarding sheep or airfields, aiding the blind or deaf, or simply helping to make folk feel better (for some time, scientists have recognised the therapeutic effects of canine pets in speeding the convalescence of human patients and actually lowering the blood pressure of people who stroke them), dogs are undoubtedly most amazing animals.

It is a privilege as well as a pleasure to own one and that privilege demands that we take the trouble to understand their workings and their needs so that they, and we, can enjoy their lives in health and happiness. Innumerable books are at hand for the dog owner, novice or professional breeder, but this is the first, in my view, that provides clear up-to-the-minute information presented in a highly accessible style for the guidance and assistance of everyone who loves and admires our best friend.

David Taylor BVMS, FRCVS, FZS

The right dog for you

Buying a dog is a huge responsibility and one of the most important decisions that any family has to make. A dog is for life and he will become your responsibility for at least the next ten years and therefore you should not rush into getting one without considering how he will fit into your lifestyle and what you can give him in return. Owning a dog is extremely rewarding but your furry friend will need regular exercise, feeding, grooming and companionship, and you must be prepared to set aside some time every day to care for him and play with him.

Chapter One

CHOOSING A DOG

If you want a puppy, impulse buying is your worst enemy: every puppy is small, pretty and vulnerable, and it is so easy to fall for a little bundle of mischief without any consideration for the future – the puppy's future or your own. Buying a puppy or an adult

Above: *Owning a dog is very rewarding and you will receive many years of happy companionship and affection from your canine friends.*

dog is one of the most important purchases of a lifetime. You will be assuming control of another creature's life and he will be dependent on you for upwards of twelve years, so you are, in effect, buying a new member of the family.

Because of the importance of the decision, it is a good idea to consult with all the members of your family from the youngest to

the eldest for each one will bear some responsibility in different areas of the dog's life. Children should be closely involved as the lessons they can learn from caring for a dog will stand them in good stead for the rest of their lives. Owning a dog now is likely to help them to be more caring to both animals and humans later on in their adult life.

Which breed?

There is a breed of dog which is suitable for every family. The UK Kennel Club registers 173 breeds of dog and obviously it will take a little research in order to discover which one is ideal for you but all the effort is well worthwhile. Probably the first consideration is where you live and the size and style of the accommodation. All dogs love freedom and are suitable for country living with the exception of only some very small heavy-coated breeds, but not all dogs are suitable for city or town life. It would not be right to condemn a large dog such as a St Bernard or any of the larger hound breeds to life in a small flat in a tower

block, but dogs, being what they are, would adapt to the life. However, the fact remains that it would not be fair and would almost certainly lead to problems, particularly concerning behaviour and temperament.

If you live in an estate where the houses are quite close together, the neighbours must be respected. They have the legal right to peace and quiet and thus a breed that is inclined to yap or bark for long periods is not suitable; neither would you want a breed that has the reputation of being aggressive to other dogs and too defensive of you and your family. Remember that unfortunately not everyone likes dogs, and therefore you would not want to willingly introduce an element into your life which will bring aggravation.

Next, consider your own attitudes; if you are super tidy, a dog with a thick double coat which tends to moult heavily would be a source of irritation. He would require daily grooming but would you have the time to do this? There are other considerations, such as is the house left empty for long periods? Is there a member of the family willing and able to walk the dog at least twice a day? Who will be responsible for feeding him and making sure that fresh water is always available?

FINDING A DOG

It has never been easier to find out about dogs, and the latest most convenient and complete way to do this is by using the Internet. It is simplicity itself to click on to the Kennel Club's own website or one of the others that relate to pets and link into the breed history, breed clubs and the breeders themselves. It is possible to communicate with breeders and owners around the world and to download photographs and articles. The Kennel Club will also provide you with the telephone numbers of any breeders close to where you live. However, if you are looking for one of the rarer dog breeds, you will have to be prepared to travel further afield.

There are literally thousands of books on breeds of dogs and there are many specialist book shops dealing in the subject. The public libraries are also an excellent source of information, and if they haven't got a particular book they will order it specially for you.

There are weekly newspapers devoted to pedigree dogs, their care, exhibition and breeding as well as some monthly magazines publishing information on every aspect of owning pet dogs.

One UK magazine even has a section on finding dogs with a list of consultants for every breed. A phone call can put you in touch with a friendly expert who is not there to sell you a dog but to give you unbiased information so you can make an informed decision.

Pedigree or mongrel?

At about this juncture you will have to decide whether you want to own a pedigree dog or a mongrel. Some authorities claim that pedigree dogs are less healthy than mongrels or cross breeds. Although this may be so with a few breeds, there is no scientific evidence that will prove the case generally. There are two reasons why a pedigree dog is a pedigree:

◆ The first is that his ancestry is known and recorded.
◆ Secondly, he breeds true; that is to say that if you mate a dog and a bitch of one breed the resultant puppies will be replicas of their parents (colour excepted).

One of the main advantages of a pedigree dog is that within close parameters you will know the size to which he will grow. You will also know the sort of temperament he is likely to develop. However, buying a mongrel is a bit like a lottery – unless you have some specialized knowledge, the little creature at eight weeks might be a giant at eighteen months; he may have inherited some nasty genes from one of his parents which may not manifest themselves until he is two years old or even older.

The Kennel Club, the Internet, canine newspapers and magazines can all lead you to find the right pedigree dog or puppy for you. Many prospective owners go to dog shows to seek out breeders but with today's All Breed Championship Shows, which are held over three days, it is as well to find out in advance on which day your favourite breed is being exhibited. A telephone call to the Kennel Club or a study of the canine newspapers will reveal the most convenient day; the smaller Open Shows which take place over one day may not schedule your particular breed.

Left: *No matter what sort of dog you choose, be it a pedigree or a mongrel, it can enrich your life and become part of your family.*

Pet shops and puppy farms

There are traps into which the unwary can fall, and the selling of puppies and young dogs is now a multi-million pound business, and unfortunately there are a few unscrupulous breeders, dealers and retailers waiting for the gullible. Most people have seen on television and read in the national newspapers of 'puppy farms'. However, these are not farms in the true sense of the word but premises on which puppies are bred with no thought to their welfare, physically or mentally, and fed on cheap and inferior foods with no veterinary attention. Their breeders are not concerned where they go or what happens to them after they leave their premises. The puppies can either be sold direct to the public via misrepresented newspaper advertisements or they can go to dealers who will sell them by any method. Alternatively, they may be sold on through pet shops.

It must be emphasised that these puppies do not have a good future, and it is most unlikely that the vendors will offer a 'back-up' in case of trouble. The puppy may become ill and his papers may be false. Therefore it is always wise to buy direct from a breeder who should be recognised by the Kennel Club, or from a registered charity. Lastly, do not buy a puppy unless you see the mother!

Rescue dogs

Not everyone wants the problems associated with rearing a puppy and you may want a rescue or an adult dog. A network of breed rescue organisations exists to help you – a call to the Kennel Club will provide the relevant phone numbers. There are many reasons for dogs to be in rescue: broken marriages, deaths or simply an owner going overseas.

A large number of these dogs come out of a happy home, are well trained and can become a fully accepted older dog in any household. However, some have been ill treated and require tender loving care before they have confidence in their new home. Because of the difficulties, potential owners should be prepared for some searching questions before the dog is handed over. You may have to pay a small fee to cover expenses. It also unusual for the Kennel Club documents to be made available; this is to stop the possibility of further abuse to the dog.

Of pedigree dogs, greyhounds have the biggest problem. Many racing greyhounds are bred in Britain and Southern Ireland – far too many dogs for the market to absorb. As a result, numerous greyhounds are abandoned by their owners if they don't make the grade. Contrary to some opinions, they can be easily trained not to chase small furry animals and can make extremely gentle and loving companions. There are specialist rescue organisations for the breed which not only rehome ex-racers but actually go to the race tracks in Spain (where greyhounds are frequently ill treated) and buy them back. These dogs are then re-homed in Britain or in Europe.

NATIONAL CHARITIES

There are national charities that never put down any dog except if he is very old and infirm and, no matter what is done to help him, can never have any quality of life. Both Battersea Dogs' Home and the National Canine Defence League (NCDL) give dogs of all breeds, including abandoned mongrels, a chance by re-training them, treating their ailments and matching them very carefully with potential owners. Owners are at liberty to return any dog who fails to fit into the new home, and further efforts will be made to re-home the dog, no matter how long it takes.

■ **Above:** *Giving a rescue dog a good home is a rewarding experience for both the dog and owner.*

Choosing a rescue dog

The problem when looking for a rescue dog is the beguiling eyes of the dogs. Every one will touch the heart but you must be practical. You will have decided on the most suitable size and how much time you are prepared to spend on grooming the coat. It is in the interests of the rescue centre to match you with a suitable dog so listen carefully to their advice, speak to the person who normally walks the dog in which you are interested, and ask them questions.

The dog may be suspicious at the start but don't worry; this is natural. He should come to you after about five minutes. However, if he shows any aggression, then beware. If he lays on his back urinating slightly, he is being submissive, which is acceptable in puppies but not in adult dogs. There is always a gamble with a rescue dog because his history is usually unknown, and great patience from all the family will be needed.

1 Sit quietly without making direct eye contact with the dog but keeping an eye on him and his reactions to you.

2 Offer him a small treat or piece of food and watch his reaction. Does he snatch it or refuse it?

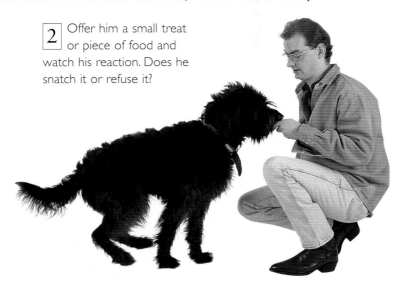

4 Put a lead on the dog and take him for a short walk. Note how he reacts to you. Then put him back in the kennel and invite him out again.

3 Ask the staff whether you can observe the dog's behaviour when he is placed with other dogs.

THE RIGHT BREED FOR YOU

Breed	Temperament	Exercise
Labrador Retriever	Affable, tolerant and easy-going with dogs and humans. Easily trained and learns quickly. Enjoys the company of children. A superb family and working dog.	An active dog. Needs lots of free running, walks, play and retrieving games.
Golden Retriever	Gentle, biddable and highly intelligent. A good working dog as well as an excellent family pet. Good with children and a great companion and gundog.	Needs frequent exercise and mental stimulation. Enjoys Flyball and Obedience.
Rottweiler	Intensely protective and highly intelligent, this is a good guarding breed. Needs good socialization and kind but firm training. Not suitable to be left with young children.	Needs lots of walking (at least, twice a day), free running and games for stimulation.
German Shepherd Dog	Highly intelligent and a wonderful guarding and working dog, the German Shepherd makes a good family pet if it is trained and well socialized. Needs kind but firm handling.	Needs and enjoys as much exercise as it can get. Excels at Obedience and Agility training.
Parson Jack Russell Terrier	Intelligent, alert and always busy, this dog loves to hunt. An easily trained fun dog who loves to live within its family pack and is good with children. Affectionate and a watchful guard dog.	Needs lots of exercise with walks, free running and playing stimulating, imaginative games.
Cavalier King Charles Spaniel	A gentle, docile and intelligent little dog. Confident and fun-loving with a friendly nature, it makes a good family pet and loves to play with children if they are not too rough.	Needs two short daily walks, free running and play – less exercise than bigger Spaniels.
Boxer	Exuberant, full of fun, loyal and affectionate. A good guard dog and a loving family dog. Good with children but can be over-boisterous with very young ones.	Enjoys exercise and needs lots of walks, free running and games for mental stimulation.
Yorkshire Terrier	Playful, inquisitive, a good companion and the perfect small pet, especially for the elderly. A spirited, game little dog who enjoys hunting and playing games.	At least two short walks a day plus playing games in the garden and running.
English Springer Spaniel	Gentle, loving and good with children. Craves affection and hates to be left alone. Highly intelligent and easy to train. A loving family pet as well as a good working dog.	Needs plenty of free running, daily walks and play. Excels at agility and flyball.
Cocker Spaniel	Gentle, intelligent, biddable and easily trained. A good companion and family dog, especially with children. A happy working dog, good at retrieving.	Needs a lot of exercise, especially free running, as well as daily walks.
Poodle	Highly sensitive, loving and intelligent, the Poodle can be easily trained and makes a delightful family pet. It is gentle with children and a good companion for all ages.	Has unbounded energy and loves exercise and playing games – can't get enough!
Dalmatian	Affectionate, anxious to please and loves human company. Devoted, loyal and very attached to children. A dog that is more suited to country than town life.	Boundless energy and needs a lot of exercise – as much as you can give.
Dobermann	Loyal, affectionate, intelligent and easily trained, its power must be controlled and it needs kind but firm treatment.	An hour a day walking plus free running and games.
West Highland White Terrier	Intelligent, inquisitive and mischievous with an independent spirit. A good family dog who loves to be involved in every activity. Relatively easy to train.	Naturally active and needs lots of exercise, especially free running and playing.

SELECTING THE RIGHT DOG

There is no magic formula for selecting the right dog from either a rescue centre or from a litter of puppies at the breeder's kennels. It is best that the entire family go together to make a choice, as everybody, including the children, should be there to express their opinion. Staff at rescue centres are deeply concerned that the right dog goes to the right family, and they will ask you about your house and garden, whether there will be anybody at home during the day to look after the dog and also whether you have any other pets. You will be shown dogs which have been carefully assessed and will be told candidly if, in the opinion of the kennel staff, there are likely to be any problems.

Before the dog is allowed to leave the kennels there will almost certainly be a home visit as the centre will wish to satisfy themselves that your home is suitable for the dog. For instance, they have to ensure that your garden is escape proof if you want a terrier-type dog and that there are no steep stairs if you wish to adopt a big, elderly dog.

One of the most difficult tasks facing any dog lover is to walk along a corridor which is lined with kennels, each containing one or more dogs; their pleading eyes will touch all hearts and in fact it is often better to let the dog make the choice. Families looking for a pet will be allowed to be in a room with the dog and this is the moment to find out if the dog likes the family. Re-homing staff often report how a dog may be indifferent to one family and yet go for another in a big way.

Dogs from rescue centres

There are disadvantages of getting a dog from one of the charities, the main one being that the dog is likely to have been a stray, either lost or abandoned by the previous owners, and nobody will have any idea of his previous life, how much training he has received, any illness he may have suffered or whether he has been abused or ill treated in any way. The staff will have gone to considerable trouble to find and correct any behaviour problems but in the privacy of a home the dog may lack confidence and be troubled by the

■ **Left:** *With kind treatment and lots of tender loving care, a dog will soon settle into his new home. Try to involve him in family activities.*

alien atmosphere. New owners will require a lot of patience until the dog understands his place and what is expected of him. It is, however, quite remarkable how quickly a rescue dog will attach himself to a new family if he is shown kindness.

The agency should supply you with the dog's veterinary record so that in the event of illness or accident your vet will know what treatment has been administered. There will also be a record of your pet's vaccinations which you will want to keep up to date. A dog's digestive system cannot cope with sudden changes of diet, and you should receive a small quantity of the dog's regular food. If you want to change his food, you should do it gradually over several days by increasing the amount of new food each day while reducing the old food.

■ **Left:** *You can usually find a dog breed that will be a good match for your personality and lifestyle. Jack Russells love to play tough and have boundless energy, whereas Border Terriers like lots of affection and are just as happy curling up next to you on the sofa as they are going out for a walk.*

Settling into a new home

When you collect your rescue dog or puppy, there is a possibility that he may be travel sick as he might never have travelled in a car before. Although this can often be controlled, it is always advisable to consult your vet on the subject. Do not be tempted to try out home remedies; you must be sure that any medicine used contains nothing that will harm the dog.

In his new home the dog must not be pressurized; he should be allowed to find his own level. Put a basket or bed in a draught-free corner with something soft and comfortable for him to lie on.

This bed must be inviolable and once he goes to it for a rest he must not be disturbed.

The children must not smother him with love to start with – a tickle under the chin, a pat on the head and a few soothing words will be sufficient. He will let you know when he wants more. Be patient, take your time and before you know it the dog will be your faithful companion.

Dogs like routine. Your dog will like to know that he is fed at the same time each day and taken out at the same time. He will have preferences for food but he should not be spoilt; otherwise you may train him only to eat chicken! Try to persuade the children not to feed him titbits at meal times as some dogs tend to fat.

■ **Above:** *A puppy will need smaller and more frequent meals than an adult dog, so feed him more often.*

The dog may have had some training or he may never have experienced it at all so it would be an excellent idea to take him to a local training class. It can be a fun evening for your children, especially if your dog is to be trained into the Kennel Club's Good Citizens Scheme which, when he passes simple tests, will win the children a certificate.

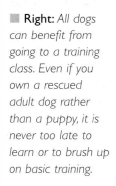

■ **Above:** *Let your children handle the new dog under your supervision. They will soon accept him.*

■ **Right:** *All dogs can benefit from going to a training class. Even if you own a rescued adult dog rather than a puppy, it is never too late to learn or to brush up on basic training.*

Pedigree puppies

You may opt to start from scratch and buy a pedigree puppy. If you have done your research you will have probably got down to a shortlist of two or three breeds you like. You should now try to find a suitable breeder. You can do this by contacting them at a dog show, but bear in mind that many of the minority breeds have only a few breeders in the country and you may have to wait or go on a waiting list for a puppy. The choice of the breeder is really important so if you don't like him or her do not buy a puppy from them. The ideal breeder has a policy of breeding sound dogs, both mentally and physically, will take advantage of all the modern veterinary technology as far as genetic tests are concerned, and will be interested in the puppy's future life. In fact, the purchase of a puppy can often be the start of a lifelong friendship.

You must be prepared for some searching questions about your lifestyle, and, in return, the good breeder will not be offended if you ask leading questions about their breeding history.

Genetic tests

From your research you will know which, if any, genetic anomalies your favourite breeds suffer. One of the most frequent in the larger dogs is hip dysplasia. The best breeders, however, have been working on this problem for many years and are succeeding in reducing the incidence in most breeds. You should have found out the average score for the

breed and the breeder will show you either the parents' scores or the mother's British Veterinary Association/Kennel Club score sheet. If the score is very much higher than the norm, you would be well advised not to buy one of the puppies, however cute. There are other genetic tests, particularly for eye conditions that affect some breeds. The Kennel Club will be happy to advise you about any genetic abnormalities which may be present in various breeds.

Choosing a puppy

Take your family to see the puppies, which should be over eight weeks old, but make sure the children are under control. There is a possibility that the puppies have never encountered children before and might be disturbed, as will the breeder.

Always ask to see the puppies' mother. This will enable you not only to see the fully-grown size of an adult dog but also, and more importantly, to make a quick judgement of her temperament.

Whichever sex you have

decided upon, ask the breeder to remove the others and then examine the puppies individually. Look for any sort of discharge from the eyes, the mouth, the anus or the vulva; if there is any present, don't take that puppy. Any runt of the litter should also be discounted. On no account, be persuaded to buy a puppy at a lower price because 'there is something minor wrong with it'. Therein lies trouble. If everything looks good, watch for the most extrovert puppy, the one that approaches you full of curiosity and happiness, and ignore any that creep about apprehensively.

Below: *Never buy a puppy without seeing the mother first. This will help you to assess a pup's eventual size, appearance and temperament.*

CHECKING A PUPPY

When choosing a puppy, ensure you examine him thoroughly before committing to a sale. Always look at his mouth, ears, nose and anus or vulva for any signs of discharge. Watch the puppy carefully for reassurance that he is contented and well cared for. Stroke him, play with him and ask to see the mother.

1 Gently examine the puppy's anal regions for any tell-tale signs of discharge.

2 Fold back the ear flap and check for any wax or discharge. The ears should not smell unpleasant.

3 Check the eyes for signs of discharge. They should be clear, bright and alert.

4 Examine the mouth and teeth. They should be white and smooth with a correct bite.

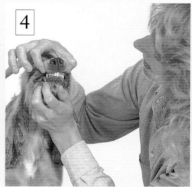

The cost

For most people the expense of having a dog has to be thought about carefully. The costs of buying and owning a dog can be considerable. The initial cost of buying a pedigree puppy depends very much on the breed but even if you acquire a cross-breed or a mongrel puppy you will still have to pay for his first vaccinations and, later on, for annual boosters. Veterinary treatment is not cheap and statistically some dog breeds need more veterinary attention than others. Fortunately, some insurance companies specialize in insuring against illness and accident in pets, thereby ensuring that you can afford to pay the veterinary fees. The cost of pet insurance varies and you will have to shop around to find the best deal for you, but paying the annual premium may save you a lot of money in the long run if your pet dog does ever have an accident or a serious illness.

A fact of life is that the bigger the dog the more he eats, and a large dog can cost a lot to feed properly although there are often cheaper alternatives to expensive dog foods. Another important element is professional grooming unless you are prepared to learn how to do it yourself. Breeds such as Old English Sheepdogs and Poodles can cost a lot of money per year to keep them in trim.

Taking your puppy home

The children will be very excited when you finally bring your new puppy home but you must try to keep them calm during the journey. The puppy is most unlikely to have been in a car before so have a soft blanket available, sit him on a lap and stroke him gently. He may be car sick so you should have a plentiful supply of tissues. Don't be cross with him if he is sick; he doesn't know that he is doing anything wrong and he should be comforted to make him think that travelling in a car is a pleasurable experience.

At first reading, all this may seem to be an awful lot of trouble but the owning of the right breed of dog can really create enormous interest and bring to your family a closer understanding of nature.

Don't forget...

Discuss a 'buy back' agreement with the breeder. Most reputable breeders will agree to have the puppy back if, for any reason, he is not suitable or your home conditions change so much that you cannot look after him.

Do not forget to get a signed and dated receipt when you hand

over the money. You should also enquire about insurance; some insurance companies working in conjunction with breeders will offer four to six weeks' free cover. This is useful as it encompasses the most vulnerable time in a puppy's life.

The breeder should give you five or six days' free supply of the food normally fed. Keeping to the same food will help to prevent stomach upsets and enable you to change the diet slowly, if required.

■ **Above:** *When you get home, make sure your puppy has a warm, comfortable bed and some toys to play with. You don't need a proper basket – a cardboard box will suffice.*

■ **Left:** *When you bring your puppy home, wrap him in a blanket or towel and sit him on someone's lap in the car to make him feel more secure.*

REGISTERING YOUR PUPPY

When you have made up your mind it is time for business. The registration of dogs and puppies with the Kennel Club is important as you will not be able to show a dog or breed without registration. The cost is normally absorbed by the breeder. At the time of buying you may be dismissive, thinking that you do not need registration, but do not be hasty. You don't know how your interests may change in the future, and many great careers in the world of dogs have started with the purchase of a first puppy. It may be that the papers have not yet been issued by the Kennel Club in which case you must ask the breeder to state in writing that the documents have been applied for and will be sent in the immediate future. When you receive the registration document there is a 'Transfer' form on the reverse side. Complete the form, return it to the Kennel Club with the appropriate fee and the dog will be transferred into your name.

Chapter Two

THE PERFECT PUPPY

Every puppy is born perfect; it takes human beings to introduce imperfections. Like children, the first part of a puppy's life is the formative part. With puppies the first year is of ultimate importance but what constitutes a perfect puppy varies considerably. Whilst some people are very tolerant of lively active puppies, others like them to be calm and laid back. However, whatever is wanted, a puppy must always be treated with affection and firm kindness – smacking and harsh treatment of any description are always counter-productive.

The perfect puppy should arrive in your house when he is between eight and nine weeks of age, although some unscrupulous breeders, puppy farmers and

dealers often try to sell them at six weeks. However, the extra two weeks are of great importance to the young puppy because it is during this time that he will learn from his mother about his own identity in dog terms and also how he should behave with his own species. He also acquires just a little more strength and maturity which will allow him to settle into a new environment with minimal stress for both dog and owner. Ideally, you should

Left: Although puppies appear to have boundless energy and love playing, they spend a lot of time resting, too.

Above: Choosing a puppy is never an easy task as they all look appealing but you must harden your heart and not be tempted to take more than one.

try to get a puppy from a breeder who allows the bitch to have her puppies in the house. In this way, they will be socialized from the moment they open their eyes and they will not be disturbed by the presence of people or any loud household noises, such as the vacuum cleaner, the television and washing machine. An added advantage is that the litter is almost certain to have been trained to defecate on newspaper which is of great help with later house-training.

BRINGING YOUR PUPPY HOME

Having made the decision to get a puppy, it can be great fun planning for his arrival. With the help of your children and other family members, you can decide on what sort of things your new puppy will need. The dog magazines are full of advertisements for suitable accessories. You may be lucky enough to have a really good pet shop close by where the added advantage is that a knowledgeable assistant will be able to point you in the right direction.

Your puppy will most certainly need just a few basic items of equipment, including a soft puppy collar, a lead, feeding and water bowls, some bedding and possibly a bed, and also some strong toys, including an artificial bone and

hide chews to chew on.

Specialist grooming tools can be bought at a specialist pet store or at one of the Championship Shows. There are always a large number of traders selling items solely for dogs. Crufts, which is held annually in March at the NEC in Birmingham, has the biggest selection in the world.

Collecting your puppy

At least two people should collect your new puppy and ideally he should travel home in the car on someone's lap. He may never have been in a car before and will be separated from his family and litter-mates for the first time ever so he will need lots of reassurance and comforting. Be sure to take a supply of tissues and a towel with you as he may be travel sick. Put a bottle of water and a bowl in the car in case he needs a drink. Don't let him out of the car at lay-bys to go to the toilet as these can be serious sources of infection.

Settling him in

The first important thing to impress on everybody is that the puppy should not be taken into a public place before having his course of vaccinations for fear of infection (see page 33). Secondly, give him his name and only use it with pleasant connotations. Your puppy should be given a place

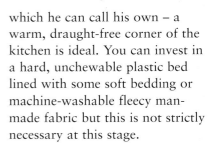

■ **Below:** *If buying a plastic basket, get a suitable size for a fully-grown adult dog.*

which he can call his own – a warm, draught-free corner of the kitchen is ideal. You can invest in a hard, unchewable plastic bed lined with some soft bedding or machine-washable fleecy man-made fabric but this is not strictly necessary at this stage.

When puppies are very young, they often have a great liking for cardboard boxes, so turn a box upside-down, cut an entry hole in it and put in an old sweater. Your puppy will love it because he feels safe inside. He can also chew the box and it can be renewed at no expense. When he gets older, you can buy a proper chew-proof dog bed of adequate size.

Whenever he goes into his box,

■ **Right:** *Puppies enjoy chewing expensive baskets and plastic beds so a cardboard box is a cheaper and more practical alternative. If your puppy chews it, just throw it away and replace it with a new one.*

leave him in peace. Instruct the children that his bed is his private sanctuary and he must be allowed to sleep without being disturbed. Like a child, a puppy needs rest. It is during these periods that his body and bones develop. Whenever you put the puppy in his box, give him the command 'In your bed' and he will soon understand what you mean.

Many people find that a puppy playpen is a very good idea. The puppy's box can be placed inside together with his toys. The floor can be covered with newspapers. A playpen will keep your puppy safe and out of the way of the children and family while still allowing him to be with you all and observe what is going on around him. He can rest or sleep, and the playpen can be moved from room to room if wished.

For the first day or two, do not hassle the little dog; let him investigate his new home in his own time. Comfort and reassure him because he will feel lonely. Don't leave him alone in the house but be with him, talk to

■ **Left:** *A playpen will keep your puppy safe and secure.*

him and play gently with him. This is an important socialization period and what you do now will set the pattern for the future, too. Don't give him any sweets and 'treats' or he will suffer an upset stomach. Leave plenty of fresh water down for him and give him the food that he is used to eating.

Feeding your puppy

The breeder should give you a diet sheet together with a small supply of the food on which your puppy has been weaned. To avoid problems, stick to the regime as closely as possible. Puppies have tiny stomachs and should be fed only small amounts frequently – as

many as four or five times a day. After two or three weeks, reduce the number of feeding times to three and slightly increase the amounts given at each meal. Every breed will differ but by the time your puppy is five to six months he should be on two meals a day. Always feed the best food available, at the same time and in the same place to establish a routine. A wide range of

FEEDING TIPS

◆ It is always unwise to feed your puppy titbits from the table. If you don't start now, he won't bother you when you are eating.

◆ Don't offer him sweets, sugar-based biscuits, cakes and chocolate. He'll eat them but they are bad for his teeth and his weight.

◆ If your puppy does not eat his food immediately, don't leave it down for long in case insects contaminate it.

◆ Don't allow him to eat the cat's food or milk, nor should you feed them together.

◆ Don't feed him cow's milk while he is still very young. Some dogs react unfavourably to it and it may cause diarrhoea. All he needs is water to prosper.

◆ If he has a diet of complete dried food he will need plenty of water, so make sure he has a continuous supply and change or top it up frequently.

◆ If you introduce new foods, do this gradually so as not to upset his stomach.

◆ Don't give your puppy cooked chicken, lamb or pork bones as these can splinter and cause serious injury. Hide chews will help with teething and cleaning teeth.

◆ Large knuckle bones can be given but train your pup to give them up to you – young dogs can soon become over-protective of their food and treats. It is wise not to let the puppy have them for too long as he may manage to chew small pieces off which can eventually become impacted in his stomach.

■ Right: *A puppy needs small, regular meals while he is very young. A bowl of fresh water should always be available.*

specially formulated food for puppies is available, including the complete dried foods, canned foods, biscuit meal and mixers. Alternatively, cook fresh meat and mix it with special puppy biscuit meal. However, the advantage of the commercial puppy foods you can buy is that they provide the right scientific balance of vital nutrients for a growing dog.

It is impossible to over-estimate the importance of giving a dog the correct food. There are hundreds of brands from which to choose, so pay special attention to the manufacturers' recommendations and be sure not to overfeed your

puppy. Dogs are running creatures and should be slim with hard muscles. Even small dogs, such as Pekingeses, should not carry any excess weight. If you are unsure about how much food your pup should be eating, then ask your vet for advice.

Do not be tempted to give him extra supplements of vitamins or minerals unless it is on veterinary advice. The modern convenience foods are said to contain all the essential nutrients and therefore there is no need for supplements. Some experts believe that to reach their full potential young adult dogs should have meat or offal as part of their diet. Whichever type of food is offered, an unlimited amount of fresh water should always be available.

Night-time

Missing the comforting presence of his fellow litter-mates, your puppy may cry during the first few nights so tire him out by playing with him before he goes to sleep. Place a hot water bottle under his

FEEDING GUIDELINES

Puppies have incredibly small stomachs and after weaning need small feeds frequently: four meals a day plus two puppy milk drinks. There is no way to know exactly how much to feed a puppy as every breed differs. A general guide using complete puppy food is 22 g (³/4 oz) per 450 g (1 lb) body weight daily, bearing in mind that medium-sized dogs double their birth weight every seven days, and larger dogs grow even faster. Every major specialist dog food manufacturing company gives guidelines and most have a telephone helpline. The best way to monitor progress is to weigh the puppy daily. Any standstill or loss of weight needs immediate investigation so make sure he is getting his proper quota and slightly increase the amount given if necessary.

bedding, put a ticking clock in with him and play the radio quietly – you are trying to fool him into believing that he is not alone.

It is best to place the box on a washable, non-carpeted floor and to surround it with newspaper in case the puppy wants to urinate during the night. Puppies rarely soil their bed.

If he howls during the night and you go to him he will think you are answering his call so steel your heart and try not to go. However, it is cruel to let him cry all night and if he is very persistent and cannot settle, you may have to take him into your bedroom. Put

■ Left: *Puppies should not have too much exercise while they are young. A short walk or run will be sufficient.*

his box by the bed and comfort him by stroking him from the bed, but on no account let him get up onto the bed because you may be setting a pattern that will be very difficult to change when he grows to his full size.

When he is relaxed, you can move his box a little closer to the door each night until it is outside, and then it can be taken back to the kitchen. However, if he does sleep upstairs, make sure that he cannot fall downstairs – his bones will not be calcified until he is about six months old and will break comparatively easily at this age. As a temporary precaution, place a child-proof stair gate at the top of the stairs. This can be used at the bottom of the stairs during the day to prevent him climbing upstairs. If he does go with you, always carry him up and down as he is likely to injure himself if he falls.

Left: *Provide your puppy with a snug bed that he can call his own. Make it comfortable with some rugs or vetbed.*

Toilet-training

Wherever you put the puppy's box, surround it with newspaper as he will not want to soil his own nest. When he is accustomed to using the paper, gradually remove some pieces and move the remainder towards the kitchen door. At the door it is then an easy matter to place it outside.

Every puppy will indicate that he wants to perform, but each one is different. One may turn in little circles whilst another one will run back and forth sniffing.

Whenever your puppy indicates that he wants to go to the toilet or finishes a meal or awakes from a sleep, put a collar and lead on him and take him outside to the place in the garden where you want him to go. Always use the same one or two words as a command and then praise him rapturously when he performs to order. Never chastise him severely when he makes a mistake in the house unless you catch him in the act. If so, use your voice, never your hand. He regards defecating, and where he wants to do it, as perfectly normal behaviour and will not understand why you are punishing him.

There are some times when the puppy should be taken into the garden which will stimulate him to perform his toilet: first thing in the morning, after every meal, after any strenuous play, after a daytime sleep and before bed every evening. With the praise system, he should soon relate it to the required performance.

LIFE EXPECTANCY

Like their owners, dogs are living longer nowadays, but few will pass seventeen years, which is eighty-four human years. The record for canine longevity is claimed for a twenty-seven-and-a-quarter-year-old black Labrador that died in Boston, Lincolnshire, though there are less reliable reports of another dog tottering up to an incredible thirty-four years!

One year of the dog's life is equivalent to seven of man's, or so the saying goes, but it isn't true. A one-year-old bitch is mature and can have pups; a seven-year-old child cannot. Many dogs reach fifteen years of age but few folk celebrate their 105th birthday. A more realistic approach has been

worked out by the French veterinarian, Dr Lebeau. He has suggested that the first year of a dog's life equals fifteen human years, the second equals a further nine human years and thereafter each dog year counts for four human years. This provides us with the table shown below.

Age of dog	Equivalent age of a human
1 year	15 years
2 years	24 years
3 years	28 years
4 years	32 years
8 years	48 years
12 years	64 years
15 years	76 years
20 years	96 years

Cats and other pets

Do not force your new puppy to accept a cat. Holding a cat near a puppy so he can smell it is not advisable – the cat will object and it could be painful for the puppy if he gets scratched. Anyway, the cat will probably find a high place to keep out of the way for the first few days. Feed them both in

■ **Above:** *This Spaniel puppy is being introduced to a pet guinea pig. Neither animal seems stressed by the encounter but you should never leave your dog alone with a small pet.*

■ **Below:** *Dogs and cats can grow accustomed to each other and learn to live happily together, even sharing a bed and playing games.*

different places and don't let the puppy eat the cat's food; it may not suit his digestion. Sooner or later the cat will venture close to the puppy, but if he gets too frisky the cat will defend itself. In this way, the puppy will soon learn to keep out of the cat's way.

In the fullness of time it is usual for a dog and a cat to live together in harmony in the same house, even after a tense start. However, this does not mean that the dog will tolerate a strange cat running across the lawn.

Take special care to separate him from any pet rabbits, gerbils, hamsters or other small animals, as they are a natural prey for a dog and it would be wise not to tempt him. When your puppy is a little older he can be introduced to any small pets under your supervision, and most dogs will learn to live alongside them.

Danger and hazards

Inside
◆ Fit stair gates at the top and bottom of flights of stairs
◆ Cover up trailing wires
◆ Unplug electrical appliances
◆ Turn off electric sockets
◆ Don't leave small chewable objects at ground level

Outside
◆ All fences should be high enough and secure
◆ Close gates and garden doors securely
◆ Attach wire netting to the bottom of garden gates
◆ Check for holes in netting and fencing
◆ Lock up poisons and sharp tools

Dogs like being outside if the weather suits them, and their garden becomes an extension of their territory. As puppies, they will explore every corner, so for obvious reasons you must make your garden escape-proof and remember that most puppies can squeeze through very small holes. As they grow, some of the taller breeds will jump 1–1.5 m (3–5 ft) if something attracts their attention. Securing wire netting on top of the fencing and then bending it over inwards towards the dog's territory solves this particular problem.

Make sure also that any gates and garden doors close securely and cannot be opened by an inquisitive dog. Nor should there be a gap at the bottom under which the dog can crawl; if so, attach fairly strong wire netting to the gate or door at ground level.

Inside the house

There are danger points inside the house, too. When they are young, long, low dogs, such as Basset Hounds and Dachshunds, and large breeds, such as Wolfhounds, should not be allowed to go up and down stairs as their vertebrae

can be over-stressed, leading to spinal disc troubles in later life. A child gate at the bottom of the staircase will put an effective stop to this activity.

Electrical sockets, plugs and trailing wires present an almost irresistible temptation to most inquisitive puppies so cover the wires, unplug those that are not in use and switch off the sockets. You could even place a piece of furniture over the socket.

With a puppy around, children have to learn to live on a higher level. Their habit of leaving their favourite toys on the floor will tempt the puppy who will pick up and chew any small plastic toy. This can be very dangerous as small pieces can lodge in the dog's stomach and even tear the lining resulting in death or, at the best, some very expensive veterinary treatment. Puppies also tend to mark their territory with urine frequently and clothes left on the floor are often targets.

Above: Small, low-slung dogs, such as Dachshunds, shouldn't be allowed to climb the stairs.

Left: Don't leave temptation in your puppy's way. This Cocker Spaniel is chewing the TV remote control!

Indoor kennels and travel boxes

One of the great training aids is an indoor kennel, which can be a wooden box with a wire front, a plastic travel box or a simple wire cage. These are all available from good pet stores and also from specialized traders. It is easy to train your puppy to go into it happily by feeding him inside the box, and he will very soon enter willingly and the door can then be closed for a short while. This will prove of inestimable value if you want some peace to vacuum the carpet or to go to the shops for an hour. However, do not keep him locked up for long. It is not cruel to box a dog for short periods as they

■ **Left:** *A sturdy wooden box with a wire grille can be used for short periods or when travelling in the car.*

like the security they experience inside it, but make sure that the container is of an adequate size. The dog should be able to stand up, stretch out and lie on his side easily.

A travel box is especially good in the car, where a wild young puppy leaping around at seventy miles an hour is not conducive to safe driving. It also offers security if your car is ever involved in an accident as the car doors can fly open, releasing a frightened, loose dog who can become a danger to himself and to traffic.

■ **Left:** *For small dogs, such as these pretty Pomeranians, a plastic travelling box is ideal for most car journeys.*

■ **Above:** *A puppy can be caged in a wire crate fitted with a small rug or blanket and containing some of his favourite toys.*

At the vet's

Tell your vet that you are going to acquire a puppy and make sure he knows which breed so that he can find out in advance about any potential health problems before you take your new puppy along for his first visit. When the puppy has settled down after a couple of days you will need to introduce them to each other. However, do not put the puppy down on the pavement between your home and the veterinary surgery and, above all, do not set him down on the floor of the surgery. There may be other dogs waiting and because yours is a puppy they are likely to be interested. Keep him well away from their inquisitive noses as there is a danger of infection, and most dogs visiting the veterinary surgery are there because there is something wrong with them.

Vaccinations

The vet will give your puppy a general examination and if he considers he is old enough he will vaccinate him. Several diseases are a threat to your dog's life, parvovirus, distemper and leptospirosis being the three main ones, and it is essential that your dog is inoculated against these. Most vets will perform the initial vaccination between ten and twelve weeks, with the booster following two weeks later. If the puppy is deemed not old enough for

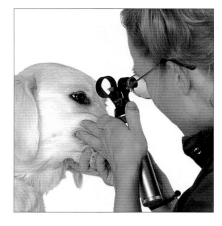

vaccinations, make an appointment at the first opportunity

Puppies should not go out into a public place until about ten days after the vaccinations are complete. Your vet will be able to advise you whether there are any potentially dangerous places locally, and, in particular, never make the mistake of putting your puppy out of the car in a roadside lay-by as these are hotbeds of infection.

■ **Left:** *The vet will give your puppy a thorough examination and will look at his eyes, ears, nose and mouth.*

Now is also the time to ask the vet any questions that might be bothering you about your dog's diet, behaviour or health and also about matters such as insurance. Puppies are vulnerable to disease and it is always a wise move to take out insurance because of the ever-escalating costs of veterinary services. There are several reputable companies that offer different levels of cover so ask your vet for advice.

■ **Below:** *When your puppy has his first vaccination, the vet will check him all over to assess his general health.*

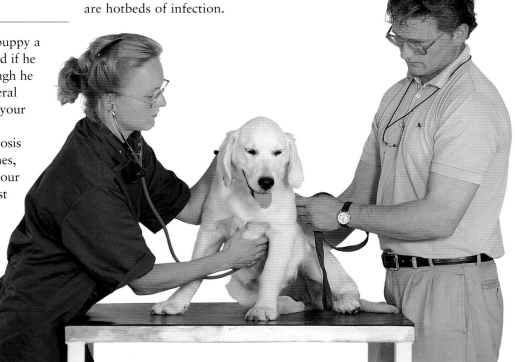

GOOD SOCIAL SKILLS

Your dog needs good social skills if he is to become a well-behaved member of canine and human society. Thus it is very important to socialize and train your puppy from the earliest age. This will help to prevent any behaviour problems occurring later on and make your dog more socially acceptable. Your dog must always be under complete control in any public place.

Lead training

The first essential accessories that you need are a collar and lead; in fact, two collars and leads. Some trainers recommend that the first collar should be very light, like a cat collar, the wearing of which will not irritate the puppy. The lead can be made of light cloth which is hardly noticeable. Thus the puppy will learn to wear a collar without being aware of it.

The second collar should be more substantial, probably made of leather, with a supple leather lead. An identification disc on which your name and telephone number have been engraved has to be attached to the collar your dog wears whenever he is outside your home. Do not engrave your dog's name on it; that would make it too easy for thieves.

Collars

A young puppy will need a lightweight collar made of nylon, soft leather or fabric. He will grow out of it quite quickly so don't bother buying an expensive one.

You can begin lead training almost as soon as the puppy arrives in the house. Let him run about wearing the collar for a

■ **Above:** *Let your puppy wander about with the lead on to get him used to it but watch him carefully in case the lead gets caught up on something.*

■ **Right:** *When a young puppy is old enough to take out after vaccinations, keep him on a lead in public places as there are always many distractions to tempt him away from you.*

little while and then add the light lead – he will quickly get accustomed to it trailing after him. Pick up the lead and follow him without applying any pressure to the lead. After a little while, assert some light pressure and try to guide him but don't make it so strong that he stops to fight it. Talk to him all the time in an encouraging way to boost his confidence.

Make certain that the collar is sufficiently tight that he cannot pull out of it, but at the same time it should not be so tight that it is strangling him. Continue the exercise outside in the garden. Make it fun and train in short bursts as puppies become easily bored, like young children.

If the teaching period lasts for too long, most puppies can think of something better to do.

When your puppy is ready to go out for a proper walk, remember that all cars and lorries appear as huge, smelly, noisy monsters to him and thus he may be afraid. Carry him in your arms around the block two or three times for a day or two before you put him down. Speak to him gently all the

■ **Left:** *To get your puppy used to traffic and road-walking, carry him in your arms for a day or two before walking on the pavement.*

while; it will help to build up his confidence knowing that you are there to protect him. Never allow him to walk in any traffic areas without a collar and lead; a dog does not understand that cars can kill him and neither does he know nor care that his presence on the road may cause an accident for which you can be held responsible.

■ **Above:** *Your pup may be reluctant to walk on the lead at first and may hang back. Don't get cross with him. Try to make it fun.*

Play and games

A young dog needs lots of things to do and his brain needs to be stimulated. In the wild, he would be taught to track animals, to fight predators and to catch prey. However, the domestic dog has none of these skills to learn and therefore you should provide alternatives. By doing so, you will minimize the chances of your puppy becoming bored and then engaging in destructive behaviour. Toys and games are the answer; most dog toys are now virtually indestructible, though not totally, as you will soon find out. Dogs, particularly Terriers, love squeaky toys and will not be content until they have found the squeak and killed it. Sometimes, however,

they may adopt a soft toy, which Retrievers or Spaniels will carry about in their mouth.

Do not play tug of war with a soft toy – you will be training your puppy to be destructive and possessive. All dogs can be taught to play with a ball but be careful that the ball is not too small. Dogs' jaws can open very wide and they can swallow quite large objects. If they should accidentally

■ **Below:** *Tug of war games are great fun for both dog and owner, but you must win the game more often than the dog does or he will never bring anything back. A powerful puppy, such as this Rottweiler, may be too strong for a child, and adult supervision is advisable.*

TOYS FOR PLAYING GAMES

1 Soft toys: Ideal for retrieving and exercises

2 Tug toys: Ideal for strong and boisterous dogs

3 Squeaky balls and toys: Fine for smaller dogs

4 Kongs: Ideal when your dog is left alone for mental stimulation

5 Rubber rings and toys: Perfect for tug and fetch

6 Frisbees and tennis balls: Ideal for playing outdoor fetch

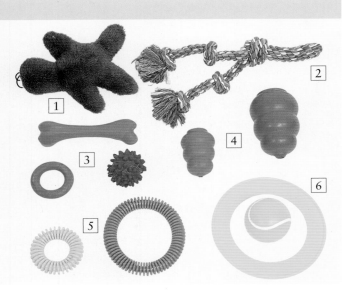

swallow a rubber or plastic ball the repercussions can be very serious. Do not give your puppy an old shoe or slipper to chew and destroy – dogs notoriously ignore the difference between old and new shoes.

Games you can play

Games for dogs are invariably those of catch, retrieve and hide-and-seek. Dogs derive the most fun out of chasing and retrieving balls. However, the one proviso is to ensure that the ball is not too small in case it slips down a dog's throat and chokes him. Start when your dog is a young puppy.

■ **Left:** *Reduce the risk of losing your best footwear by not giving your puppy any personal items to chew or play with, especially shoes, socks and children's favourite toys.*

Throw a ball just in front of him, then make a fuss of him when he returns it and persuade him gently to 'drop'. When he is proficient at retrieving, hide the ball for him to find, close by to start with but gradually increasing the distance.

Another good game is to teach your dog to 'find your child'. Some dogs adore to push a football with their nose, and kids can play footie with their pet. Quoit rings are fun to throw and pull but the ultimate throwing game is with a 'Frisbee'. Dogs get great exercise running and leaping for it.

Good pet shops will have a variety of toys, and you should choose those that are said to be indestructible with no metal or plastic. The 'Kong' is particularly good: a hollow eccentrically shaped ball which can be stuffed with small food titbits. Your dog will chase it happily for hours, trying to get the food out. Nylon bones keep dogs occupied as well as keeping their teeth clean.

■ **Below:** *Most puppies enjoy playing 'fetch' with a ball. It allows them to run freely and have some fun.*

Socialization

When a puppy faces something he has never encountered before his first instinct is to run, and it is up to you, his owner, to socialize him in such a fashion that he will not be scared of anything. He should not be over-protected from any household noises, and it is a good idea to get him accustomed to the sound of such appliances as the vacuum cleaner, dishwasher, radio, television and washing machine. In fact, even dropping a dustbin lid about 5 m (15 ft) away from him is not a bad idea.

After his vaccinations, you must introduce him to the people who visit your house regularly: the postman, the milkman and the refuse collectors. Let your friends and neighbours handle him and, when he is old enough, take him into town or to the market and let him mix with people, always on the lead and under your control.

Puppy socialization classes are sometimes a good way of getting him used to meeting other dogs as well as a wide range of people. Ask your vet for the details of your nearest class. They are now widespread in most areas.

■ **Left:** *This West Highland White Terrier puppy is meeting some older dogs. Most adult dogs will not be aggressive to young puppies.*

■ **Left:** *If friends come to visit with their dogs, encourage them to handle and play with the puppy. It is important to introduce your puppy to as many new people as possible.*

■ **Right:** *Puppies will get most of their normal daily exercise requirements from general play and activity with you at home. Therefore make sure that your walks aren't too long at first. Use them to help your new dog develop social skills and reinforce his training, especially lead training.*

Exercise

Young puppies get all the exercise that they require from their own exuberance when running and playing, and there is no need for formal exercise. In fact, it could harm a puppy's development if he is forced into too much activity at too young an age. The age at which it is necessary varies from breed to breed, but the average is probably at between five and six months – the breeder or your vet can advise. For a large dog, such as an Irish Wolfhound, too much exercise can be positively harmful for a growing puppy whose bones are still growing. It is also a good idea to start taking your puppy for short walks on the lead.

You can teach your puppy some simple but essential commands, such as 'Sit', 'Stay' and 'Come', at home (see page 70). More formal training can begin when he is about six months of age and it is advisable to attend obedience classes at your local Dog Training School where there will be some knowledgeable trainers on hand.

■ **Above:** *Like many other giant breeds, Irish Wolfhound puppies should not exercise excessively before the age of six months. Let them play in the garden rather than take them for long walks.*

Social responsibilities

Behavioural scientists have proved that without doubt the ownership of a dog is beneficial to adults and particularly to children, but in the light of today's social attitudes an owner must train a dog to fit into modern society's perception of what constitutes acceptable social behaviour. The law is becoming unreasonably harsh when dealing with those it considers transgressors.

The 1991 Dangerous Dogs Act in the UK has given the courts the power of what is in effect a mandatory death sentence on any dogs which are judged to have contravened its stipulations. Nobody wants a dangerous dog on the loose but under this law a dog does not have to be deemed dangerous in the accepted sense; the police have only to accuse it

of looking dangerous for it to suffer the death penalty. A reverse of the burden of proof applies which means that the dog is guilty before being found guilty which effectively prevents a defence no matter how trivial the alleged offence. Thus it behoves every dog owner to make certain that they do not fall foul of this law.

Councils and local authorities are also taking a tougher stance by introducing new dog 'no-go' areas, especially on beaches and parks, and are also enforcing new 'dog fouling' by-laws under which dog owners can be fined should they allow their dog to foul public places without picking up the mess. There are many hygienic methods of doing this and various gadgets can be obtained from pet shops to pick up dog faeces.

Owners would be wise to always carry something with which to scoop dog mess up, even if it's just a plastic bag, when they're out walking their dogs.

At the time of publication of this book there is no legislation requiring a dog owner to either license or register a dog. However, a special committee is sitting in the UK to examine the situation and report their findings. If they find in favour of registration, all owners may have to get their dogs tattooed or micro-chipped for the purposes of identification and will have to pay a fee for this.

However, despite these minor obstacles, sharing your life with a dog more than compensates for all the difficulties for he will be your loyal friend and companion through all your tribulations.

Good dog behaviour

When we take a dog into our family we want him to be acceptable to everyone who comes to our home, whether they are friends, our children's friends or callers on business. We do not want our new family member to be a nuisance to us or anyone else, either in the car or when walking on the street or in the countryside. Our dogs have to learn good manners and we have to teach them — by patient repetition, by watchfulness for instinctive behaviour which has to be controlled, and by teaching the dog to trust us. First of all, we must understand the dog's senses, the way in which they work and how they are controlled.

Chapter Three

COMMUNICATING WITH YOUR DOG

The dog is probably the best communicator in the whole of the animal world; perhaps this is why, for hundreds of thousands of years, dogs have been the favoured companions and workmates of the human race. And from the earliest days of the dog/human relationship, dogs were not only used to help with hunting, guarding and herding but were also regarded with great affection.

Right: *We have taken over the role of pack leader and in return for shelter and food, dogs give us loyalty and affection.*

This relationship is supported by the finding of the skeleton of an elderly human, clasping the skeleton of a puppy of about five months. These remains were discovered at a burial site in Israel where the grave was dated as 12,000 years old. It may be that this puppy was in fact a tamed wolf. However, it has now been established that all modern dogs are descended from wolves which indirectly offered themselves to our ancient ancestors as suitable candidates for domestication by becoming part of a human community.

The man/dog relationship

Professor James Serpell wrote in his book, *The Domestic Dog* (Cambridge University Press), that all the archaeological evidence indicates that the dog was the first species to be domesticated. There was a mutual advantage bargain to be made; the wolf that came in from the cold instinctively helped man in hunting and pulling down quarry and in tracking wounded animals. In return, gradually relinquishing its wild state, the wolf had the benefit of shelter and food and, eventually, shared company and a tolerable pack leader.

It is probable that relatively few wolves were domesticated in this way. Those wolves that did form a relationship with the primitive tribes would have mated with other like-minded wolves. Many generations of mating within this small gene pool would have gradually produced an animal that bore little resemblance physically or temperamentally to the wild wolf; the dog was emerging as a separate and individual animal. And the dog has never left man's side, at least in the Western World. Where there is a break in the dog-man relationship now it is brought about by man's intransigence, never by the dog choosing to be wild again.

Although some dogs may, on impulse, break out of their homes, whether they are impelled by an over-riding desire to seek a willing mate, or to revel in the fast chase of some quarry, these dogs will invariably come home again,

provided that they have not been injured in a road traffic accident. A dog who has temporarily lost touch with his owner through yielding to the temptation to chase some quarry in woodlands or through open country will usually return to the place where the owner and dog were last together, or to the car park where the walk started. Very few dogs want to be on the run permanently, and there are, in current records of dogs rescued from cruel and neglectful homes, many examples of dogs who seem devoted to harsh and unkind owners.

In Britain and across most of Europe, there are no wild dogs, and no feral dogs – dogs that have deliberately chosen to live and breed far away from the homes that once sheltered them, as feral cats choose to do. Dogs rarely change their

homes deliberately or voluntarily, by leaving one home and applying at another for food and shelter, as many cats quite often do. So can this very special relationship and devotion, as strong as ever today, be reinforced by the ease with which man and dog communicate and the pleasure that both species can take in their exchanges?

The reason why many families make the effort to have pets – and pet ownership, however enjoyable, can indeed be an effort in today's busy life – is because the dog can become the separate and inviolate confidant of the whole family.

Children can gain a tremendous amount of comfort and stability from having a canine best friend who shares their disappointments, misunderstandings and troubles yet never blames them, never tells their secrets and never transfers his allegiance to any other person.

■ **Left:** *Your dog will always be your devoted companion, giving you his love and affection and never judgmental.*

■ **Above:** *A working dog, such as this young Retriever with a pheasant in his mouth, learns to work with his owner as part of the human pack.*

This unique friendship is especially valuable in the modern world where many traditional human relationships are no longer permanent. The high level of mutual communication that we have with our dogs is the basis of real friendship on a special level between dogs and their owners.

DID YOU KNOW?

The Australian aborigines use dingoes (wild dogs) for warmth on cold nights by sleeping with them clasped in their arms. Women, when not carrying their young children, will often 'wear' a dog draped across the lower back with the head and tail in the crook of their arms as a kidney-warmer.

COMMUNICATION MECHANISMS

Dogs have many ways of communicating with us; they have voices, facial expressions, manipulation of ears and lips, body language, a neat use of paws and a very visible signalling mechanism with their tails. Dogs usually have very acute hearing so that they can hear our slightest whisper. They use their warm pink tongues to dry tears or to beseech us to notice them; they will raise our spirits by playing simple games very enthusiastically, and their coats give us tactile pleasure. And dogs are closer to us than we will ever be to them; they have so many hours in which to watch us, to assess our facial expressions and our behaviour, and to interpret our moods.

The dog's voice

Dogs have an extraordinary vocal repertoire; they can talk to us in a myriad of ways which we can interpret and understand provided we take a close interest in them. The dog's vocalizations range from a murmur, usually directed straight to the human ear, through to a whine, a pleading bark, a serious warning or an aggressive bark, an attention-seeking bark, a low growl or a very deep intense growl, and also a muted howl ranging in intensity over several notes. The latter quite musical howl is usually made as a protest against strident noise from some outside source, such as television signature tunes. The classic long howl is usually made from a sitting position with the dog's head and throat thrown back into an almost vertical line so that the voice travels as far as possible.

The howl, which is particularly annoying or distressing to the neighbours, is thought to be a rallying call to the pack, triggered by loneliness. Dogs do not howl when they're in pain; in fact, a dog suffering physical discomfort from an injury is almost always completely silent. Nor does a howling dog forecast a tragedy in the neighbourhood. These two old-fashioned country beliefs still surface sometimes, even among urban people when they want to complain about noisy dogs causing them disturbance.

Singing is a talent only a few dogs express; some dogs vocalize in a cadence of notes when they are very pleased, such as when their owner has arrived home after an absence. These dogs can be taught to respond as a duet when their owners sing back to them, and both the dog and the human can enjoy this harmony. The murmur, made with mouth closed and straight into the human ear, is a demonstration of greeting and affection. Enjoy this spontaneous expression by your dog; he certainly will not murmur to a stranger or someone he is not fond of or does not trust to handle him gently. Puppies in the nest murmur into the dam's ear, which is usually turned back to allow maximum access; the puppy also relaxes the outer flap of its ear, one of the signs of pleasant

Left: *Dogs make a wide range of sounds, ranging from barks and growls to howls and murmurs. Some dogs can even 'sing' along with their lucky owners.*

submission. All puppies are born completely without hearing though they can vocalize at birth using the humming murmur for pleasure and satisfaction, usually while feeding from their dam, and also telling the world when they are unhappy, hungry, cold or ill by using a thin, high-pitched wail.

The ear canals do not develop until nearly three weeks after the birth. As soon as the puppies can hear they start to use their voices, ranging through sharp little barks at the arrival of the breeder and food, to growls and mini-roars when playing competitively with their litter-mates.

Whines

Your dog will direct his whine at you, too. The whine is used to ask you to fulfil his need or wish of some kind, whether to have the door opened or for biscuits to be handed out. Enjoy the fact that

your dog is communicating with you and also that you can interpret what he is asking for. You will not want to comply with every whined wish but when you do so try to make it a happy time because your dog asked and you understood what he wanted.

If the request is obscure, make an effort to find out what the dog wants: touch this or that object and show the dog things that he normally uses. Is it the food dish, his lead, or a toy? You will get a very positive response of tail wagging, dancing on hind legs or another expression of joy when you find the key to the pleading whine. Less vocal dogs will stand and stare silently at the object they want made available to them; these are usually serious canine requests but can also be converted into a game in which the dog has to tell you what he wants and then you grant the request.

Sound sensitivity

Howling in response to a loud noise or a particular musical sound, such as a strident trumpet or violin, seems to mean that this noise is actually painful to a dog's very sensitive hearing. Remember that dogs' ears are much more acute and more discerning than our own. Sound sensitivity of this degree may often coincide with a fear of fireworks and thunder.

Dogs can hear sounds on a much higher register than we can appreciate, so very high-pitched sounds can inflict actual pain. Dogs will often show fear and resentment, even anger, at some pieces of household equipment which make a painful sound for them. Many breeds with pricked-

■ **Above:** *A dog's hearing is extremely sensitive and many prick up their ears and swivel them to locate sounds.*

up, wide-open ears, such as the German Shepherd Dog, can suffer acutely in a household which is drenched with loud sounds.

Fear of thunder is made more acute if a family member is also nervous of the noise; being brave and not reacting to storms will help your dog and may help you, too. Because his first instinct is to run away from an overpowering sound, provide a refuge when you know a noise is going to occur: either a covered crate which will insulate the dog from the noise, or access to a bedroom perhaps where he can dive under the bed, or even a cupboard which is insulated by its contents.

Try not to act with any urgency or fear but always make your actions quite matter-of fact and calm, and then your dog will imitate your mood.

■ **Right:** *You will soon recognise the sounds your dog makes and learn to understand what he is trying to tell you. His body language will also provide you with clues.*

Deafness

While thinking about the sounds that can inspire fear in dogs, we must remember also that some puppies are born deaf, in one or both ears. White-coated dogs are more likely to be affected by this inherited fault. Even partially deaf dogs should not be bred from.

Susceptible breeds, including Dalmatians, Border Collies, white Bull Terriers and white Boxers, should be tested as puppies before they are sold at eight weeks old. The old-fashioned way of testing by dropping a tin dish behind the puppy is too inaccurate to be of any use in deciding the future of a puppy – the puppy may see the movement or feel the air vibration as the testing object falls. The definitive computerized test, called

■ **Right:** *White dogs, like this Boxer puppy, are susceptible to deafness.*

the Brain-stem Auditory Response Test, is quite painless and can be used on puppies from five weeks of age. Your veterinary surgeon can refer you to a specialist in testing for hearing capacity.

In old age, dogs may lose some of their hearing capacity just as humans do, or chronic ear disease may have the same effect, but these dogs will usually know all they need to know about their owners and their way of life so partial deafness is not a tragedy for them. There should never be any need to shout at a dog.

Even stone-deaf puppies can be trained, by the use of human facial expressions, hand gestures and body language, to be happy and safe companions. You can obtain an excellent short guide to training a deaf puppy (see Useful Addresses, page 190).

Sight

Dogs that live in a human family keep their eyes on their owner and other caretakers all the time. Dogs watch us constantly; they can predict what we are going to do next, and even what we are thinking of doing. You have made, as your ancestors did long ago, a mutual agreement with the dog to live and work together. Your life has no secrets from your dog; even a half-asleep dog is well aware of everything you do and is poised to accompany you in whatever you choose,

■ **Right:** *Dogs learn a lot about us and how to communicate and respond to us from our facial expressions and the hand signals we use.*

however boring an expedition it may be from the dog's natural inclination. Since your dog's eyes are almost always on you,

Right: *The dog's eyes are extremely expressive and are almost always on you. Respond with a smile and you will see his face soften.*

enjoy the cheering habit of some mutual smiles. When you catch your dog's eye, you will notice that the whole face softens: the lips spread instead of being tense, and the ears drop. It does you good to smile back! Both you and your dog are at peace with the world! And if you are not very happy at the time, then the knowledge that your dog has sympathy and comfort to offer you can be helpful and cheering.

However, a long, hard stare right into your dog's eyes is a challenge signal and should only be used when it is obvious that the dog is about to do something that is normally forbidden. Never 'hard stare' an angry or a hostile dog or one who is defending his own territory. It is better to watch the dog with an oblique glance while planning your next move.

A puppy's eyes are open and its sight is fully developed by about fourteen days after birth. Unless a dog has a particular sight defect, it can usually see better than humans in dim light or darkness. At a distance, dogs see moving objects best, so if you are calling your dog from a long way away, use hand signals.

A dog's field of vision

Dogs see differently from us and they have a larger field of vision whereby they can see things to the sides and rear. Their accuracy in judging distance is determined by the amount of overlap.

Right: *Whippets were bred for the chase and to focus on their prey, and thus their field of vision is very narrow (only 200 degrees).*

The mouth

In both humans and dogs, the mouth is a very important organ of relationship. Young puppies will lick around the mouth of their mother to entreat her to disgorge partly digested food for them. Puppies playing together often use open-mouthed biting as part of their play strategy. They will also try to lick around the lip and chin area of their owners, and it may be that this impulse is the origin of leaping up to people's faces in greeting, a habit that we do not wish to encourage.

Some breeds, particularly the Retrievers, sometimes have the ability to produce a grin of greeting, with the open mouth showing the teeth, much akin to a human smile. We have to learn to differentiate between this grin and the true angry snarl grimace where more teeth are bared and the mouth is wide open.

■ **Left:** *Some dogs can smile and look happy. Just take a look at this cheerful Pomeranian!*

Scent recognition

Dogs have around fifty times the capacity for detecting scents as humans possess; scenting is very important to a dog's way of life. The enormous number of scent-detecting cells in the dog's nasal area allows it to detect a far wider range of smells than we can, and also enables dogs to be sensitive to faint scents. Dogs learn a great deal about their world and the other animals and the people who pass through it by savouring the distinctive scents which are left behind on the ground, on fallen leaves and on gate-posts. Dogs habitually do their own scent marking by depositing urine and faeces and also by leaving traces from the sweat glands on their feet. Another animal inspecting such a scenting post is like a human being reading the local newspaper; he instantly finds out what animal has been that way, how old he was, what species, where he was going, on what purpose and whether the passing animal was looking for a mate, for food or a place burrow. Where several dogs are kept together in a household, it can be noticed that the leader of the dog pack will 'counter-sign' urine deposits made by the other dogs, all the animals seeming to deliberately urinate on the same patch.

The scent of the dog's owner and the rest of the household are important to a dog, and an

■ **Left:** *Terriers and Spaniels are more likely to be on the scent trail of their 'prey' rather than checking which other dogs have strayed into their 'territory'.*

■ **Right:** *When dogs meet and greet each other, they do so by smell. Each will sniff the other dog.*

important means of recognition of a familiar person in different clothes or in an unusual place. This talent is also used by search and rescue dogs who are given their scent-clue by being allowed to smell the sweat on a garment that the victim has used. Human footprints also emit individual smells, and an adult dog can successfully follow a trail on grass, four hours after it was laid. Many dogs seem to dislike strong perfume, perhaps because it masks the natural scent that they need to recognise.

Dogs are used in France and Italy to find the subterranean truffle fungus; and in Holland and Denmark to detect gas leaks. They are more accurate than the most sensitive odour-measuring machines and are used everywhere to search for humans, explosives and drugs, often in incredible conditions. An amazing German Shepherd Dog of the Cairo police in Egypt successfully followed the track of a donkey that was made four-and-a-half days previously.

Tail signals

Where a dog has its full tail, it is a very valuable adjunct both to communication with humans and with other dogs. A tail can be wagged in pleasure, particularly on greeting, but if it is held out stiffly behind the dog it is usually part of an aggression pose. When a dog with a tail that is normally 'teapot handle style' is truly and happily relaxed, the tail will straighten out, all except for the last tiny curl.

■ **Below:** *Although the Staffordshire Bull Terrier is holding his tail up it is held quite stiffly and, together with the fact that the ears are down, indicates that the dog is ready to take a defence posture. In contrast, the jaunty Jack* Russell *is enthusiastically greeting the somewhat apprehensive Great Dane whose tail is drooping down between his legs. The Terrier's tail is up and wagging and his ears are pricked as he jumps up at the larger dog.*

HUMAN/DOG COMMUNICATION

In an ideal situation, we should start communicating with a new puppy while he is very young and still with the breeder and the rest of the litter. If you are able to visit the litter frequently, it is a good

idea to do so and once you have chosen your puppy, take every opportunity to get to know each other in order to build a firm foundation for a happy transfer to your own home. Ask if you and your children may hold the puppy; let him sniff at your faces and hands. Make sure as many people as possible talk to the puppy in gentle but natural voices. If

■ **Above:** *The first meeting can often be a nervous and tentative affair as you and the puppy get to know each other better. Be patient, get down to his level and let him sniff your hands and face. He will soon relax.*

you have decided on a name, by all means use it, but if the choice is still open, just call the little dog 'puppy'. Most dogs will respond to 'puppy', used occasionally, for the whole of their lives. Let your new puppy become familiar with the voices of all the members of your family. Always use a light

and pleasant voice, never a deep resonance which could easily be confused with a growl.

Possibly the most important act of communication, once you have the new puppy in your home, is to call your puppy to you often. Always crouch down to receive him with open arms and make sure he knows that coming to you is worthwhile, either by giving him a small food reward or a lot of fuss and praise. This is the foundation of all human/dog communication so make it worthwhile to your dog!

■ **Above:** *Puppies crave company and affection and will always respond with enthusiasm to their new owner.*

■ **Left:** *Play with your puppy every day and praise him lavishly when he comes to you when you call him. Make a fuss of him and reward him with a hug or a favourite titbit.*

Chapter Four

CURING COMMON PROBLEMS

We, as dog owners, can create some behaviour problems in our dogs. We ask so much of them; we expect them to share our lives and our homes and cars yet we also expect this pack-orientated animal to be content to be alone when we do not want canine company. We want the dog's services as a warning of intruders;

Right: *Boredom or lack of mental simulation, especially in active breed types like the Boxer, can sometimes lead to destructive behaviour.*

however, we do not want him to create any unnecessary noise, and nor do we expect our dog to spoil any of the possessions. When a dog fails to live up to the canine image we have created, we say he has a behaviour problem, meaning the dog does not always behave in the way we want and expect.

A new industry, employing a large number of variously qualified animal behaviourists, has arisen around the need to stop dogs doing what comes naturally to them – chewing, gnawing, barking and urine marking on the dwarf conifers. It's possible to achieve modification of some of a dog's more annoying behaviour traits if we try to analyse what is causing the behaviour and why the dog finds it necessary to do it. Whatever the problem is, it's not done to annoy us, that's for sure. The dog does whatever he feels he must in the prevailing situation, and probably our annoyance at his behaviour is only peripheral in the dog's thoughts.

The first night in your home

After all the fun and the cuddles and kisses of the day, your new puppy will find himself absolutely alone for the very first time in his life – no mother, no brothers and sisters, and not even the scent of where they have been. He is in a strange room with no familiar

noises, and he will feel abandoned, lonely and frightened. Cruel, yes! You could say that, but you did make the rule – no dogs in the bedrooms – and you are starting as you mean to go on. As a side effect of this, however, you may be instilling into your puppy a

long-lasting insecurity, a phobia about being left alone.

Your most constructive plan alteration is to take the puppy into your bedroom, keeping him in a deep box or in the wire crate you have bought for him. Put the box beside your bed so that you

■ **Right:** *Always take your puppy out into the garden first thing in the morning.*

can just put a hand down to soothe the puppy when he cries. In this way there is no break in building trust and confidence between you and the puppy. He will surely wake at first light, and you then have the opportunity to rush him downstairs and into the garden, so that you are continuing the house-training.

This first-thing-in-the-morning visit to the garden is the one that always gets immediate results, so capitalize on it. The puppy will enjoy a little game afterwards or you may want to feed him early. No matter; let the puppy shape your day while he is new to your home. When he has confidence in you and knows your rooms and your household scent, you may want to move him downstairs. However, in many ways it is advantageous to have your dog close to you at night anyway.

House soiling

It is both disconcerting and annoying to find that your dog, who may have been perfectly house-trained for a long time, has suddenly started to urinate or worse in the house, overnight or when you are out.

Is your dog unwell?

First of all, think illness. Are there any indications that the dog is not well; is he perhaps drinking more, does he have diarrhoea, is it inevitable that he cannot wait as long as you expect him to? Can you make it possible for him to get outside when he needs to? Have you made any

change in the feeding menu; is there the possibility that the formula of the food you give can have been altered? Then think

disturbance. Are there workmen or visitors in the house, or even another animal introduced? Are there any new noises from the surrounding properties?

Many dogs are great creatures of routine and they can feel very disturbed by any domestic changes. Their expression of anxiety may be demonstrated in an intestinal disturbance. Watch carefully for a few days and then, if there is no improvement, consult your veterinary surgeon.

■ **Left:** *Check that your dog's diet has not changed recently. This may cause him to soil inside the house.*

Build an outside run

It is a good idea, if at all possible, to create for your dog his own exit from the kitchen or the utility room in which you keep him when you are busy or out of the house. You could build a small yard-type well-fenced concrete run for the dog to which he has access through a dog door. He will soon learn how to utilize his run and he will also have an alternative environment for when you're out; quite the opposite to being shut inside the house. Our dog yard is also used as a clothes drying area and for storing flower pots, quite a dog's delight, but damage is surprisingly minimal.

Dogs that are house-trained will expect to go outside to be clean when they need to do so, either overnight or when you are out during the daytime. You must be prepared to make some allowances, especially for the time in the autumn when the house doors are shut up again, having stood open for practically all the summer.

The dog has to ask to go out at this time, and younger dogs may find this concept difficult to grasp, so you may have to go back to an hourly or two-hourly routine of putting-out for a while until your dog adjusts.

Elderly dogs

Remember also the disabilities of old age: elderly dogs tend to drink more and they need to urinate in considerable quantities. If they also suffer from arthritis, they may find it difficult to get up from their beds. Understand and do not grumble but plan to make their life easier for them.

Male dogs

Some male dogs may perform urine marking indoors if they feel that some provocation warrants it – a bitch in season in the house or next door, or even a new baby coming into the home. In fact, any creature with a completely different smell may trigger off the dog's need to mark the premises as his own.

Cleaning up

You must clean up all indoor mistakes thoroughly but do not use an ammonia-based product as that will compound the smell of urine. Supermarkets now sell a number of floor, upholstery and carpet cleaners which are specially formulated for cleaning up our pets' mistakes and they do work very effectively.

Summary

You cannot eradicate the soiling behaviours mentioned other than by investigating the cause and doing what you can to alter the situation. You may well indicate to your dog that you are not pleased but otherwise the dog should not be blamed.

■ **Left:** *You may have to face the fact that even though your elderly dog is still fairly fit and active, he may start to suffer from the ailments that come with old age. If he drinks more, he may find it difficult to hold his urine and soil inside the house.*

Play biting

It can be a great disappointment, especially to children, when their new puppy that they just long to cuddle just seems to be intent on biting them constantly. Those tiny sharp teeth can inflict some quite painful bites, so have we got a potentially dangerous dog here? The answer is quite firmly 'No!' The puppy will be teething, quite a painful process especially in dogs with short faces.

When you get your puppy at around eight weeks old, he should have his first set of baby teeth, but the second, and permanent, teeth will be coming through until he is about four months old. The pain of teething causes the puppy to need to gnaw, unfortunately often at your hand or ankles. There is little that you can do about this, except to have some hard nylon bones handy to push into the puppy's mouth to gnaw on. Our most recent puppy had a passion for undoing shoe laces – some twenty times a day we had to retie them! Then suddenly she stopped needing to do this and gave up the annoying habit – we never found out why. Perhaps it was a particular tooth that had eventually erupted.

You should express displeasure at hand biting; a sharp 'Ouch! No!', probably over-exaggerating the pain felt, as well as giving

■ **Above:** *Short-faced dogs like this Pug can find teething especially painful and you should check their mouths regularly for infection or damaged teeth.*

the puppy something more suitable to bite, will be the best deterrent.

Never let this puppy-biting stop you doing something you want or need to do to the puppy, such as handling or grooming him. If it is really necessary, you can resort to a basket muzzle, which you can put on at such times.

Your vet can supply a suitable muzzle, even for the difficult to fit short-faced breeds.

■ **Left:** *All puppies go through a spell of play-biting, especially when they are teething. When your puppy bites you, cry out in pain so that he realises he is hurting you.*

EDIBLE CHEWS TO HELP WITH TEETHING

1 **Treated real bone:** Ideal for strong and boisterous dogs, will keep them occupied for a long time
2 **Real hide strips:** Strong taste and smell will tempt most dogs but they can become smelly over time
3 **Rawhide strips, bones and toys:** Ideal for most dogs, and especially good for teething dogs as they won't damage the dog's mouth or teeth as they soften easily
4 **Compressed chews and bones:** Most dogs love these but don't give too many at a time as they can upset a puppy's tummy. They also crumble quickly

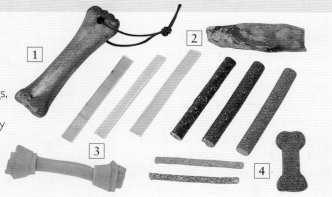

Car travel

It is absolutely essential that your new dog gets used to car travel. Even if you have no need for a car yourself, you will inevitably have to take the dog to a veterinary surgeon and perhaps further afield if you are referred to a specialist practice. Many taxi firms now refuse on principle to carry dogs because of the possibility of hair shedding – dogs do sometimes shed excessive quantities of hair through excitement or fear.

If a friend is kind enough to offer you transport, you want to be confident that your dog will behave well in their car.

Your new puppy should ride home comfortably in someone's arms or, if the driver is alone, in a deep box placed in the front of the passenger's seat. A tired puppy will sleep solidly for many miles, but water should be offered as the atmosphere close to the engine can get dry. In the following days, take the trouble to accustom the puppy to the car very gradually. Park the vehicle in the shade and let the puppy explore the car, then sit on the back seat and attract the puppy to sit with you, perhaps to fall asleep.

The car needs to be perceived as a restful, contented place, so try to keep the excitement rating low, as some dogs do tend to get over-excited when in the car and subsequently will behave badly.

You have to decide where the dog will travel when he is older. If you have chosen a large breed, you will probably consider buying one of the specially constructed and shaped dog crates that are specially designed to fit into the

■ **Right:** *Let your puppy explore the car before you take him on a journey in it. Don't allow your puppy to run around in the car. For his own safety, he should be put in a crate either on the rear seat or in the back of the car. The crate should be well ventilated and always shielded from direct sunlight.*

car luggage area. The advantage is that your dog will have plenty of room, and the wire construction of the crate will act as some protection for him if there should ever be a rear-shunt incident. A smaller dog can ride in a small

■ **Left:** *A specially constructed wire crate that will fit snugly into the back of your car is a good investment. It will protect your dog, keeping him safe, when you're driving.*

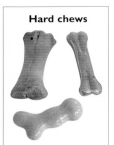

crate placed on the back seat. In either system, the crate may be covered with a light sheet to protect against sunlight and also to prevent the dog watching the road and perhaps objecting to other dogs who are walking or riding past his car.

Drive very gently on the first few 'learning' outings, going only a short distance at a time with a break for a talk and a cuddle at some point during the expedition. Maybe drive to a friend's house nearby and then give your puppy a little time to enjoy exploring their garden before getting back

into the car for the return journey.

If you have a saloon car, then the space needed to crate a very big dog on the back seat may be formidable. The answer is to buy a car harness for the dog, which will fasten on to the attachment for the seat belt. The fastening attaches to a comfortable harness but this must never be attached to a collar or neck chain.

Early in life many dogs tend to drool or be actually car-sick. Dogs are best taken in the car on an empty stomach (very empty), possibly twelve or more hours

after their last meal. Then when the ride's over the dog can be fed as a 'reward'.

If the dog is distressed in the car, do not sympathise. Just clean him up and drive on. Hopefully, he will get over these anti-car sickness reactions in quite a short time, just as children have to. In the meantime, fasten a waterproof bib around him so cleaning him up is not such a problem.

■ **Above:** *No young puppy likes to be left at home alone. Don't leave him for too long and give him some toys and chews to keep him occupied.*

Home alone

Being alone in a room for a short time is another of the lessons that a puppy should learn in his first weeks in your home. Puppies need quiet and rest in any case, so being left along in the kitchen or utility room is a good beginning. Make sure the 'time out' is quite short and do not introduce any element of retribution for bad behaviour.

Tidy up the room unobtrusively before putting the puppy in, remembering that he will purloin and probably chew any object that you have recently handled and which has your scent on it. Line the puppy's crate with some soft material, including perhaps an old garment which you have worn, and leave a soft toy and a nylon chewing bone where they can be found. The door of the crate should be left open. Leave also a small untippable bowl of water. Perhaps leave the radio on, tuned to a talk station so the puppy hears a human voice. Put the puppy into the room, perhaps with a tiny piece of biscuit as a present, then quietly shut the door and walk away. No goodbyes ever, whether you are going out

for ten minutes or two hours.

Dogs are natural pack animals and do not like to be left alone, but most have to endure this experience and they do come to accept it. If your puppy cries when you shut the door, just say, 'Quiet, quiet' and walk away. When he has been quiet for, say, five minutes, open the door and let him out. Your behaviour at this stage is critical; do not make a great fuss of the puppy, just take this whole routine as an ordinary

■ **Left:** *Get your dog accustomed to sitting quietly while you are busy doing other things. It's always a good idea to let him have something he can chew on, such as a nylon chewing bone.*

day-to-day experience. It is also probably a good idea to follow the 'time out' by going into the room used with the puppy and finding something to do there, so that you and the puppy can be companionable together in a quiet situation and he does not link this room with always being left alone. Next day and every day, repeat this routine until the puppy accepts short periods of solitary confinement happily.

As the puppy grows, his owners will probably need to be away for longer periods. It is very important to make your exit and your return very low key. Having unobtrusively tidied the room in which the dog is to be left, making sure that all cupboards are firmly closed, shut the dog in, remembering to leave the radio on quietly, and possibly closing the blinds so that people cannot peer in. Just go, quietly and undemonstratively, without

SINS OF SOLITARY CONFINEMENT

It is really not fair to blame your dog for what he has done in your absence; certainly it is too late to think of a reprimand for something that may have been done an hour ago. So say nothing, but take note, and plan what you can do to prevent more damage occurring again in the same place.

Table or chair legs chewed?
You can buy a liquid, unpleasant to taste but quite safe to paint on wood. Probably the veterinary nurses at your local practice can recommend a suitable product for you to use.

Cupboard open and contents scattered?
This is your fault! You must devise a better fastening.

House plants pulled down and chewed?
Remove them to a safer place – the room where the puppy is going to have to stay alone needs to be stripped of all temptations.

House-training broken down?
If the dog cannot get outside, remember to put down a pad of newspaper in the area which has been soiled.

any impassioned goodbyes which will only make the dog feel that this is a big event.

Your return should be just the same: come into the house, take off your coat and let your dog out of confinement but do not make too much fuss of him. It is a good idea if you both have a short walk around the garden together or a little play, but do nothing that will heighten his excitement.

The barking and/or howling problem

It is normal for dogs to bark a warning when they sense that there are intruders upon their territory. Most of us want our dogs to warn us if there are strangers about or tradesmen approaching the door. But dogs, even tiny dogs, seem to become incensed if anyone approaches their property, and a warning bark can become a tirade and escalate into a howl, and that is when the neighbours start to complain. We want the dog to bark but not to go on incessantly.

For advice on teaching your dog to stop barking and be quiet, turn to the training routine 'Stop barking' on page 78.

■ **Left:** *It is natural for a dog to bark as a warning to people approaching his territory, but he must not bark excessively or your neighbours may complain.*

If your dog barks when you are out, he may have good reason to bark – for instance, if the doorbell is rung or if the telephone rings. Having an answerphone on which you leave a message can be useful for calming your dog; he can hear your voice telling him to be quiet. What your callers may think is another matter! However, if your neighbours complain, you may want to point out that your dog's barking is actually a deterrent to potential intruders and is helping to protect their property, too. Persistent barkers may respond to more exercise, especially in busy town situations where the dog can quickly acclimatize to noises that would cause him to bark if he were left at home alone.

Stop doing that!

There will always be times, within the house or out in the garden, when your dog starts to perform undesirable actions. Digging in the carpet, for instance, standing up on his hind legs to reach a laden table of food, pulling at a cushion or scratching at the back door – an endless list of unwanted behaviour. It is very useful to be able to stop the dog in his tracks without declaring your presence, and this is where an empty can or an already charged water pistol comes in handy. You can throw the can close to the dog without any intention of hitting him, or direct the water pistol at his hind end. It is the startle factor and the projectile that comes from an invisible source which do the trick. Try not to let the dog see the action you are taking. Magic works very well on dogs.

Jumping up

Excitement seems to project a dog into jumping up towards the face and mouth of newcomers, just as very young puppies jump up to the mouth of their mother to get her to disgorge food. It is embarrassing when a dog insists on mobbing a visit or when they have just arrived, but it is difficult to control an enthusiastic dog at this time. Work out a routine to suit you, your house, and your dog. Many people put the dog in the kitchen or another room before letting people in; you say 'This Way, this way' and the dog troops in, knowing that he must not be at the front door when it is opened. You are still making it clear that you have a dog to protect

■ **Left:** *If your dog bothers you and jumps up when you are sitting at the table eating or drinking, it is best just to look away and ignore him. If he cannot get your attention, he will soon give up and stop the behaviour.*

■ **Above:** *Jumping up is an annoying habit – and potentially dangerous if you happen to own a large, boisterous dog. Discourage your dog from jumping up at you and shut him in another room when opening the door to visitors.*

you, as the caller will be able to hear your commands to the dog. In many cases, it is advantageous to let the visitors enter the house and sit down, preferably at a table so that they have some protection when the dog does come in. Ask visitors not to interact with the dog at this stage, and not to make eye contact; let the atmosphere cool until all the excitement has died down. You may then want to put your dog into his crate where he can see and be seen, or perhaps attach a lead to his collar so that you can keep him at the 'Sit' and 'Down', under your control while you talk to your guests.

Safety first

Beware of leaving any dog with guarding instincts alone with a visitor; he might object to the visitor harmlessly handling an object in the room – even an old magazine is sacrosanct to a dog guarding his owner's possessions.

Summary

Careful and thoughtful management of your dog early on will pay out dividends later on; you should end up with a dog who enjoys life to the full but also understands where he stands in the household hierarchy. And you will have the pleasure of knowing that your dog is obedient and anxious to please you but not cringing – a confident, happy dog, created by your sensitive and compassionate training.

USING DOG ABILITIES

Your dog is more agile and more clever than perhaps you will ever realise. Playing with dogs is fun for people, too; we get so little opportunity for carefree play! Dogs enjoy hide and seek, hunt the slipper and other games that stretch their mental powers; seeking hidden objects is well demonstrated by sniffer dogs which find secreted drugs or guns. Your dog, especially if he comes from one of the scenting breeds, can specialize in finding other objects, such as your car keys. Dogs enjoy solving puzzles, too. As an exercise, block the way through a door with some boxes and see how your dog works out his own solution to creating an exit for himself.

You may even want to set up a mini agility course in your garden: a flexible tunnel that the dog has to crawl through, a ladder to climb and a suspended tyre to jump through.

Wrestling with big dogs seems an irresistible game for the young and fit, but remember that a large dog will always win. It is better not to play rough games with dogs with dominant tendencies. Never end the game in such a way that your dog thinks he has won; always end when you say so. 'That's enough' or 'Finish' can be the words you use, but say them calmly, not on a note of panic. Reward the dog when he stops the game on command and bear in mind that you are playing with fire to allow such a game at all. However, it is not a good idea to put yourself in competition with the dog when he has all the attributes to win the contest.

■ **Below:** *Playing games such as hide and seek with your dog will stimulate his mind as well as exercise his body. Mental stimulation helps to prevent boredom and can prevent unwanted behaviour problems developing, many of which may be caused by having nothing to do. Try to make time to play with your dog every day.*

Chapter Five

TRAINING IS FUN

You can make training fun! Like any kind of education, whether it is designed for children or puppies, sometimes the going is hard and sometimes you or your dog may despair of ever getting it right, but the joy of having a well-mannered, happy dog who is a credit to you in any situation is a joy that can scarcely be matched.

The trained dog is a happier dog, too, not always getting into trouble because he has behaved badly without being aware that he is doing so; not always being shut away because he is a nuisance. The dog who has been trained to be a tolerable member of our society flourishes in the approval of his owner and his owner's friends.

The dog is unable to reason that because he is well-trained he gets to go on a lot more outings than the badly-behaved dog, but this is definitely the case. If you can trust your dog to behave well, he can go to the countryside, to parks and interesting beaches. He can walk through spring-time woodlands, and visit all the places where other dogs can be met and enjoyed. The trained dog has a wider social life, and so will you! If both you and your family take

a pleasure in obedience training you may decide to take the skill to further lengths; for instance, you may want to join a local class for more advanced training or even proceed to competition level. However, this progression will have to be deferred until you and your puppy have mastered the initial kindergarten stage.

Get a language

Before you bring your new puppy into your home, draw up a short list of the words that you will use in training him. Make the words as simple as possible, easy to say and distinctive from one another.

You may want to make your word for 'go and pass urine or defecate in the garden, or on the patio' a special and secret code word, so that you can use it anywhere in public without any embarrassment. The Guide Dogs for the Blind Association use the words 'Hurry up!' – as good a praise as any for the purpose. However, remember if you adopt these words not to use the phrase at any other time.

Your language list should then continue with the puppy's name, followed by 'Come!' Usually, just calling his name will suffice, and you can use hand signals to back up your request.

Right: *Your dog or puppy will enjoy training sessions if you make them fun and keep them short. He will always be ready for walking on the lead!*

USEFUL COMMANDS

Here are some useful commands that you should use with your dog. You cannot teach your puppy all these words at once. Introduce them slowly and he will soon learn to respond.

◆ 'Bed' (get in your bed!)
◆ 'Down'
◆ 'Sit'
◆ 'Stay'
◆ 'Good dog'
◆ 'Give it to me'
◆ 'Come on'
◆ 'Outside'
◆ 'Quiet' (to stop barking)

'No!', said sharply, is a very important word; the one you will say when the puppy is about to do, or is actually doing, something that you do not wish him to do.

It's important to make sure that all the members of the family use the same words for the same actions, at least for a year or two. When the dog is an adult and is familiar with what he may or may not do, it's possible to vary the commands a little or, indeed, to do without commands at all.

Most dogs respond to a variety of names later in life – affectionate nicknames – on the basis that it doesn't matter what you call them as long as you call them!

House rules

In the early days of puppy ownership, you should decide what your dog is allowed to do with regard to such basics as going upstairs or not, lying on the furniture or not, or being temporarily enclosed in a crate when the family is busy, when high-powered cooking is going on in the kitchen or when there is any crisis in the home. Decide what precautions you will always take when opening the front door so that there is no risk of the puppy slipping out. All the family must agree on what is forbidden to the puppy; it is no good if most of the family keep the him off the sofa but Auntie allows him to snooze there with her in the afternoons.

Danger zones outside

Talk to all the family about the hazards of the house and garden. What about getting the car out – could the puppy be underneath? Get into the habit of checking up on the puppy, always knowing where he is. What about callers leaving the gates open? Is the swimming pool securely fenced against puppy access? What about hazards within the garden: are there insecticides, poisons and, most of all, slug bait? This is a very dangerous substance, whether it is laid for use or in store in the shed. If there is any possibility that the puppy could escape into

■ **Left:** *It may look cute when your puppy climbs up to look out of the window but when he becomes an adult and more conscious of territorial rights, damage may well be done. Do not tolerate 'chair climbing'.*

your neighbours' garden, ask them if they will be kind enough not to use slug bait. Reinforce your fencing, remembering that the puppy may dig underneath or, later on, go over the top.

Check also that there are no old cans of paint or varnish lying around, and that all the outside drains are properly covered. There is a case recorded of a puppy who got trapped in a drain while some boiling water from a washing machine flooded over him.

A puppy will always investigate everything he comes across, so never think that 'he won't touch that' because the odds are that he will. It is not easy to keep a new puppy off your cherished flower borders or seed beds. The easiest way is to make or buy very low wicker hurdles to make temporary barriers. Puppies find great joy in digging up what you have just lovingly planted and bringing their trophies proudly in to you. Spring bulbs are very dangerous if chewed, as are buttercups, azaleas, foxgloves and discarded foliage from privet and green Leyland Cypress. Knowing what your puppy is doing and stopping him doing it is inevitably a relatively full-time occupation.

Tags and collars

Your puppy must wear a collar with an identity tag when he is away from home, but make sure that it is removed when he is in the garden or in your home, so there is no risk of his becoming hooked up on protruding branches and the like. Never leave a puppy or even an older dog confined in a room on his own while wearing a collar. I know of one unfortunate

dog who got her collar caught on the brass door knob of an old-fashioned cupboard and was in immediate danger of strangulation when she was discovered.

Danger zones inside

Indoors train yourselves to be tidy: hang the teacloth high up out of the puppy's reach; do not leave electric plugs in sockets that are live; and remember that electric leads are very chewable. Be aware that the on-off switches on the cooker hot-plates can be switched on easily by canine paws so you should always turn off the heat-source at the mains before you leave the puppy loose in

■ **Right:** *Another hard day working in the garden. Puppies love to explore and investigate and will happily dig up your flowerbeds and border plants. Train them not to do this at an early age.*

either the kitchen or utility room.

Buy a child-gate for the stairs to prevent the puppy from going up. If he should accidentally climb the stairs, always help him to come down safely step by step. A tumble down the stairs at a young age could not only injure a young puppy but also make him feel inhibited about climbing any kind of steps later on in life.

■ **Left:** *There are many hazards lurking in your home and garden. Almost everything in this garden shed poses some sort of danger to a dog. Never risk your dog having access to household or garden chemicals. It only takes a few seconds for him to lick a chemical or paint container or chew an electric flex.*

HOUSE-TRAINING

This is probably the subject that warrants priority in most households. However, it can also be the most difficult attribute to teach, although every dog varies in its ability to grasp what it is you want done because to the dog there are many inbuilt facets in the acts of urination and defecation. As we have said before, territory marking is important to both dogs and bitches, as is pack-marking – eliminating on the same patch as is used by other dogs of the same breed or the same family. Male dogs do not usually use the leg-lifting marking stance for urination until they reach puberty, perhaps at twelve to eighteen months old. Bitches usually squat to urinate all their lives but may also lift a leg sometimes, especially when marking.

When you first bring your puppy into your home, carry him through into the garden and put him/her down on the patch that you would like to be used for elimination purposes. Try to pick somewhere near the house, as you will be spending quite a lot of time there! You may decide that paving is most easily cleaned, or you may want your puppy to use the grass. Remember that on clay soil bitch urine bleaches the grass in circles but on chalk soil this is not noticeable.

Your puppy will be anxious to urinate after the journey and so you will get a successful result almost straight away. Now say the word you have decided upon and praise your puppy.

You have to start watching your puppy now so that if at all possible you can prevent him soiling in the house. You must always keep the doors to your formal rooms shut unless you are actually in them, so the puppy does not have the opportunity to 'mess all over the house', as complaining owners say.

Taking your puppy out

When a puppy, or a young adult, wakes from sleep and straight after feeding are good times to take the dog outside to be clean. And do please note the emphasis is on taking the puppy out. This means that you go too, rain or shine! It is absolutely useless to push the puppy outside and then leave him to his own devices. He will not be learning anything, except perhaps to wonder why he was suddenly pushed outside in the cold. Go with your puppy; every hour on the hour is a good regime. Stay near the place you have chosen for the pup to use and say the words you have chosen. It takes time but when learnt, house-training is there for life, except perhaps in illness.

Using newspaper

If the weather is bad and the pup is very small, you may decide to use newspaper. This is what the litter would have used when they were still in the whelping box. Although this only postpones the ordeal of garden training until later on, it can be helpful if the weather is bad. Alternatively, you may wish to try out a relatively new product: sheets of white paper backed in plastic which are said to be impregnated with a scent that encourages urination. These are very helpful in winter. To train your puppy to use the newspaper, do the following:
1 Place thick pads of newspaper near the garden door.

Right: *When a puppy, or a young adult, wakes from sleep and straight after feeding are good times to take the dog outside to be clean. Be patient! In the end, the penny will drop!*

2 When your puppy starts sniffing or running around in small circles (both indications that elimination is imminent), pick him up and put him on the newspaper.

Puppy crates

A folding crate made of plastic-coated wire is a modern blessing in helping to keep a puppy, or an older dog, safe and happy. These crates fold down to a flat pack in just a few seconds and are just as quickly erected wherever they are most needed. Puppies and grown dogs love their crates – they are to the dog the equivalent of the primitive den, a safe house from which the dog can see everything that goes on but is out of harm's way. Comfortably furnished with fleece bedding, with possibly a

BE PATIENT

House-training can be a trying procedure; its success largely depends on a human watching the puppy for indications of its needs. Obviously some breeds are quicker to learn and house-train than others – the smaller toy breeds are notoriously slow but the puddles are smaller! When you feel that you are not winning in the house-training race, remember that puppies are a great deal easier to train than human babies. A puppy does not produce involuntary urination during sleep after four weeks of age whereas a child will not be dry overnight until it is four years old. Most puppies are house-trained by the time they are seven months old although the human child takes four years to reach this stage.

Left: *A puppy playpen or crate will not only keep your puppy safe for short periods but will also stop him soiling the house. A wire crate makes a wonderful substitute for a primitive den, and has the advantage that the puppy can see and be seen while being safe from harm.*

rug thrown over the top to cosy-up the inside, the door of the crate can stand open all day for the dog to use as he wishes, or it can be quickly shut and fastened if you want absolute assurance at any time that your dog is totally safe from any potential dangers or unsuitable encounters.

Your first experience of using the crate may well be on the puppy's first night in his new home. The crate may be set up in your living room or bedroom, possibly with a well-wrapped hot water-bottle for comfort, so you have the advantage of keeping the puppy within your observation and yet not intruding too much on your own space. Remember that the puppy will need to be given the opportunity to pass urine and faeces.

Every hour on the hour is a good time schedule to aim at when training your puppy. His natural instinct, and the regime which his mother instituted when he was with his litter-mates, is to get away from his bed for this purpose. If the crate you buy is a large one which will suit the puppy and be very useful for the rest of his life, then it should be possible, while he is still so small, to fill one end of the crate with some newspaper to serve as a place for elimination.

Below: *It may be a good idea, especially during periods of cold, wet weather, to train puppies to urinate on pads of newspaper.*

GET DOWN TO TRAINING

Reward titbits

Dogs respond well to food rewards and it's a good idea when training to keep some small titbits in your hand or pocket. Use dried food, cheese cubes or tiny pieces of cooked, roasted liver.

Literally! Bend or crouch down as near as you can to your puppy's height and communicate on his level. From time to time, pick him up to give him an opportunity to converse with you face to face but on your terms.

You are already training your puppy to interact with you and with other members of the family; the message he gets is that little food rewards and lots of petting and approval come from these people as does the mutual play experience. Life is good with these people and they can be trusted not to hurt or tease him, and to create a secure environment as a basis for further socialization experiences. Let your puppy meet a wide variety of people and carry him outside the home so that he can see and hear the rush of traffic while he is safe in your arms. Remember that until your vet has completed his series of vaccinations and given them time to take effect it is not a good idea to put your puppy down on pavements that are frequented by other dogs or take him to fields or parks used by other dogs.

HEAD COLLARS

A comfortable nylon head collar, such as the Gentle Leader (shown below), will help you to control your dog when walking on the lead and in training. It doesn't hurt the dog and allows you to direct his head and body in the right direction and prevents him pulling.

1 To fit the head collar, push the noseloop over the dog's nose and jaw.

2 Take the collar band round the dog's neck and fasten securely at the back.

■ **Below:** *Get down to your dog's level and praise him enthusiastically when he responds to your commands. Make him want to please you and come to you. If wished, keep a small titbit hidden in your hand.*

■ **Left:** *A well-
trained dog who
walks on the lead
at your side without
pulling is a pleasure
to take out.*

'Sit'

Teaching your dog to sit when he responds to your call is a very useful move, because the sit is a calming finish of the run or gallop

1 Kneel or crouch on the floor to be nearer your puppy's level.

2 Hold the reward over his head so that he must look up to see what you have got for him. Tell him to 'Sit'.

3 He should go into the 'sit' position naturally because he cannot look up without losing his balance. Give him the reward and praise him.

towards you. When your puppy comes in response to your call, the next thing he must learn is to 'sit' on arrival, either in front of you at your feet or by your side. The puppy knows the attitude of 'sit' well – he has been doing 'sits' spontaneously since he was four weeks old. What you have to teach him is the word that you use when you want him to go into this position. A small reward will be necessary to get your puppy's attention initially; special dog treats are ideal. It's a good idea to teach this command while your puppy is still young and eager to respond. The 'sit' is a position that dogs assume readily of their own accord many times a day. The head is held high, the front legs are straight, and the hind legs are folded in a jack-knife position.

Training tips

◆ Never use force at any time when teaching your puppy any basic commands; it is unnecessary and unproductive. Some gentle pressure on the hindquarters is enough to show the puppy what you want him to do.
◆ Never give your puppy the reward until he has assumed the 'sit' position or performed the behaviour you want him to adopt.
◆ As he learns to comply with your command, do not always give the reward but continue to

■ **Right:** *Be careful not to hold the titbit too high or you will encourage your dog to jump up to snatch the reward. Obviously, this is counter-productive.*

GENTLE LEADER – 'SIT'

You can use a Gentle Leader or another head collar to teach the dog to sit. Pull the lead gently forwards and upwards. As your dog's nose goes up, his rear end will go down. Say 'Sit' when it touches the floor and reward him.

praise him and show that you are delighted with your clever puppy.
◆ If your puppy does not assume the 'sit' position immediately, just run your hand down his back in a stroking action and press very lightly at his hip level so that he folds his legs correctly.
◆ Use the word 'Sit' often so the puppy realises what he has to do to get the reward. Then it's 'Good dog' and down comes the reward.

'Stay'

When your dog will go into the 'sit' and 'down' positions when you ask him to do so, you may want to move on to teaching him to 'stay'. This may be a difficult task as the dog's natural instinct is to be with his owner and you are going to ask him to remain at a distance from you, perhaps in distracting circumstances. It's best to put a collar and lead on your dog when teaching 'stay' so that you have some control over him.

1 Begin with the dog in the 'sit' position beside you. Hold your hand up, with the flat of your hand towards the dog, and give the command 'Stay', controlling the dog if needs be by use of the collar and lead every time he attempts to move.

2 Then move yourself, just one pace or two away, and continue giving the 'stay' signal. Keep eye contact with the dog all the time. Praise him and then call him to you.

After a lot of practice you will be able to move a yard or two away, or even further, and the dog will be comfortable that he still has the security of your presence even though you are standing a short distance from him.

Training tips

◆ Do not forget to praise your dog when he has remained correctly in the 'stay' position, and then you can formally break that control by using some release words of your choice – 'OK' will do.
  ◆ Always give the command to break the 'stay'. Never allow the dog to wander away, and do not do so yourself. Later you may want to introduce a distraction, such as some other person walking by, or another dog coming on the scene.
◆ If your dog 'breaks' before you have released

him from 'stay', then take him back to the position he was in originally and start the exercise again. Perhaps you may wish to enhance the reward a little by offering a titbit so that your dog realises that complying with your wishes is well worthwhile.
  ◆ If you intend to train your dog up to competitive obedience level, he must learn to 'stay' for fifteen to twenty minutes, probably along with other dogs but with their owners out of sight.

IMPORTANT

Never forget that the well-meant use of 'stay' may put your dog in danger: he may bolt into a dangerous situation, he may be attacked by another dog, or he may even be 'rescued' by a well-meaning stranger. 'Stay', even when perfected, has limited use for the pet dog outside the home, but it is a useful ploy to keep a dog in a static position while you open the front door or move around the kitchen with a hot pan.

Come when called

When you start out on some more formal training for your puppy or, indeed, an older dog, try to arrange that he does not have the opportunity to get things wrong. Success always pays as far as puppies are concerned, and if your puppy comes straight to you when you call him, welcome him enthusiastically with cries of pleasure. Stroke him and pat his chest and flanks, but don't raise your hand above the puppy with the object of patting the top of his head, as a hand coming down towards a dog can be perceived as a frightening gesture. From time to time, but not every time, quickly produce from a hidden source – a pocket or a waist bag, for example – a tiny food reward.

If your puppy does not come to

TRAINING TIPS

◆ Keep the training sessions short. About ten minutes twice a day, preferably just before meals, is enough formal training while your puppy is young, but if you are teaching 'come when called', every time that you need or want to call the puppy is an opportunity for training him.

◆ Never chase a puppy as a game or because he is tantalizing you by not coming to your call. The odds will be in his favour as he is likely to be faster and more agile at dodging, and trying to catch a laughing puppy can be very frustrating. The best thing to do in these circumstances is to walk away; this takes the advantage away from the puppy, who will find it more attractive to follow you in the end.

◆ The same tactics may be applied when an older dog will not return to you on an off-lead walk. If your dog has this tendency to test your patience and tolerance, practise calling him and putting him on the lead long before it is time to go home, and then after a short time let him off again. Repeat this process so that your dog does not associate the putting on of the lead with the end of pleasure.

1 First of all, tell your dog to sit. Raise your hand with a titbit inside it.

2 Move slowly away, with your hand raised, and keep your dog looking up at your hand.

3 Call your dog to you at the same time as you drop down to his level, which is similar to an invitation to play. Praise him enthusiastically when he reaches you and give him the titbit.

you when you call him, then say nothing but walk away to another place and call him again from there. Remember that you are the clever one with devious ideas, so never let the puppy think that he can defy you or evade you. Nor should you ever get cross, shout or deliver any physical punishment to a puppy no matter what he has done. Just arrange things so that the pup does get his task right and then reward him with lots of praise or even a titbit because dogs learn by finding out what behaviour pays best for them.

Remember that rewards work only if they are given within

seconds of the puppy having done what you have asked him to do. Five minutes later is too late, as the puppy will not then connect what he did with the gaining of a reward, and you may in fact be rewarding behaviour that you did not wish him to do.

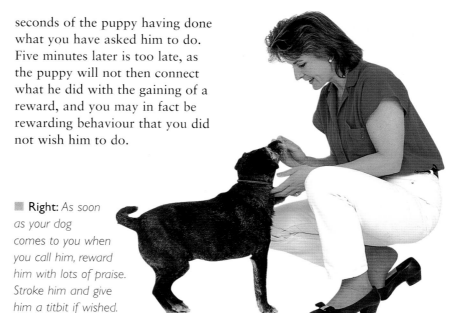

■ **Right:** *As soon as your dog comes to you when you call him, reward him with lots of praise. Stroke him and give him a titbit if wished.*

RELUCTANT PUPPIES

If your puppy is incorrigibly naughty about coming when he is called, then try putting a collar on him and attaching a long line or piece of rope to it. When he takes no notice of your call, gently haul him in towards you by means of the line and then praise him and give him a reward within seconds of his arrival. All manoeuvres must lead to the conclusion that coming to you when you call that magic name ends in good things.

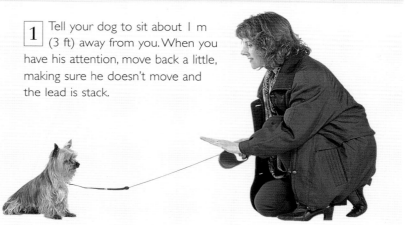

1 Tell your dog to sit about 1 m (3 ft) away from you. When you have his attention, move back a little, making sure he doesn't move and the lead is stack.

Extending leads

A lightweight modern extending lead is ideal for training your dog to come when called. You can gently reel it in as your dog comes to you.

2 Call him to you while gently retracting the lead and showing him the titbit.

3 Reward him immediately with lots of praise and a titbit.

'Down'

This is the next command to be taught. The puppy is required to fold his legs in the 'sit' position, but also to extend his front legs until they are parallel with the ground. The neck is extended and the head is held up high. This is another 'resting' pose which the dog does not mind taking up when he understands what you want him to do.

It's important to limit the words that you use. Take care not to say 'Get down' when you mean to reprimand a dog which is jumping up to greet you.

If you ever want to take part in competitive obedience displays, your dog must be accustomed to a precise word of command for each action he performs.

Training tips

◆ Like the 'sit', this command will have to be repeated many times and in many different situations before it is engraved on your dog's mind but this is easy to practise wherever you may be.
◆ Remember the importance of body language and raise your hand, palm towards the dog, to reinforce the fact that he must stay in the 'sit' or 'down' position until you give your command to release him.
◆ When you are able to add 'stay' to the 'sit' or 'down' exercise you have taught the basics of training which you can elaborate as you wish. Remember you and your dog learn together; congratulate each other when you get it right.

1 Get the puppy to go into the 'down' position by putting him first into the 'sit', holding a reward in the appropriate position above his head. Let him sniff the hand holding the reward.

2 Gradually lower and draw back the hand holding the reward, but keep the reward within your puppy's field of vision throughout.

3 When he moves his front legs forwards to be nearer the reward and his elbows touch the ground so that his body is extended, say 'Down' and give him the reward. Praise him.

Retrieve

This is an action which comes naturally to many dogs; you can start your puppy playing retrieve games as early as eight weeks old. Start indoors, and reserve a specific playtime with the puppy, say about twenty minutes' play before a meal is due.

1 Show the puppy an interesting toy of a suitable size for him to pick up. Make sure that he gets the scent of the toy, and also your scent.

Training tips

◆ Praise and encourage the puppy when he brings back the toy and say 'Give it to me' in a light, happy voice so that he knows that this is play. However, never say 'Give it to me' when he runs off with something you did not intend him to have.

◆ If the puppy is reluctant to come back to where you are, use a long cord attached to his collar and gently pull him in to you. However, most young animals are eager to come to the person who has taken over as their foster-mother or pack leader.

◆ If an older dog, who knows about retrieving, is available it is useful to allow the dog to join in, but do not allow the toy to be picked up and pulled between the two animals, making every game a tug of war, because this is not what you want.

◆ You can develop the retrieve indoors further by deliberately throwing the toy into a 'difficult' position – under a cupboard or on to a low table. Your dog must find the toy by scent.

◆ When the playtime is over, make sure you secure the object that has been played with and put it in a drawer out of sight; this will make the dog more keen and interested for a game next time.

◆ Later your retrieving game can move outside, adding even more interest. As your dog grows up and gets more confident, he may be reluctant to give the toy to you; the remedy is for the human player to go down into a crouching position, offering a small reward biscuit in a hand held out to the dog and giving a lot of praise when the article is given up – the dog will usually drop the toy in front of you.

◆ Don't forget to use a happy voice and happy face to greet the dog. Even if he has not carried out the command as well as you would wish, never get angry or lose your temper. Training a dog is a lesson in owner control, too!

2 Now send the toy skidding across the floor and give the command 'Go fetch'. Almost certainly the puppy will chase after it.

3 As the puppy picks up the toy, say 'Come'. When he brings it back to you, say 'Give it to me' and take it out of his mouth and praise him. Reward him, if wished, with a titbit.

Lead training

'Walking to heel' with your dog off the lead is a somewhat outmoded practice now, and this quasi-military exercise is no longer wanted or needed for the pet dog. What we are aiming for is a dog that will walk quietly by our side on a lead, neither pulling too far forwards or deviating backwards or from side to side. In today's heavy traffic conditions, it is almost never the action of a responsible owner to allow a dog to walk without any lead control on any type of road, even on a supposedly quiet country lane. It is essential that you train your dog from the earliest possible age to walk happily on a lead at your side. If your dog is a pleasure to walk, you will both enjoy going out together and he may even end up getting more exercise.

Make your dog a pleasure to walk

Start with the puppy on a light but firm leather collar. Never use any form of chain collar as it has been found that jerking on a check or choke chain can do serious damage to a dog's throat and larynx. For a few days, just attach the lead to your puppy's collar and leave it loose while he is eating or walking round the garden with you. Make the lead a pleasant thing, not something that your puppy feels obliged to fight. Start formal lead training when you are not going out anywhere! Inside the house or in the garden is ideal, but never when you are on some sort of errand.

Training tips

◆ When you have taught your dog to concentrate on what you want him to do regarding walking by your side, you will want to introduce a command to remind him – you can use the word 'Heel' or 'Here' or 'Steady'.
◆ When he has reached the stage of walking by your side on a

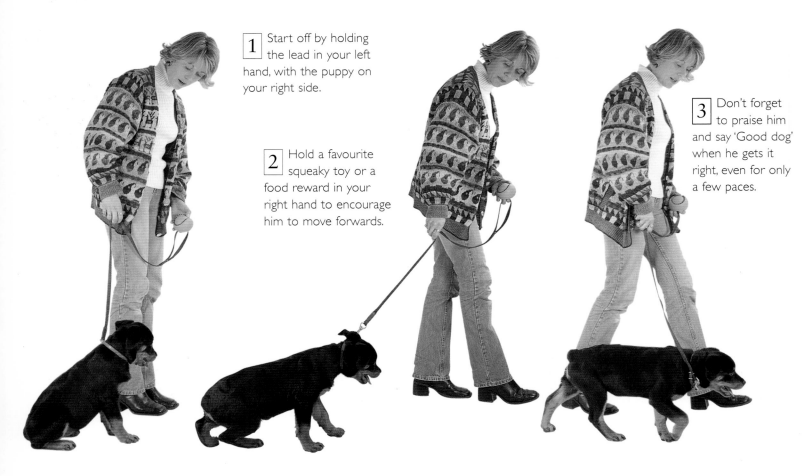

1 Start off by holding the lead in your left hand, with the puppy on your right side.

2 Hold a favourite squeaky toy or a food reward in your right hand to encourage him to move forwards.

3 Don't forget to praise him and say 'Good dog' when he gets it right, even for only a few paces.

public pavement, remember always to have a plastic bag in your pocket, ready to pick up any faeces which your dog may pass. You should even do this on open land if the faeces has been dropped on a footpath where people habitually walk. Dispose of the bag in a discreet spot if there are no bins designated especially for this purpose in the area.

◆ Once your dog is walking steadily, use the 'sit' command when you meet someone coming in the opposite direction or when a loose dog rushes up to you. Keep your dog in the 'sit' position and continue to reassure him until the loose dog is reclaimed by its owner.

◆ Even if your puppy is really

■ **Below:** *If another dog approaches your puppy, keep him in the 'sit' position and reassure him until the loose dog is reclaimed by his owner.*

small, never pick him up when confronted by another dog; the intruder may jump up and you could be caught off balance. Additionally, snatching your dog away from another member of the

canine race tends to build up into a nervous reaction to other dogs. Puppies are usually sacrosanct to adult dogs; a puppy is unlikely to be savaged but will be treated to a curious in-depth inspection.

Leads

A leather handle with a chain that clips on to the collar is ideal for large dogs, but a heavy swinging chain can hurt a smaller dog.

Nylon leads are light and are easily wrapped around your hand to bring the dog close to you for better control.

Cord and rope leads are more comfortable to hold easily for strong pullers, but they do get wet and dirty.

4 Inevitably, the puppy will want to pull forwards; this is when you turn around and walk the other way. The lead should always be slack, never taut.

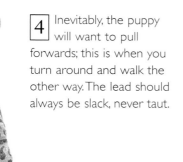

GENTLE LEADER

The Gentle Leader is an excellent form of head collar which gives the owner full control while teaching walking manners. It is also excellent for preventing a dog from lungeing sideways at other dogs he passes in the street. By controlling your dog's head and nose, you can direct his whole body.

'Give it to me'

Whenever your dog succeeds in bringing a thrown or requested object back to you at your command, never go into 'tug of war' mode. It may be a precious object you want back in one piece! Instead, praise your dog enthusiastically for coming back to you and encourage him to give it to you without having to fight for it. If wished, you can reward him with a favourite titbit.

1 When your dog brings an object back to you, don't try to pull it out of his mouth. Praise him lavishly and then tell him firmly to 'Sit'.

2 When he is sitting in front of you, put your hand on the object and say 'Give'. If necessary, open his mouth with your free hand. Praise him when you have the object.

'Stop barking'

It is useful to teach some dogs to stop barking and be quiet. Probaby the most useful command is the word 'No!'. However, if the dog is barking as a warning of intruders, use calming words like 'all right, all right' and then praise him if the barking was warranted.

1 When your dog barks, say 'No!' and get him to go into the 'Sit' position. Dogs rarely continue barking when sitting.

2 When your dog sits down and stops barking, praise him enthusiastically and reward his good behaviour with a favourite titbit, if wished.

'Bed'

Sending a dog to bed should never be used as a punishment. Dogs love their beds and should regard them as a safe place where they can lie and sleep or sit and watch in safety and undisturbed. If you want him out of the way, tell your dog to get in his bed but do so in a happy voice and give him a titbit or favourite toy and praise him when he has settled. Make the bed comfortable with a rug or a fleecey blanket and position it in a draught-free place which is out of direct sunlight.

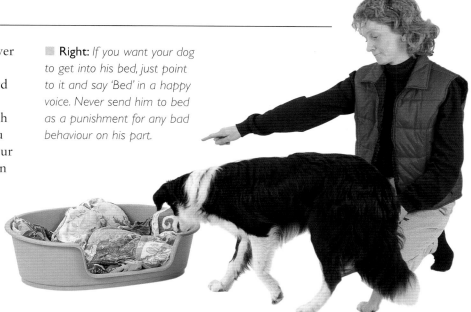

■ **Right:** *If you want your dog to get into his bed, just point to it and say 'Bed' in a happy voice. Never send him to bed as a punishment for any bad behaviour on his part.*

TRICKS TO TEACH YOUR DOG

Most dogs enjoy learning tricks and commands, which stimulate them. Teaching your dog new things will strengthen your understanding of each other and enrich your lives.

'Give a paw'
This is an endearing action. Visitors dote on a dog who gives them a paw in a handshake gesture. You can encourage the voluntary paw-giving that some dogs want to do; in others, you may have to pick up the paw several times. Reward your dog with lavish praise and a titbit when the paw comes up naturally. Always practise this command from the 'Sit' position.

'Come on'
This is the command you will use in the garden or in open countryside when you want your dog to follow you without being on the lead. You must never be so confident in your training skills that you allow your dog off the lead on a road, not even in a country lane where the traffic is very light.

Other tricks and commands
There are many commands and tricks you can teach your dog. He will show you the words he recognises and you can work them into a trick.

■ **Right:** *When the dog offers you his paw, hold it lightly in your hand. Reward him with a titbit.*

Caring for your dog

Your dog will become your life-long companion and you will have to care for him on a daily basis. Not only will you have to feed, exercise and groom him but you will also have to play games with him and arrange for him to be well looked after if you go away on holiday. You also need to know how to keep your dog fit and healthy and thereby prevent many common health problems as well as how to treat them if they occur. In this section, there is expert practical advice on every aspect of looking after your dog.

Chapter Six

DAILY CARE

Recent studies have shown that one of the most important facets of a dog's life is his involvement in the life of the family; the more involved he is, the more integrated he will become, and the more he is spoken to the more he will understand what is expected of him. The dog is a hierarchical animal and he is happiest when he knows his position within the pack – in this case, the human family with whom he lives.

Within the framework of his breed he will, almost certainly, wish to please his 'pack leader'.

Below: Grooming is just one of the many things that you will have to do for your dog. Children will enjoy helping.

It is not fair, however, for you to attempt to persuade a dog to do something or behave in a way in which he is not temperamentally suited; for instance, if he is not genetically a guard dog he should not be forced into guarding. He will do his best but will be unhappy and this unhappiness may manifest itself in a way that's untypical of the breed.

The daily care of your dog is dependent on the breed and the purpose for which the dog was acquired. Thus a companion dog will be treated differently to a dog who was acquired for showing, and he'll be treated differently to a dog who is a working gundog.

Your responsibilities

It is socially irresponsible to allow a dog to run free without the control of his owner. Such dogs can form packs and terrorize their entire neighbourhood; their faeces can contaminate the streets and can cause infections to children. The 1991 Dangerous Dogs Act penalizes owners severely if their dog is adjudged 'out of control'.

For a dog to be a social asset he has to be trained to behave himself in human company as well as in canine company. This requires daily lessons. The length of time it takes depends on the skill of the teacher and the dog's intelligence. So take your dog to training classes that specialize in teaching the Kennel Club's 'Good Citizens' scheme. Your dog will be taught everyday good manners, and children can enjoy learning, too – they receive awards as they achieve higher levels. You can reinforce this training with daily, short training sessions at home.

In peak condition

To stay healthy, fit and happy and to succeed in any activity, a dog needs to be operating at the peak of his condition, and this can be achieved only with the correct feeding, exercise and mental stimulation for the breed. The show dog probably needs more attention at home than pet dogs and working dogs for not only must he be trained to perform in the show ring but he'll need more time spent on his presentation and grooming. The amount of time spent will depend on the type of coat. Lhasa Apsos and Afghan Hounds, for instance, require more grooming than most Terriers.

However, whatever breed of dog you own, you must be prepared to exercise and play with him every day and to groom him at least once a week, depending on his coat type. He will also need to be fed a well-balanced diet which contains all the vital nutrients he needs for good health.

GENERAL HEALTHCARE

Any dog who comes from a caring breeder who pays due concern to the breed's genetic potential for anomalies, should, with regular healthcare, lead a long and healthy vet-free life. For full health, the four main considerations for a dog are:

■ Worming
■ Correct feeding
■ Correct exercise
■ Mental stimulation.

Regular examinations

You should examine your dog regularly. Whenever you groom him is a good time for this. Look especially at the eyes, ears, mouth and genital area for any unusual discharges. If you do notice something odd or out of the ordinary, consult your vet. After any country walks, examine your dog's feet and body for cuts, abrasions, ticks and fleas. If anything is judged to be serious, again consult the vet.

■ **Left:** *Chewing on chews, hard biscuits and bones will help to clean your dog's teeth and keep them strong and healthy.*

Dental care

A puppy's baby teeth will fall out during the first few months but in some toy breeds the baby teeth will persist and the second teeth will not dislodge them. If this happens, veterinary treatment is necessary to remove the first teeth and in order to allow sufficient room for the adult teeth to come through.

Like humans, all dogs produce tartar and plaque. It is thought that this is because of our modern feeding regimes. Should these substances be allowed to build up, they will trap pockets of bacteria which cause gum disease, tooth rot and bad breath in the dog. It may even become necessary for your vet to remove the deposits under a general anaesthetic.

If you start when your dog is young enough, it is relatively easy to train him to have his teeth cleaned; it just needs patience and kindness at the beginning. There are toothpastes that are specially formulated for use with dogs and brushes which are designed for a dog's mouth. Never use your own human toothpaste which is formulated specifically for our use; dogs find these toothpastes offensive.

Hard biscuits are good for a dog's teeth, and there are plenty of chews that are designed for cleaning teeth which are now available from most pet shops. Chewing on a bone is a classic remedy but you should only give your dog big raw marrow bones – never cooked chicken or lamb bones or little bones of any description as they can splinter and pierce the dog's stomach lining, causing death.

If you do give your dog bones, make sure you teach him to give them up to you when requested to do so, otherwise he may become possessive and aggressive.

Caring for eyes

The eyes of some breeds, such as Pugs, protrude slightly and are set forward in the skull. This makes them very vulnerable to scratches from playing in the bushes and running through the undergrowth.

When grooming your dog,

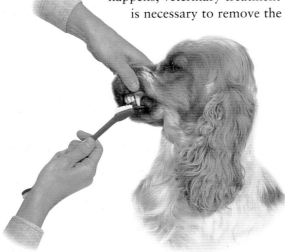

■ **Below:** *You can clean your dog's teeth with a special toothbrush and dog toothpaste. Start doing this when he is still a young puppy.*

examine him carefully for marks on the eyes themselves. Check if there is any excess tear staining of the coat or any deposits in the corner of the eyes. If there is any evidence of scratches, ulcers or infection, such as conjunctivitis, go immediately to the vet. Even if there is no evidence of injury, there may be particles of dust in the eye. If so, bathe the eye gently with some cotton wool soaked in Optrex. Tear staining on a white coat can be removed with special products available from pet shops.

Feet and claws

Should your dog develop a limp when out walking, examine his feet. If there is any damage, then pressure bandages should be applied immediately if the cut is deep, and any significant cut should receive urgent veterinary

WORMING

Both dogs and bitches should be wormed regularly once every six months with a proper veterinary vermifuge. Not to do so can seriously affect the dog's health, resulting in depression, weight loss, hair loss and, in extreme cases, even death. Ask your vet for advice on worming your dog. Note that the faeces should always be disposed of hygienically to protect children from infection. Remember also that it is an offence not to pick up a dog's mess should he defecate in a public place.

■ **Below:** *It is a good idea to trim the long hair growing between the pads of some dogs, especially if it gets matted. Use an ordinary pair of scissors.*

treatment. Check your dog's feet regularly, trimming the hair if necessary. Leave some between the pads but keep it clean. Grass seeds can embed themselves into the pad and migrate up the dog's leg so always check for these in the summer months.

Claws should be kept short. However, great care should be taken when cutting claws as there is a sensitive part containing a vein and to cut into this causes great pain and an outpouring of blood. Before undertaking this task, watch an expert, a caring dog breeder or a vet and ask them to show you how to trim them.

Ear hygiene

Some breeds are more prone to ear infections than others, and dogs with erect ears suffer less than those with floppy ears, the reason being that erect ears allow the circulation of air. Floppy ears trap warm, moist air which is ideal for the breeding of bugs. The first indication of infection is when the dog persistently shakes his head and scratches an ear

deeply and slowly. When this happens it is almost certain that you are already too late to apply home remedies and a visit to the vet is indicated.

The vet will probably prescribe ear drops which should clear up the ear condition fairly quickly. However, failure to do so will certainly result in a dog becoming so irritated that his general health will deteriorate.

You can keep your dog's ears clean by wiping them once a week with an ear cleansing liquid which is available from pet shops or the vet. The excess hair inside the ears of some breeds can harbour mites and so it should be plucked out with your fingers. Do not cut it or the hairs will fall into the dog's ear. Long ears should always be cleaned and combed after exercise, and these dogs should be fed in a tall, narrow dish so the ears are not immersed in their food.

■ **Left:** *You can clean your dog's ears with a specially formulated cleanser. Just aim into the ear canal and squeeze the container gently.*

■ **Left:** *Massage the ear gently with your hand. If wished, use some cotton wool soaked in cleanser to clean the accessible parts of the ear.*

FEEDING YOUR DOG

Feeding, walks and play are the highlights of your dog's day. As he has no control over what he is given to eat, it behoves everyone to give the most nutritious food they can afford. Canines are among the most remarkable of animals as far as food is concerned: they can live on the most unlikely foodstuffs or, rather they can subsist on them, but incorrect or bad feeding will inevitably result in some health problems, such as skin disorders, hysteria, obesity, wasting of the muscles and a shortening of life.

■ **Below:** *A quick test to assess if your dog is overweight is to run your hands down his flanks; if his ribs are not easy to feel or he has no visible waistline, he may be overweight.*

Food requirements are different for every breed and for individual dogs within a breed. They are based on size and energy output, and thus a Hound or a Gundog working in the field needs more food, calories and protein than a sedentary dog of the same breed.

Equipment

Before the advent of complete diets and store-bought frozen foods, kennels needed a great deal of equipment to provide suitable

■ **Right:** *It is very important to feed a dog correctly from puppyhood onwards if he is to be really fit and healthy.*

food. Convenience foods of today obviate a need for any equipment excepting deep freezers and can openers. Most kennels of any size feed a manufactured complete diet or canned foods. If you feed your dog one of the complete diets, remember to store it in mouse-proof containers.

The type of feeding dish has some importance: dogs with long ears, such as Cocker Spaniels and Basset Hounds, should be fed from a tall, narrow dish so that when feeding the dog's ears fall outside the dish keeping them clean and free from potential infection and making it easier to groom them. The very big breeds, such as Great Danes and Irish Wolfhounds, are quite often fed from elevated bowls. The bowl is fitted inside a metal frame which lifts it about 60 cm (2 ft) above the ground. This is thought to ease digestive problems.

Types of dog food

There is a bewildering array of dog food available today, each one claiming to be the ultimate nutritious food for feeding to your pet. However, for the novice dog owner, it is probably more advisable to take guidance from

either your vet or the breeder of your puppy or dog.

◆ **Complete dry food:** This is one of the most popular convenience foods. It is mostly composed of cereals and their by-products, meat from various sources, soya and vegetables, vitamins, oils, fats and minerals, but there may be colourants and preservatives, too. They can be marketed in many forms, such as biscuits, pellets, meal or extruded products.

◆ **Semi-moist foods:** These contain up to twenty-five per cent moisture and, to avoid refrigeration, some preservatives. The composition is similar to that of most other commercial dog foods.

◆ **Canned foods:** These are often more than seventy-five per cent moisture but the best of them are nutritionally complete with similar ingredients to the other dog foods. Unless otherwise stated, most of these foods contain preservatives and colourants. Canned food is mainly made up of meat, offal and tripe, which are augmented by the addition of vitamins and minerals. This food is often accompanied by extruded pellets which are better known as a 'mixer'.

Feeding your dog

The argument as to whether it's better to feed once or twice a day has raged for centuries. Modern thought is that if a dog has food in his stomach he is more likely to be calm and content, and therefore the advice is twice a day. It gives the dog two high points in his day. Most people divide the food into three parts: one part is given in the morning and two parts in the evening. Unlimited fresh water should be available at all times, whatever type of food is served.

Table scraps are not considered suitable food, although there is no reason why meat and vegetable scraps (but not potato or onion) should not be added to a dog's food providing it is not extra to his normal amount.

Some people like to prepare their dog's food themselves. Meat can be served either raw or lightly cooked and accompanied by some vegetables, rice or even pasta. The amounts fed will vary but, as a rule of thumb, a 10 kg (22 lb) dog should have 300 g (10 oz) of meat, 75 g (3 oz) of rice and a similar amount of vegetables plus some vegetable oil and brewer's yeast. The problem is that there may be a deficiency of some minerals and vitamins and it may be necessary to add a high-quality supplement. However, take veterinary advice because over-supplementation may cause health problems.

Most dogs will eat all that is placed in front of them but they should not be allowed to put on excessive weight. Ideally a smooth-haired dog's ribs should just be visible. His calorific input should not exceed his output. Printed

PRE-NATAL AND POST-NATAL FEEDING

A good-quality, balanced diet is of prime importance for a pregnant or post-natal bitch. You should gradually increase her food by about twenty per cent in the last three weeks of the pregnancy and feed it as four meals. As the pups grow inside her, her womb presses on the stomach so several small meals are essential. After the birth, increase the food slowly to about three times the norm, depending on the number of puppies she needs to feed. However, if she has only one or two, she won't need much additional food to produce the milk. After the beginning of the weaning process the amount of food she consumes should be progressively reduced.

quite clearly on all commercially prepared food packaging are the approximate amounts to be given but bear in mind that each dog is different. Thirty per cent of pet dogs are overweight, and obese dogs need special attention as extra weight can reduce their life span. Your vet will recommend a special diet and proper exercise. It is better not to give a dog of any age sweet biscuits, sweets and cakes. Chocolate should be on the banned list as chemicals in it can cause circulatory problems, particularly in small breeds. Give only the treats that are specially formulated for dogs which are available at your local pet shop.

Caring for elderly dogs

Some elderly dogs behave with the vigour of a much younger dog, in which case the usual feeding regime can be followed. However, when the day comes that the dog is not so keen on going for a walk or will only run after a ball a few times before lying down, then it is time to consider his requirements.

Take him to the vet to find out the reason for his deterioration. It may be a failure of his kidneys in which case the vet will advise you to reduce the protein and calorific content of your dog's food. He will also recommend some appropriate supplements. The old dog should not be rejected; every effort should be made to stimulate his mind and make him feel wanted.

He should be gently persuaded to take some exercise; it stands to reason that his intake of food will lessen as his activity becomes less. Give him the food you know that he likes, make an extra fuss of him, and don't be angry with him if he makes a mistake.

■ **Above:** *Scrambled egg is ideal food for an elderly dog or one recovering from a stomach upset.*

■ **Left:** *This elderly Cocker Spaniel has a raised bowl so that he does not have to bend right down to the ground to eat. This is thought to aid digestion.*

GROOMING

There are several good reasons why you should groom your dog regularly. The act of gentle grooming, the passage of a comb pulled through the hair and the brushing, gives a pleasurable feeling to the dog and it assists in the bonding process. It also gives the groomer the opportunity to examine his pet – to look for any skin conditions, cuts, abrasions or discharges. For good hygiene reasons, you must be prepared to pay special attention to the rear ends and muzzles of Old English Sheepdogs and other hairy breeds.

Some coats tangle and matt easily. They are uncomfortable to the dog and a hot bed of infection, an ideal place for bugs to breed which will irritate the dog. Some moulting dogs suffer from matting unless the dead hair is removed; in bad cases this is very painful for an affected dog.

Some breeds require a daily grooming session, whereas others need weekly attention. Smooth-coated dogs only require a twice-weekly brush and polish. Regular grooming, particularly at the time of moulting, will prevent hairs covering carpets and furniture.

Pet grooming and advanced preparation for dog shows can be learnt by anyone. The breed clubs will have grooming charts and will give you advice, and most breed books contain chapters on show preparation and the tools required.

Grooming equipment

■ **Above:** *Shaggy, long-haired dogs will need more grooming than smooth-haired breeds. If your dog has a thick, long coat be prepared to put aside time every week for a long grooming session.*

The amount of equipment you require is in direct proportion to the number of dogs and type of coats. The owner of one or two Poodles, for instance, would need hairdresser's scissors, a good class clipper and several blades, a hair dryer and the correct brushes and combs. Such specialist equipment would be enough to maintain a good-looking coat even to show standard. Show people would have a grooming table, a restraint to stop the dog leaping off and a trolley to carry the grooming gear.

Owners of dogs with wire coats would have the same equipment in addition to stripping knives of various types and sizes, special palm brushes with very short teeth and even a rake for

TOOLS OF THE TRADE

The basic grooming tools are designed for different coat types and the ones you buy will depend on the breed of dog that you own.

1 Wide and fine-toothed combs
2 Soft pin brush
3 Bristle brush
4 Stripping comb

5 Thinning scissors
6 Pointed-end scissors
7 Nail clippers
8 Brush

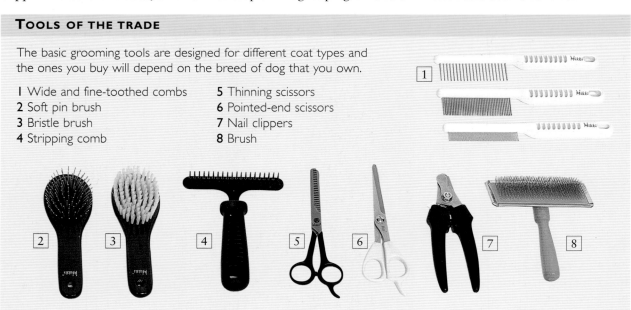

controlling the dog's undercoat.

People who keep many dogs and show them may use a drying cabinet, which is a special box with a wire front in which there are air ducts allowing the hot air to circulate. This speeds up the drying process considerably after bathing a dog for showing. They might also invest in a special bath which makes life easier by having a built-in movable shower head, re-circulating water and a side opening. The dog does not have to be lifted in – he just steps in.

Coat types

Strictly speaking, there are as many coat types as there are dog breeds and there are different types within the breeds. The first division is into three types:
◆ Short-haired (e.g. Dobermann).
◆ Medium-length (e.g. German Shepherd Dog)
◆ Long-haired (e.g. Yorkshire Terrier).
These divisions can then be subdivided into smooth, rough, wire and curly. A further division is soft, medium and harsh. In order to groom all the different types correctly, they all demand special treatment and handling.

With a few exceptions, they all have an undercoat of various textures, thickness and colours.

Some dogs are born with the colour that stays all their life; others change. The Kerry Blue Terrier starts black and finishes blue/grey. Yorkshire Terriers start black and tan and finish blue/grey and golden tan. Puppy hair is fluffy and bears no relationship to the adult hair. Although it can be removed, it's best to wait for it to drop out naturally with brushing.

■ **Above:** *If you own a Dobermann with its distinctive glossy, short-haired coat, grooming your dog will be minimal.*

Short-haired dogs

The hair on short-haired dogs is invariably smooth and relatively thin and usually has a very fine undercoat. It is the easiest coat to care for, needing only a brush to remove any dead hairs and a polish with a hound glove or a chamois leather which distributes the coat oils and gives it a shine.

Although to the touch these short coats appear to be silky, a closer examination will show that the hair is really quite harsh. The fact that it lies flat and close gives the impression of silkiness but stroke it in the opposite direction to the way in which it lies and it is quite spiky. The short coat of a Bullmastiff is said to be hard. The coat of the Shar Pei is described as short and bristly. Most of these coats are self cleaning: they do not absorb water and when they dry any mud or dirt falls off. The smooth-coated Collie has a medium-length smooth coat which, although dense, is harsh to the touch. It is waterproof by virtue of the thick undercoat.

Medium-haired dogs

Dogs with medium-length hair will require more grooming than short-haired dogs but less than long-haired breeds. Most dogs in this category will only need brushing and combing two or three times a week to keep their coats in good condition and to remove mud and tangles.

Long-haired dogs

Long coats are some of the most time-consuming ones to keep in good condition. The softer they are, the more they tangle and the more dirt and debris they pick up. It is not really feasible to keep a long-haired dog in full coat as an ordinary pet. The flowing white coat of the Maltese, the floor-length

■ **Below:** *A long-haired Shetland Sheepdog will need regular grooming on a daily basis to keep his coat healthy, free from tangles and in good condition.*

coat of the Yorkshire Terrier, the sweeping locks of the Shih Tzu present difficulties which can only be solved by the special attention given by breed fanciers.

Most pet owners will keep their long-haired dogs in a short cut, known in some breeds as a 'puppy cut'. It is quite simple to train the dog to stand on a table and, using a pair of good sharp scissors, give him the rough shape of the breed. Dogs prefer to have short hair than to have knotted long coats. Once a year perhaps, they can go to the professional groomer to be shaped properly. Old English Sheepdogs are difficult to maintain and the coats matt very easily. Therefore they are often taken to the grooming parlour to have all the hair shorn off in the manner of a sheep.

■ **Above:** *The adult Yorkshire Terrier has a silky long-haired coat which will need regular grooming even if you don't show your pet dog.*

■ **Right:** *It is easy to hand-strip a Terrier. Just take a few hairs between your thumb and forefinger and pull them out gently. This will not hurt your Terrier.*

Rough-haired dogs

This type of coat consists of harsh, stand-off outer guard hairs and a soft undercoat, whose thickness will vary according to the breed. The Spitz-type dog, such as a Chow Chow, has a very thick undercoat whereas the Rough Collie has much less. All these breeds should be groomed regularly. Dirt and dust gather in the undercoat which should be deep combed.

The area surrounding the anus can become unhygienic and the underneath of the male dogs can be stained with urine. These dogs moult copious amounts of hair which, if left, can get knotted and cause irritation to the dog.

Poodles and wire-haired breeds

Poodles and Wire-haired breeds do not moult. If a Poodle's hair was left to grow it would become corded or felted. Most people keep Poodles in a 'puppy cut' – it is scissored all over to a length of about 5 cm (2 in) with the face, feet and rear end trimmed close to the skin. With practice, most owners can manage this but those who cannot should take the dog to the grooming parlour every eight weeks. For maintenance, the dog should be brushed and combed every day.

Wire-haired breeds need special attention. If the hair is cut it tends to lose its texture and the colour will gradually fade. The proper treatment of the coat is to hand-strip or pluck it. This is an art that can only be achieved with practice and an understanding of the coat growth. For example, the hair on the body of a Welsh Terrier should be just over 2.5 cm (1 in) in length, the neck hair thicker, the head hair very short, and the furnishings on the legs profuse. To achieve this, stand the dog on a table. Hold the skin where the hair is to be removed

■ **Left:** *This Jack Russell Terrier has the rough coat which is typical of many Terriers. It is water-resistant.*

with one hand and, with a stripping knife in the other hand, trap a few of the longest hairs between your thumb and the stripping knife. Pull the hairs out evenly and smoothly without any jerking. Slowly, over several weeks, the required shape appears. Most owners do not go to this trouble; instead they take their dog to the groomers every three months and they clip it into shape.

■ **Above:** *To keep a Poodle in good condition, you will have to trim him regularly or visit the grooming parlour.*

■ **Left:** *Sometimes with very heavily coated breeds, such as this Old English Sheepdog, the coat can be shorn off to varying lengths, depending on how much time you want to spend grooming your dog after a walk in the country!*

Grooming your dog

Grooming your dog should be a pleasurable experience for both of you. Develop a grooming routine when your dog is still a puppy and he will soon come to accept and enjoy this time you spend together. Depending on the breed, you can groom him on your lap, the floor or up on a table.

■ **Right:** *To groom a Poodle's head, brush or comb upwards from the root of the hair. Be careful not to hurt the dog.*

Brushing out tangles

To remove really matted tangles, it is sometimes a good idea to tease them out with your fingers before gently pulling a brush or comb through them.

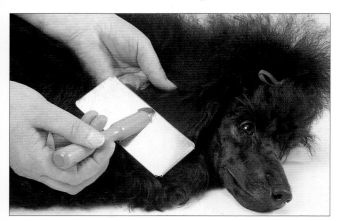

Brushing long ears

Dogs with long ears should have them brushed every day and also checked for tangles and foreign objects, especially after a walk. First tease out any thick tangles at the end of the ear flap with your fingers before you start. Then start at the top of the ears, slowly but smoothly brushing down to the ends. A hand placed under the ear flap at the base of the ear will help avoid pulling on the sensitive skin around the ear opening.

Keep the inside of the ears, especially folded ears, clean with a veterinary product. Excess hair is best plucked out with your fingers as scissoring may allow hairs to fall into the ear.

■ **Above:** *Use a comb to ease out any matted hair and tangles on the ear feathering of Spaniels.*

■ **Left:** *Use a brush to groom the long hair on a Poodle's ears and then tease out tangles with a wide-toothed comb.*

Tails

There are many different styles of dogs' tails, many of which do not require much attention. Very hairy hanging tails probably need most grooming. Carefully cut the hair away from where it touches the dog's anus with sharp scissors, preferably those with a slight curve. Otherwise give the area a routine brush and comb. Keep the folds of skin clean on very short tails, such as the Bulldog's. Wire-haired breeds should have the underside of the tail kept short.

■ **Above:** *When grooming feathering on a tail, use a wide-toothed comb. Don't be rough – always be gentle.*

Rears

Virtually every medium- and long-haired dog needs to have his or her rear end kept clear of excessive hair for obvious reasons. Great care must be asserted as the area is most delicate. Curved scissors prevent accidental 'digging in'. Bitches can suffer staining of the hair on the hind legs, which is known as 'culottes'. Excessive hair growth on the male's penis sheath should be cut very carefully for hygiene purposes.

■ **Above:** *After grooming the dog's tail, check his rear as the hair may need trimming to keep it short.*

Using a slicker

To groom short-haired Hounds and Terriers, you will need to use a slicker or hound glove. Made of rubber, it glides through the coat and massages the skin underneath.

■ **Left:** *You can use a rubber slicker with a handle or a hound glove which fits snugly over your hand for grooming Terriers and Hounds.*

Bathing

It is rarely necessary to bathe the Gundogs, Hounds or Terriers. If they get covered in mud, wait for it to dry and simply brush it off. It is not recommended to wash dogs very often as bathing will remove the oils and other skin secretions that keep a dog's skin and coat healthy. If you do need to bathe your dog, you should follow these simple guidelines.

Bathing your dog

1 Sit a small dog in a bowl or sink and splash with tepid water or pour over him, using a jug. Protect his ears to prevent any water getting inside them. Use a bath for larger dogs.
2 Use a baby shampoo or special dog shampoo to lather the coat, protecting the dog's eyes and ears.
3 Rinse all the shampoo out of the coat, especially around the dog's rear and under his legs.
4 Gently rub your dog dry with a towel and then dry with a hair dryer if he will accept it – some dogs are frightened of the noise that they make.
5 Make sure that your dog is thoroughly dry and don't let him lie in a draught until he is dry.

■ **Left:** *After rinsing thoroughly, wrap the dog in a towel and rub him dry. If he does not mind, dry him off with an electric hair dryer.*

■ **Left:** *Another way to dry your dog is to put him inside a clean zip-up towelling bag after towel-drying him. This will keep him snug and warm until he is thoroughly dry all over.*

EXERCISE

Dogs are running animals and they do need some regular free running for their physical and mental well-being. The amount needed is dependent on their size, conformation, breed and age. When exercising your dog, you need to follow a few basic rules, which are as follows:

◆ Always keep your dog on the lead in public places; it is an offence to allow a dog to be out of control.

◆ Use an extension lead; this allows you to control your dog and, at the same time, gives the dog some freedom.

◆ Never let a dog loose near traffic, no matter how light the traffic and how obedient the dog. However well trained he is, he should be on a lead, not just walking at your side.

◆ Always have a reflective strip on the dog's lead at night so that it will show up in car headlights.

◆ Never allow a dog to run loose near sheep or other livestock; farmers are likely, and legally entitled, to shoot the dog.

◆ Ensure that your dog obeys the commands 'come' and 'sit'; they can save a dog's life.

■ Above: *If your pet dog has been properly socialized he can 'work out'.*

How much exercise?

Hounds, Gundogs, Working and Pastoral dogs generally require a great deal of exercise. They are built to move over great distances and thus a stroll round the block twice a day is unlikely to keep these breeds in their optimum condition. It follows that they are best kept in the country where there is plenty of space for them to run. Swimming is also great fun for most dogs; Gundogs, in particular, enjoy water. You must understand that dogs kept alone do not have the motivation for running about unless they hunt, and it is up to you, the owner, to provide the motivation. Most dogs can take as much exercise as their owner can give, but if you live in a built-up urban area then two good walks a day and a run out at the weekends are the very minimum that you should give your dog.

Don't forget that gardens are also good for exercising dogs, and thirty minutes' playing with a ball or a Frisbee is good exercise for your dog's mind and body.

Terriers, Utility and Toy dogs

Dogs from the Terrier Group and also some from the Utility and Toy Groups are busy, busy dogs who like exploring gardens,

■ Right: *Springer Spaniels need lots of exercise but take care that you don't over-exercise young puppies while their bones are growing.*

sniffing about in the bushes and trees, play-hunting, looking for mice or rats and trying to catch the birds. However, they will still enjoy walking out – seeing new things and smelling new smells. A walk twice a day, and a long run in your local fields or woods and a swim at the weekend do the dog and his owner a great deal of good. These types of dogs are usually very playful up to old age; an hour spent with the children in the garden playing 'catch' or 'hide and seek' as well as exercising them occupies their mind and keeps them out of mischief, especially the Terrier breeds.

Tiny breeds, such as Pekingeses, Chihuahuas and Pomeranians, will need very little in the way of formal exercise – just their normal activities plus some playing in the garden are sufficient. However, they love to go out on excursions, even if it means carrying them.

What surface is best?

There is an ongoing discussion as to which surface is best for dogs: exercise on hard surfaces, such as roads, or soft ground, such as grass. Generally speaking, softer ground is much better because it cushions the impact of the feet and is obviously less stressful on the muscles; it also smells better and there is no chance of being poisoned by exhaust fumes.

However, there are some good reasons for exercising a dog on hard surfaces. For one thing, the nails tend to overgrow if the dog only runs on grass; by walking on pavements the friction against the abrasive surface helps keep the claws short. Long claws force the dog's foot back, causing strain on

the joints of the foot; eventually the pain can cause the dog to limp and he may even be unwilling to go out. Country dwellers would do well to check their pets' claws regularly and either have them trimmed by their vet or do it themselves, providing they have the necessary expertise.

Good movement

The correct movement of a dog is important to dog exhibitors and there are exercises to improve it. The speed at which a human being walks is not the natural pace for most dogs, and they have to learn to walk in a way that is foreign to their conformation. Controlled walking on a lead on hard surfaces will achieve this aim, and it will also harden the leg muscles and strengthen the joint sinews. Dogs generally should have tight feet but, unfortunately, this is not always the case. To tighten the feet, show dog owners will walk their dog on a gravel surface so that the dog will have to clench his toes to stop small pieces of gravel getting up into the tender part of the foot. Eventually the muscles develop and the foot stays tight.

GOING AWAY

It would be an act of cruelty to leave a dog alone in the house, even with sufficient food and water, whilst the owners go away on holiday. Almost certainly it would attract the attention of the police and animal welfare charities and would warrant court action. There is no reason why a pet dog should ever be left at home; he can either be taken along or left in boarding kennels.

What is needed is more research. There are hotels and guest houses that will accept dogs. The tourist information services in towns are always pleased to help and many issue a booklet containing the names of any establishments that will welcome dogs.

Some holiday towns prohibit dogs on their beaches at certain times of the year; the information

services will advise. There are many beaches a little way from the fashionable ones where a dog can run and swim as he pleases. Keep your dog under control in public places and always have enough plastic bags handy to pick

■ **Above:** *Many dogs enjoy car travel and happily accompany their owners on holiday. Many hotels welcome dogs.*

up after the dog – some town authorities are extremely hard on owners who fail to do so.

Travelling

Buses and coaches will only accept dogs at the driver's or conductor's discretion. If the dog occupies a seat, a fee may be charged. Dogs travel on trains

■ **Right:** *Rather than travel alone in the back of the car, your dog can be put in a travel box with a front wire grille on the front seat. For safety's sake, the seat belt can be wrapped around the box and secured.*

free of charge providing they are under control and do not occupy a seat. When flying in Britain and some European countries, dogs are not allowed to travel in the cabin; they travel in appropriate-sized boxes in the cargo section and you are charged a fairly high fee for the privilege. Details are available from the airline or from agents who specialize in the transport of animals.

In a car it is always best to put a dog in a travel box, which is safer for both the dog and driver. Get the dog used to the box by feeding him in it with the door open at first. After a day or so,

close the door. Quite soon the dog will accept and enjoy being in his own box. Go through the same procedure in the car and then drive the car slowly for a couple of hundred yards each day for a week. Go somewhere the dog connects with pleasure: the park, the beach or open ground where he runs. If the dog is travel sick after this training consult the vet, but do not use human remedies.

Feeding the travelling dog

Do not change the dog's food when on holiday; he may suffer an upset stomach. If ordinary and

BOARDING KENNELS

If you decide to place your dog in boarding kennels, you should visit the kennels and inspect them first. If the proprietor is not willing to permit you to do this, then find another kennel. Look for cleanliness, lack of smells and smart attendants. Make sure they exercise the dogs regularly and feed them properly. Check which vet calls on a regular basis and phone him if you're uncertain. Put in writing any special feeding or medication that your dog may require and make sure that he is fully vaccinated, especially against kennel cough.

easily available complete diet or canned food is the norm for a dog there is no need to take food with you. If he needs special food – for instance, he may be elderly with a kidney dysfunction – you would be wise to take the right food with you. For a day out there are food carriers that are specially designed to hold a day's food and water, keeping them hygienic and cool. Frequent stops to allow the dog to stretch and relieve himself should be made; if the day is hot, offer him water regularly.

Hot days

All dogs suffer badly from heat, especially thick-coated, short-nosed and black ones, so on hot days take ice packs or bags of frozen peas to place on the heads of overheated dogs. Never, under any circumstances, leave a dog in a car in the sun. Even with the windows open, he can be 'cooked' to death in a short time. If a dog shows heat distress his tongue will loll fully out, he will pant deeply and be unwilling to move. Pack him with ice, immerse him fully in cold water and then get him to a vet as a matter of urgency.

Elderly dogs

Unless an old dog is full of vigour it would not be fair to take him

■ **Right:** *With a dark thick coat and short nose, this Lhasa Aspo will have to be watched carefully on hot days when you are travelling.*

on a long journey. It's no problem if he is used to particular boarding kennels and you are satisfied with the service and treatment. If not, he can be placed in the home and care of a trusted friend whom he knows and who will feed and exercise him in the way that he understands. Alternatively, you can engage the services of a dog sitter. Advertised in the pages of the canine press are people who make a living by staying in dog owners' homes and looking after their animals. Be sure to take up their references before making a decision. You should not rely on a neighbour popping in to feed and exercise him – he is not their dog and they can too easily forget.

PET PASSPORT SCHEME

From early in the year 2000 it has been possible for dog owners to take their pets on holiday in the EU countries and some other designated rabies-free countries. However, there are some stringent rules to follow:
◆ A microchip must be inserted.
◆ The dog must be vaccinated against rabies.
◆ The dog must be blood tested thirty days after vaccination.
◆ You must have a MAFF PETS (Re-entry) certificate confirming the above six months after the blood test gives positive results.
◆ Twenty-four to forty-eight hours before your return, the dog must be treated against ticks and other parasites and have a veterinary certificate to prove this.
◆ You must sign that the dog has not left the qualifying countries. Everything must be in order on your return; if not, the dog will have to go into quarantine. These regulations are subject to change. You must obey any local regulations applying to the countries you are passing through and the country in which you are staying. For instance, if you stay in France for more than one month your dog will have to be tattooed according to the French law.

The nearest MAFF office will advise of the exact requirements as far as British and foreign regulations are concerned. Your vet should be able to advise about any unusual diseases with which your dog may come into contact and the steps you can take to avoid them.

Take your dog's usual food with you and break the journey regularly so he can relieve himself. Dogs are often better received in Europe than in Britain but not all hotels accept them. The local Tourist Information Office will be the best guide.

Chapter Seven

HEALTHCARE

The arts of medicine and surgery that relate to the dog, whether it's a Cruft's champion or a rescued foundling, are now very highly sophisticated veterinary specialities. The actual health problems that can afflict the species are being intensively researched and much is known about both how similar and how different dogs are compared to other animals or to humans when they are unwell or in trouble.

An intricate machine needs a skilled mechanic. So do not be tempted to tinker with your dog. Our aim in this section of the book will be to explain certain symptoms and what you should do about them, and to give you some simple, useful first-aid with an emphasis on the 'first'. It is very important that you seek veterinary help for all but the mildest and briefest conditions. The basic principles behind the commoner diseases of dogs, are outlined, together with the ways in which the vet counter-attacks these afflictions.

However, in all of your pet's ailments, whether they are mild or serious, you will normally have to be prepared to do something, usually acting as a nurse, and there are some essential nursing techniques to be learned. These are explained later in this chapter (see page 126) so that you are armed with the knowledge and also the basic skills to look after a sick dog with loving care.

■ **Left:** *The specialist terminology for the dog's anatomy is shown here.*

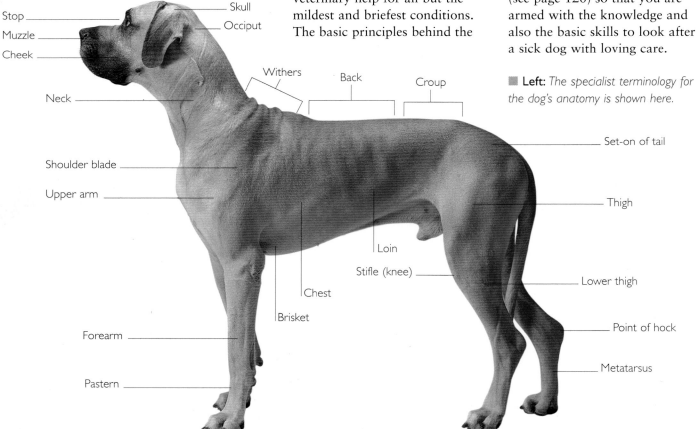

Stop — Skull
Muzzle — Occiput
Cheek —
Neck —
Withers — Back — Croup
Shoulder blade —
Upper arm —
Set-on of tail
Thigh
Loin
Stifle (knee) —
Lower thigh
Chest
Brisket
Point of hock
Forearm —
Metatarsus
Pastern —

WHAT TO LOOK FOR

As already advised, it is a good idea to examine your dog regularly and to check for any warning signs of potential health problems. If you know what to look for, this is a good way of preventing ill health or identifying tell-tale symptoms early enough to treat them effectively before they become more serious. Check your dog over once a week – when you are grooming him is usually a good time to do this. If you handle him in this way from an early age, he won't mind you opening his mouth and peering into his ears and eyes when he grows older and bigger.

A healthy dog should always look healthy, be bright-eyed and full of energy and always ready for a walk or a game. He should not be too fat nor too thin and should have a healthy appetite. Any changes in his normal appearance, temperament and behaviour should be analysed carefully as they may be clues to present or future health problems. Watch out especially for persistent scratching and licking, which may be caused by parasites, allergies, injuries or skin inflammation.

WARNING SIGNS

Here are some of the signs of poor health that you should look out for. If you think your dog is unwell, contact your vet.

- Loss of appetite
- Asking for food but not eating
- Eating more without weight gain
- Sudden weight loss
- Increased or excessive thirst
- Reluctance to exercise
- Limping and holding up a paw
- Decreased agility
- Pain on movement
- Discharge from eyes and nose
- Persistent cough
- Bad breath
- Yellowish-brown, cracked or missing teeth
- Bleeding, swollen or sore gums
- Persistent scratching
- Obsessive licking
- Skin inflammation
- Skin abscesses
- Dull coat
- Bloated abdomen
- Dragging the hindquarters
- Diarrhoea
- Vomiting
- Constipation

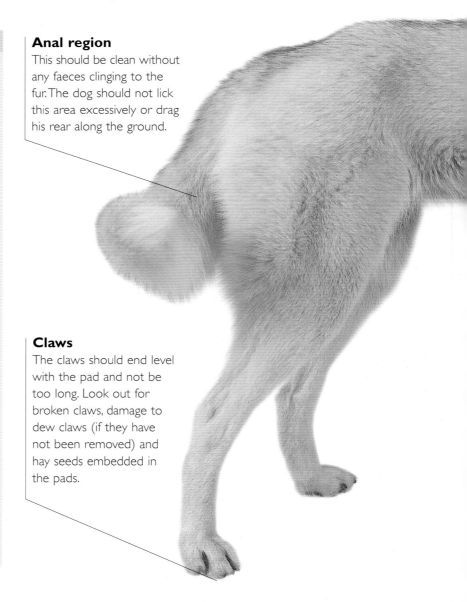

Anal region
This should be clean without any faeces clinging to the fur. The dog should not lick this area excessively or drag his rear along the ground.

Claws
The claws should end level with the pad and not be too long. Look out for broken claws, damage to dew claws (if they have not been removed) and hay seeds embedded in the pads.

Ears

They should be responsive to any sound. The insides should be pale pink with no visible wax nor an unpleasant smell. Your dog should not shake his head excessively nor scratch his ears too often.

Eyes

The eyes should be bright, alert and without any signs of discharge, swelling or tear stains. A tiny amount of 'sleep' in the inner corners is quite normal.

Nose

The nose of a healthy dog should be cold and damp without any discharge. Occasionally there may be a little clear fluid.

Teeth

Healthy teeth are white and smooth, not yellow, which is a sign of plaque and tartar formation. The breath should not smell unpleasant and there should be no loose or missing teeth or inflamed or bleeding gums.

Body

The dog's body should be firm and well-muscled. He should not carry excess weight nor be so thin that his ribs stick out.

Coat

The coat should be in good condition and should smell pleasantly 'doggy'. It should be glossy and pleasant to touch. When you part the hairs, there should be no signs of fleas' droppings or sore or bare patches.

CHECKING YOUR DOGS'S WEIGHT

Feel your dog along the flanks. You should be able to just feel his ribs under his skin. However, they should not be visible.

HEREDITARY DISEASES

There is a wide variety of diseases in dogs, as in humans, that can be inherited, and these may occur in both pedigree and cross-bred animals. Caused by genetic faults or aberrations, they may appear to a lesser or greater degree in any individual of a particular breeding line, or they may even be absent altogether in some litter members or whole generations.

The genetic background to this type of ailment can be highly complicated and it is the concern of the professional dog breeders, veterinarians and geneticists. Screening tests are available for tendencies to some hereditary diseases and potential owners of dogs, particularly pedigrees, should discuss the lineage and history of the dams and sires concerned and of the specific breeding kennel involved with the breeder and their vet before purchasing a puppy. Although some hereditary diseases are treatable, the underlying genetic faults cannot be eliminated.

Here are some of the best known hereditary diseases with the breeds most commonly affected. This list is not exhaustive.

HIP DYSPLASIA

Hip dysplasia is one of the most common inherited diseases and affects many breeds. In a normal, healthy dog the hip is a 'ball and socket' joint and allows a wide range of movement. The rounded end at the top of the femur fits tightly into the cup-shaped socket (acetabulum) in the pelvis. In hip dysplasia a shallow acetabulum develops with an irregular, distorted femur head and slack joint ligaments. There can be excessive movement between the femur and pelvis, leading to a malfunctioning joint that will gradually become arthritic.

◆ Early symptoms
If a puppy develops severe hip dysplasia he may have difficulty walking. Getting up from a sitting position may be painful and he will cry out. When he runs, he may use both hind legs together in a 'bunny hop' or look as though he's swaying. These symptoms may be identifiable from five months onwards. Mildly affected puppies may show no signs at all of hip dysplasia at this age, but later on they will begin to develop arthritis at about eight years of age.

◆ Hip dysplasia scheme
The British Veterinary Association and the Kennel Club run a joint scheme (the BVA/KC hip dysplasia scheme) based on hip scoring. The vet submits the X-ray, bearing the KC registration number of the dog, to the scheme. Each hip is scored from 0 to 54, making a total of 108 maximum between the two hips. The lower the score the better, and 0:0 is the best score possible.

You should not breed from a dog or bitch with a higher hip score than the average for the breed if Hip dysplasia is ever to be reduced or eliminated from that breed. When buying a puppy, check that both parents have been X-rayed, scored, and achieved a low score. This does not guarantee that the puppy won't develop hip dysplasia, but it does reduce the chances.

◆ Treatment
If mild hip dysplasia is treated in a growing puppy with anabolic steroids, limited exercise and diet, he will often grow into a healthy adult. However, you may have to restrict his exercise later on, too. In severe cases, surgery is available.

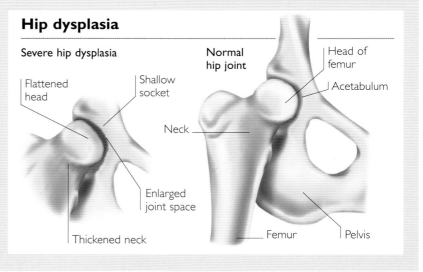

Hip dysplasia

Severe hip dysplasia

Flattened head

Shallow socket

Enlarged joint space

Thickened neck

Normal hip joint

Head of femur

Acetabulum

Neck

Femur

Pelvis

COMMON HEREDITARY DISEASES

Disease name	Nature of disease	Breeds most commonly affected
Bone/skeletal diseases		
Hip dysplasia	Deformation of hip joint	Labrador, other Retrievers, German Shepherd
Elbow dysplasia	Deformation of elbow joint	German Shepherd, Afghan Hound
Osteochondrosis dessicans	Disease of joint surfaces, particularly shoulder	Larger breeds, including Border Collie, Golden Retriever, Great Dane, Labrador Retriever
Wobbler syndrome	Malformation of neck bones	Great Dane, Dobermann
Eye diseases		
Entropion	Inturned eyelids	Many breeds but particularly Shar Pei
Ectropion	Out-turned eyelids	Clumber Spaniel, St Bernard
Cherry eye	Enlargement of gland in third eyelid	American Cocker Spaniel
Progressive retinal atrophy (PRA)	Degeneration of retina with progressive loss of sight	Irish Setter, Springer Spaniel
Collie eye	Another degeneration of the retina	Collie, Shetland Sheepdog
Glaucoma	Increased pressure within the eye	American Cocker Spaniel, Poodle
Cataract	Cloudiness of lens in the eye	Poodle, Labrador Retriever, Golden Retriever, American Cocker Spaniel, Beagle
Cardiovascular diseases		
Subaortic stenosis	Narrowing of the aorta with effects on heart	Boxer, German Shepherd, German Short-haired Pointer, Newfoundland
Pulmonic stenosis	Narrowing of pulmonary artery with effects on heart	Beagle
Ventricular septal 'hole in the heart' defect		Bulldog
Patent ductus arteriosus	Heart defect	Poodle, German Shepherd, Collie, Shetland Sheepdog, Pomeranian
Bleeding disorders		
Haemophilia	Clotting defects	Many breeds
Von Willebrand's disease	A special form of haemophilia	Golden Retriever, German Shepherd, Dobermann and Scottie
Neurological diseases		
Cerebellar atrophy	Degeneration of the cerebellum in brain	Many breeds, including Rough Collie, Kerry Blue, Gordon Setter
Deafness		Border Collie, Boston Terrier, Bull Terrier, Collie, Dalmatian, English Setter, Old English Sheepdog
Hydrocephalus ('water on the brain') and epilepsy		Both can occur in many breeds and are suspected of having a genetic cause
Hormonal diseases		
Hypothyroidism	Underactive thyroid gland	Beagle, Dobermann, Golden Retriever
Cushing's Disease	Overactive adrenal glands	Poodle

GOING OUT OF TUNE

Like Alice I shall begin at the beginning and look at the mouth of the dog and then together we shall wander from head to tail through the various systems of the canine body.

Remember that many common diseases and health problems can be avoided if your dog is looked after properly and receives regular exercise and a high-quality diet. By checking your dog regularly for tell-tale signs of illness or poor health, you can prevent many occurring or treat them at an early stage before they become serious. You should also ensure that your dog is vaccinated against canine distemper, canine parvovirus, leptospirosis and infectious canine hepatitis.

The mouth

Common symptoms

- Salivating (slavering)
- Pawing at the mouth
- Exaggerated chewing motions
- Tentative chewing as if dealing with a hot potato
- Bad breath

What you can do

This important sharp end of the animal should be inspected from time to time to see that all is in order. Cleaning of the teeth once or twice weekly with cotton wool or a soft toothbrush dipped in salt water (or toothpaste from a tube kept specially for your pet) will stop the build-up of troublesome tartar.

Special dog toothpaste, in various flavours that appeal to the animals, is now available. Giving chewable things like 'bones' and 'chews' made out of processed hide (available from the pet shop) and the occasional meal of coarse-cut, raw butcher's meat will also help. Providing bones of any kind does not keep tartar down.

The teeth and jaws

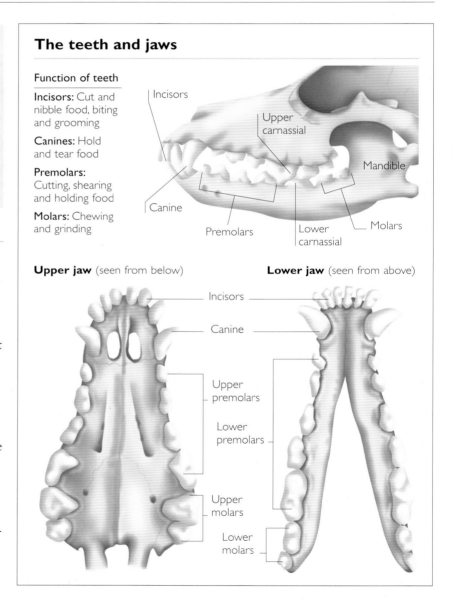

Function of teeth

Incisors: Cut and nibble food, biting and grooming

Canines: Hold and tear food

Premolars: Cutting, shearing and holding food

Molars: Chewing and grinding

Incisors

Upper carnassial

Canine

Premolars

Lower carnassial

Mandible

Molars

Upper jaw (seen from below)   **Lower jaw** (seen from above)

Incisors

Canine

Upper premolars

Lower premolars

Upper molars

Lower molars

Tooth anatomy

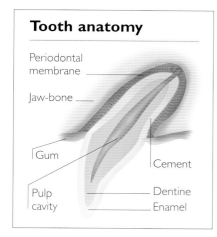

Periodontal membrane

Jaw-bone

Gum

Cement

Pulp cavity

Dentine

Enamel

Tartar

When tartar, a yellowy-brown, cement-like substance, accumulates, it does not produce holes in the teeth that need filling. Instead it damages the gum edge, lets bacteria in to infect the tooth sockets and thus loosens the teeth. Tartar always causes some gum inflammation (gingivitis) and frequently bad breath.

If your pet displays any of the symptoms described, then open his mouth and look for a foreign body stuck between his teeth. This may be a sliver of wood or bone stuck between two adjacent molars at the back of the mouth or, quite commonly, a bigger object jammed across the upper teeth against the hard palate. With patience, you can usually flick such foreign bodies out with a teaspoon handle or a similar instrument.

Gingivitis

Bright red edging to the gums where they meet the teeth, together with ready bleeding on even gentle pressure, are the prime signs of gingivitis. Tap each tooth with your finger or a pencil. If there are any signs of looseness or tenderness,

wash the mouth with some warm water and salt, and give an aspirin tablet. There is little else you can do without professional help.

Broken tooth

Sometimes Fido breaks one of his teeth, perhaps by fighting or by chewing stones (a bad habit that some dogs get into). The large 'fang' teeth (canines) are most often the ones damaged. These injuries do not usually produce any signs of toothache, root infection or death of the tooth. Treatments used in human dentistry, such as fillings, root treatments or crowning, may be necessary and are all possible.

Ulcers and tumours

Mouth ulcers, tumours (juvenile warts are common in young dogs) and tonsillitis need veterinary diagnosis and treatment where they are the cause of some of the symptoms listed above.

At the vet's

Canine dentistry is easily tackled by the vet. Using tranquillizers or

The teeth and jaws

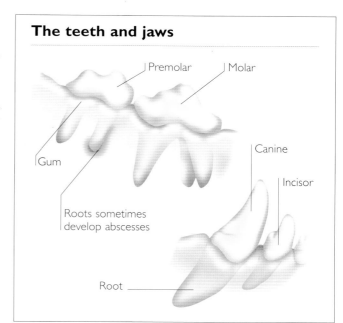

Premolar

Molar

Gum

Canine

Incisor

Roots sometimes develop abscesses

Root

short-acting general anaesthetics, your vet can remove tartar from a dog's teeth with special scrapers or the modern, ultra-sonic scaling machines. Antibacterial drugs, including antibiotics, may also be prescribed by the vet if encroaching tartar has provoked secondary gum infection.

Bad teeth must be taken out to prevent root abscesses and socket infection from causing problems, such as septicaemia, sinusitis or even kidney disease, elsewhere in the dog's body.

■ **Left:** *Periodically check the lip pouch on soft-mouthed dogs, such as Cocker Spaniels, as they may contain leftover food which can cause bad breath and lead to infection.*

The eyes

Common symptoms

■ Sore, runny or 'mattery' eyes
■ Blue or white film over the eye
■ Partially or totally closed eye or eyes

What you can do

If only one eye is involved and the only symptom is watering or a sticky discharge without marked irritation, you can try washing the eye with boracic acid powder in warm water once every few hours, followed by the introduction of a little Golden Eye ointment (obtainable from the chemist) onto the eyeball. If any symptoms in or around the eyes last for more than a day, take the patient to the vet.

Distemper

Particularly in young dogs, two mattery eyes may indicate distemper (see page 109).

Eye conditions

Persistent watering of one or both eyes can be due to very slight

The eye

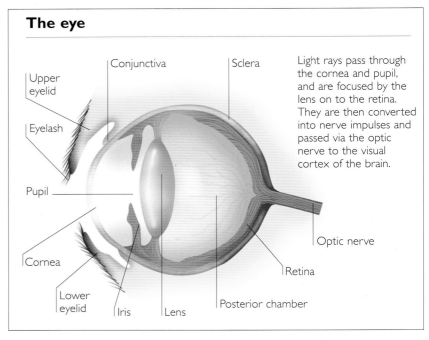

Upper eyelid
Eyelash
Pupil
Cornea
Lower eyelid
Iris
Lens
Conjunctiva
Sclera
Optic nerve
Retina
Posterior chamber

Light rays pass through the cornea and pupil, and are focused by the lens on to the retina. They are then converted into nerve impulses and passed via the optic nerve to the visual cortex of the brain.

infolding (entropion) of the eyelid, or blocked tear ducts. A blue or white film over one or both eyes is normally a sign of keratitis (inflammation of the cornea); this is not a cataract but requires immediate veterinary attention. Opacity of the lens (cataract) is a blue or white 'film' much deeper in the eye. It usually occurs in older animals but may be seen in young pups (congenital cataract) and also at other ages (diabetic cataract).

Inflammations of the eye

These are treated by the vet in a variety of ways. Antibiotic injections, drops and ointments are available, plus other drugs to reduce inflammation and surgical methods of tackling ulcerated eyes under local anaesthesia. Problems due to infolding or deformed eyelids, foreign bodies embedded in the eyeball and even some cataracts can be treated surgically nowadays.

GIVING EYE OINTMENTS

There is an important technique in applying ointments to animals' eyes.

1 Hold the tube parallel to the eyeball and pull the lower eyelid down slightly. Let 1 cm (½ in) of the ointment fall onto the eyeball or inside the lower lid.

2 Now hold both lids closed for five seconds to allow the ointment to melt and begin dispersing.

The nose

Common symptoms

- Running, mattery nostrils
- The appearance of having the human common cold
- A cracked, sore, dry nose-tip
- A dog 'with a cold', particularly if both eyes and nose are mattery, may well have distemper

What you can do

Don't let the nostrils get caked and clogged up. Bathe them thoroughly with warm water and anoint the nose pad with cold cream. If there is the 'common cold' symptom, seek veterinary advice at once. Old dogs with cracked, dry nose pads need regular attention to keep their nostrils free and to deal with bleeding from the cracks. Bathe the nose frequently, apply cod liver oil ointment twice or three times daily and work it well in, and give six drops of Abidec (from the chemist) or multivitamins as prescribed by the vet. The vet may use corticosteroid preparations on tough cases of sore noses.

Rhinitis and sinusitis

Sneezing, a mattery discharge from the nostrils, head shaking and, perhaps, nose bleed may indicate rhinitis (inflammation of the nasal passages) or sinusitis (inflammation within once or more of the sinus chambers in the skull). Bacterial, viral or fungal germs, foreign bodies, growths, tooth abscesses or eye disease can be the cause, and treatment again depends on precise diagnosis.

SINUSITIS

Like humans, dogs possess air-filled spaces in the bones of their skulls (sinuses) which can become diseased. Infections or tumours can occur in these cavities. Sometimes an infection can spread into them from a bad tooth root nearby. The signs include sneezing, persistent nasal discharge that may be purulent or blood-tinged, and head shaking.

The veterinary surgeon can X-ray the head to investigate the problem and treatment can involve anti-bacterial or anti-fungal drugs., surgical drainage or dental work as appropriate.

The ears

Common symptoms

- Shaking the head, scratching the ear
- Pain on touching the ear, bad smell, discharge from the ear
- Tilting the head to one side
- Ballooning of the ear flap

What you can do

Where the symptoms suddenly appear, an effective emergency treatment is to carefully pour a little warmed (not hot) liquid paraffin into the ear – but do this outside in the garden. Acute inflammation will be greatly soothed by the oil. Don't stuff proprietary liquids into an ear; you don't know what you may be treating. Most of all, avoid those so-called canker powders as the powder bases of these products can cause added irritation by forming annoying accumulations that act as foreign bodies.

Prevention

Clean your dog's ears once a week. If it is a breed with hair growing in the ear canal (such as a Poodle or a Kerry Blue) pluck the hair out between finger and thumb. Don't cut it. Using 'baby buds' or twists of cotton wool moistened in warm olive oil, clean the ear with a twisting action to remove excess brown ear wax. See the vet early with any ear trouble. Chronic ear complaints can be very difficult to eradicate.

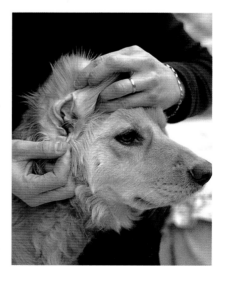

- **Left:** *Check your dog's inner ear flap once a week and carefully pluck out any unwanted hair.*

Anatomy of the ear

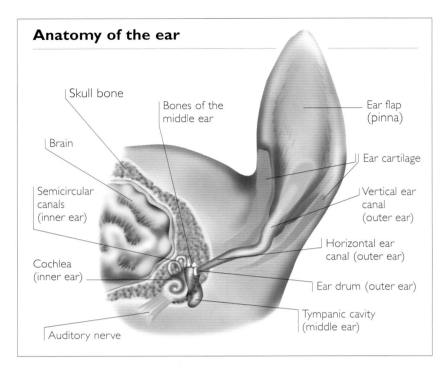

- Skull bone
- Brain
- Bones of the middle ear
- Ear flap (pinna)
- Ear cartilage
- Semicircular canals (inner ear)
- Vertical ear canal (outer ear)
- Horizontal ear canal (outer ear)
- Cochlea (inner ear)
- Ear drum (outer ear)
- Tympanic cavity (middle ear)
- Auditory nerve

Grass seed in the ear

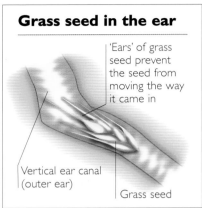

'Ears' of grass seed prevent the seed from moving the way it came in

Vertical ear canal (outer ear)

Grass seed

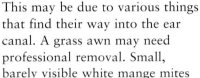

■ **Below:** *To remove surface wax from a dog's ear, gently use some twisted cotton wool. If the dog is holding his head to one side, you may suspect a foreign body in the ear. If so, seek your vet's help without delay.*

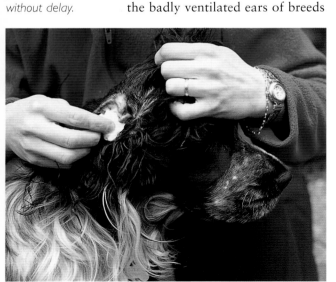

Ear irritation

This may be due to various things that find their way into the ear canal. A grass awn may need professional removal. Small, barely visible white mange mites which live in dog's ears cause itching and allow bacteria to set up secondary infections. Sweaty, dirty conditions, particularly in the badly ventilated ears of breeds such as the Spaniel, provide an ideal opportunity for germs to multiply. The vet will decide whether mites, bacteria, fungi or other causes are the main source of inflammation, and will use antiparasitic, antibiotic or antifungal drugs as drops or injections. Where chronically inflamed ears are badly in need of drainage, sophisticated plastic surgery under general anaesthetic is often performed.

Middle-ear disease

Although tilting of the head may be due simply to severe irritation on one side, it can indicate that the middle ear, the deeper part beyond the eardrum, is involved. Middle ear disease does not necessarily result from outer-ear infection but may arise from trouble in the Eustachian tube which links the middle ear to the throat. It always requires some rigorous veterinary attention with the use of antiflammatory drugs, antibiotics and, more rarely, deep drainage operations.

Ballooning of an ear flap

This looks dramatic and serious but isn't. It is really a big blood blister, caused by the rupture of a blood vessel in the ear flap. It generally follows either vigorous scratching where ear irritation exists or a bite from another dog. It is treated surgically by the vet, who may drain it with a syringe or open it and then stitch the ear flap in a special way to prevent further trouble.

Aural haematoma

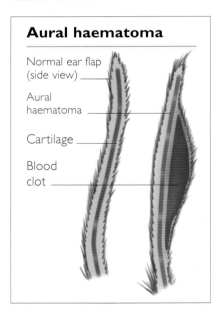

- Normal ear flap (side view)
- Aural haematoma
- Cartilage
- Blood clot

The chest

Common symptoms

- Coughing
- Wheezing
- Laboured breathing

Dogs can suffer from bronchitis, pleurisy, pneumonia, heart disease and other chest conditions. Coughing and sneezing, the signs of a 'head cold', possibly together with mattery eyes, diarrhoea and listlessness, may indicate the serious virus disease, distemper.

Distemper

Although commoner in younger animals, it can occur at any age and shows a variety of symptom combinations. Dogs catching distemper can recover although the outlook is serious if there are symptoms such as fits, chorea (uncontrollable limb twitching) or paralysis, which suggest that the disease has affected the nervous system. These may not appear until many weeks after the virus first invades the body, and can be the only visible symptoms.

What you can do

Make sure you have your dog vaccinated against distemper at the first opportunity and keep the annual booster dose going. At the first signs of generalized illness perhaps resembling 'flu' or a 'cold', contact the vet. Keep the animal warm, give him plenty of liquids and provide some easily digestible nourishing food. If necessary, spoon in invalid food such as meat jelly or glucose and water. Give an aspirin, but don't waste your time or money on patent 'cures'.

The vet, using clinical methods of examination, can confirm or deny the presence of distemper. Being caused by a virus, the disease is very difficult to treat. Antibiotics and other drugs are used to suppress any dangerous secondary bacterial infections. Vitamin injections strengthen the body's defences. The debilitating effects of coughing, diarrhoea and vomiting are countered by drugs which reduce these symptoms.

Other types of chest disease can be investigated by the vet using a stethoscope, X-rays, laboratory tests and electrocardiographs.

Coughs

Where troublesome coughs occur in the older dog, give $1/2$–2 codeine tablets three times a day, depending on the animal's size, but see the vet.

Heart disease

It is common in senior canine citizens and often responds well to treatment. Cheap drugs, such as digitalis and theophylline derivatives, can, under careful veterinary supervision, give a new lease of life to those dogs with 'dicky' hearts.

It is useful in cases of heart trouble and indeed in all older dogs to give vitamin E in the synthetic form (50–200 mgm per day depending on the animal's size) or as wheat germ oil capsules (2–6 per day).

Bronchitis

Inflammation of the tubes that conduct air throughout the lungs (the bronchi) can be caused by a variety of bacteria and viruses, parasitic lungworms, allergy, inhalation of dust, smoke or foreign bodies or by overdoing

The respiratory system

The larynx, trachea, lungs and bronchi, together with the nose, make up the dog's respiratory system. Air is inhaled through the nose, filtered and passed through the larynx into the trachea. It enters the lungs through the bronchi, which subdivide into bronchioles and end in alveoli, or air sacs. Oxygen and carbon dioxide are exchanged in the alveoli.

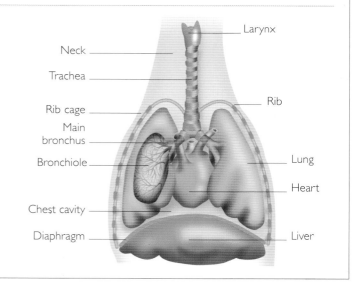

Neck · Trachea · Rib cage · Main bronchus · Bronchiole · Chest cavity · Diaphragm · Larynx · Rib · Lung · Heart · Liver

the barking. Specific therapy is applied by the vet after making a diagnosis and sometimes, in the case of foreign bodies, surgery or the use of a fibre-optic broncho-scope is necessary under general anaesthetic.

Kennel cough

This condition is caused by a bacterium (Bordetella) or viruses (Canine parainfluenza virus, Canine herpes virus, Canine adenovirus) or a mixture of these. The signs are a dry cough, often

with sneezing and a moderate eye and nostril discharge. Laboratory tests are available for confirmation of diagnosis and dogs can be protected by Kennel cough vaccines administered by injection or, in some cases, as nasal drops, after four to six weeks of age.

Pneumonia

There are numerous causes of pneumonia in dogs, the commonest being infections by micro-organisms such as viruses or bacteria. Migrating parasitic

worm larvae and inhalation of foreign bodies are less frequent causes. The signs are faster and/or more laboured breathing, cough, a raised temperature and, sometimes, nasal discharge. By using the stethoscope and tapping the chest the vet can quickly make a diagnosis and begin treatment with antibiotics, corticosteroids, 'cough' medicines and other medication aimed at relieving symptoms. Pneumonia, whenever diagnosed, or even suspected, always demands immediate professional attention.

The heart and circulatory system

As with human beings, dogs can suffer from heart ailments and these can either be congenital (the animal is born with a defect such as a 'hole in the heart' or an unwanted 'extra' blood vessel,

most commonly in the form of a patent ductus arteriosus) or be acquired (developing during life as a result of infection, trauma or the animal's advancing years, etc.).

Signs of heart and circulatory

problems can include early tiring when the dog is exercised, fast or laboured breathing, a rapid pulse, swelling of the tummy (due to an accumulation of dropsical fluid or enlargement of the liver), cough, particularly during the night, pale or unusually highly coloured gums and weight loss.

The veterinary surgeon will use the stethoscope to detect any heart murmurs, blood tests, the electrocardiograph, X-rays and perhaps other specialized medical equipment in order to arrive at a diagnosis.

Treatment again depends on precise diagnosis and dog owners should seek professional advice early on. Heart stimulant drugs, diuretics to dispel any fluid accumulations and preparations that dilate the breathing tubes and stimulate respiration are widely used. A good low-salt diet and, where necessary, slimming down of the patient may well play an important role in the handling of such cases.

How the heart works

The dog's heart consists of two pairs of chambers: the atria and ventricles. Deoxygenated blood enters the right atrium and is then pumped out through the right ventricle to the lungs where it is oxygenated. This blood flows into the left atrium and from there through the left ventricle to the body's organs.

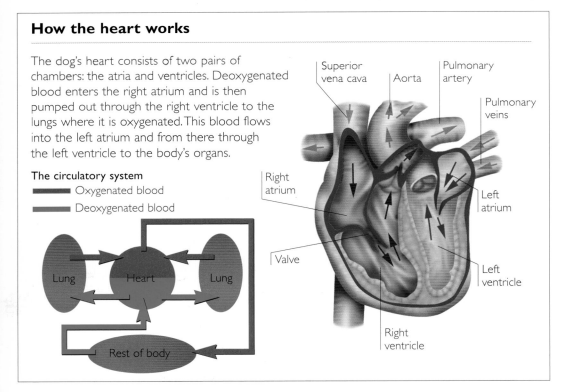

The circulatory system
▬▬ Oxygenated blood
▬▬ Deoxygenated blood

Lung   Heart   Lung

Rest of body

Superior vena cava   Aorta   Pulmonary artery

Pulmonary veins

Right atrium

Left atrium

Valve

Left ventricle

Right ventricle

The stomach and intestine

Common symptoms

■ Vomiting, diarrhoea, constipation
■ Blood in the droppings

There are numerous causes for any of the symptoms listed above and sometimes more than one symptom will be observed at the same time. I shall only deal with the commonest symptoms and not attempt to describe all the diseases that can involve the abdominal organs.

Note: Any symptom persisting longer than twelve hours despite sensible first-aid treatment needs urgent veterinary attention.

Vomiting

Vomiting may be simple and transient due to a mild infection (gastritis) of the stomach or to simple food poisoning. If severe, persistent or accompanied by other major signs, it can indicate the presence of serious conditions, such as distemper, infectious canine hepatitis, leptospirosis, a heavy worm infestation or an obstruction of the intestine.

Diarrhoea

This may be nothing more than the result of a surfeit of liver or a mild bowel infection. It may be more serious and profuse where important bacteria are present, in certain types of poisoning and in some allergies.

Constipation

This can be due to age, to a faulty diet including too much chomped-up bone, or to obstruction.

Blood in the stools

This can arise from a variety of minor and major causes: from nothing more than a bone splinter scraping the rectal lining to the dangerous leptospiral infection.

What you can do

By all means, try to alleviate the symptoms, but if they persist you must contact the vet no later than the following day.

With both vomiting and diarrhoea, it is important to replace liquids lost by the body. Cut out solid food, milk and fatty things. Give a little fluid – best of all, glucose and water or weak bouillon cube broth – and often. Ice-cubes can be supplied for licking. Keep the animal warm and indoors. For vomiting, administer 1–3 teaspoons of Milk of Magnesia, depending on the dog's size, every three hours.

Don't use castor oil on constipated animals. Give liquid paraffin ($1/2$–2 tablespoons). Where an animal is otherwise well but you know it to be bunged up with something like bone which, after being crunched up, sets like cement in the bowels, get a Micralax enema from the chemist. This disposable, small, ready-loaded enema is very easy to use; just take off the top and insert the nozzle into the animal's rectum. Then squeeze, using half the contents for a toy breed and the full enema for all other sizes.

Abdominal conditions in general will need veterinary attention. Diseases such as contagious canine hepatitis and

The digestive system

Rectum
Pancreas
Duodenum
Gall bladder
Liver
Anus
Colon
Spleen
Pylorus
Oesophagus
Small intestine
Stomach

Above: *If your dog refuses to take his medicine, you may have to give it to him through a syringe (needle-less). If he resists, you can make a temporary muzzle and then administer the fluid into the cheek pouch behind.*

leptospirosis require intensive medical attack with antibiotics, transfusion to replace fluid, vitamins and minerals.

Acute abdomen

The sudden onset of severe pain, vomiting with or without diarrhoea and the collapse of the dog into shock is a major emergency that necessitates immediate veterinary attention. The cause may be a powerful, rapidly-developing infection, obstruction of the intestine by a foreign body or a twist of the bowel itself, torsion (twisting) of the stomach, acute kidney, liver or uterine disease or poisoning. Successful treatment depends mainly on quick diagnosis.

Flatulence

'Windy' dogs may be the product of a faulty or changed diet. Often flatulence is associated with food that is too low in fibre although, paradoxically, too much fibre can cause a similar effect.

What you can do

Generally, adjusting the diet to one of high digestibility and low residue will do the trick. Helpful medications available from the chemist are bulking agents such as Celevac and dimethicone preparations (Asilone, etc.). Adding bran to the dog's food will alleviate many cases.

Malabsorption

Some dogs with chronic diarrhoea (often rather fatty looking), associated with a strong appetite but loss of weight are not able to digest or absorb their food normally. The causes may be due to enzyme deficiency (liver or pancreas faults) or disease of the bowel walls.

The vet will employ a variety of tests to establish the cause and will then prescribe the appropriate therapy. Animals deficient in pancreatic enzymes can be given pancreatic extract supplements with their food.

Polydipsia and polyphagia

Polydipsia (drinking more that normal) and polyphagia (eating more than normal) can be associated with diabetes, disease of the adrenal glands, kidney disease and other conditions. Careful examination of the patient together with laboratory tests on blood and/or urine samples are necessary to pinpoint the cause and so lead to the correct treatment.

Salmonella infection

The newspapers are full of 'salmonella scares'. Salmonella is a type of bacterium that occurs in a wide variety of strains (serotypes) which may cause disease in, or be carried symptomlessly by, almost any species of animal. Sometimes

---

PARVOVIRUS INFECTION

Only recognised for the past twenty-two years, this virus disease is spread via the faeces (droppings). It only affects the Canid family which includes dogs, wolves and foxes (although the latter are fairly resistant to it). The incubation period is five to ten days and the symptoms vary from sudden death in young pups, through severe vomiting, foul-smelling diarrhoea (often bloody), absence of appetite and depression to mild, transient bouts of diarrhoea.

The vet can confirm a diagnosis of parvovirus by means of a laboratory test of the faeces.

Professional treatment includes the use of fluid replacement, anti-vomiting and anti-diarrhoea drugs (such as the ever-useful kaolin) and antibiotics to combat secondary infections.

Puppies can be vaccinated against parvovirus from twelve weeks of age (older dogs and pups over twelve weeks of age) or six to nine weeks (young pups under twelve weeks; these will, however, need re-vaccinating at twelve weeks). Combined vaccines that give 'all in one' protection against Distemper, 'Kennel cough', Infectious canine hepatitis and Parvovirus are available.

salmonella can be found in the droppings of apparently normal healthy dogs. Dogs can contract salmonellosis with signs of diarrhoea (sometimes bloody), vomiting, stomach pain and collapse, sometimes ending in death, by eating infected food (meat, eggs, etc.), or by coming into contact with rodents or their droppings or other infected dogs or, more rarely, reptiles or birds.

Diagnosis is made by the vet sending away samples for bacteriological culture and identification. Treatment is by means of specific antibiotics, fluid replacement, etc. It is worth remembering that salmonella infection in animals may be transmissible to humans.

Anal glands

Common symptoms

■ Rubbing the bottom along the floor or suddenly chasing the rear end as if stung by a bee

Two little glands, one on each side just within the anus, cause a lot of trouble for dogs. Worms are usually blamed as the cause but they rarely are. The anal glands are at the root of the problem, since they tend to get blocked up and impacted. By rubbing his rear end on the floor the dog will often clear the glands and relieve his irritation. However, if the glands become infected, anal abscesses can result which may mean antibiotic therapy from the vet and, in chronic cases, surgical removal of the glands.

What you can do

Exercise the glands by ensuring the dog produces bulky motions. Add fibrous foods, e.g. vegetables, to the diet. Mix a teaspoonful or two of bran or IsoGel granules with meals once a day for bulk. Learn from the vet how to clean out the anal glands by squeezing them with a pad of cotton wool.

The liver

The liver is the largest organ in the dog's body and one performing dozens of varied functions essential for life. It can be the site of a number of 'distinct' diseases.

Hepatitis

Hepatitis, or inflammation of the liver, comes in two main forms: acute and chronic.

Signs of acute hepatitis can include vomiting, loss of appetite, abdominal pain and sometimes, but not invariably, jaundice.

Chronic hepatitis is more subtle with a more gradual onset and longer duration. Signs can include weight loss, a swollen tummy due to fluid accumulation, jaundice, poor appetite and sluggishness.

The causes of both kinds of hepatitis are, once again, many and varied and include viruses, bacteria and certain poisons. The vet will use urine and blood tests, X-rays, ultrasound and sometimes a procedure called needle biopsy to investigate a faulty liver. Treatment will depend on the cause.

What you can do

Apart from specific therapy which is prescribed by your vet, it is always important to support undamaged liver cells and encourage their multiplication by giving a correct diet. This normally should contain high-quality protein and plenty of carbohydrates including sugars.

Vitamin supplementation is helpful as is the administration of silymarin preparations (milk thistle) which are available from health food shops.

Chronic liver disease

Characterized by jaundice, loss of weight, fluid accumulation in the abdominal cavity and sometimes neurological symptoms, chronic disease of the liver can follow hepatitis, hormonal disease, tumour development or cirrhosis.

The vet will diagnose and treat this condition as in chronic hepatitis.

Infectious canine hepatitis

This condition, which is caused by a virus is also known as Rubarth's Disease. It is a serious disease that can present the symptoms mentioned above in Acute hepatitis as well as a blue-white 'film' of the corneas of the eyes in the later phases as a dog recovers.

Treatment is as for acute hepatitis (see page 113) in general. Antibodies can be injected in the form of canine gammaglobulin preparations. As ever, prevention is better than cure and all puppies should be vaccinated against the disease.

This can be done by means of a vaccine that also protects against other important infection such as canine distemper when the puppy is three months of age. It may be used at an earlier age only on veterinary advice but will, in that case, need repeating at twelve weeks or a little later. Booster vaccinations should be given annually to maintain protection.

Leptospirosis

There are two main types of Leptospiral infection that affect dogs. One of these, Leptospira icterohaemmorhagiae, attacks principally the liver and the other, Leptospira canicola, is associated with interstitial nephritis of the kidneys. Both are bacteria. Symptoms of the two forms can sometimes resemble one another.

The liver form, often picked up from contact with rat droppings or urine and with an incubation period of five to seven days, produces fever, vomiting, thirst, painful abdomen, diarrhoea (often bloody), increased redness and blood-flecking of the gums and jaundice. Treatment, which must be given quickly, includes specific antibiotics, antiserum, fluid therapy and drugs to suppress vomiting and diarrhoea.

Again, vaccination, along with the canine distemper shot, and annual booster doses will give excellent protection against this serious ailment. Leptospira icterohaemmorhagiae can infect humans so care and good hygiene are absolutely essential when you are handling canine Leptospira patients.

Jaundice

Yellow gums, mouth lining and eye membranes often indicate a significant liver problem but there are other possible causes including certain blood disorders, poisons that destroy red blood cells and disease of the pancreas.

Jaundice always requires immediate veterinary attention.

■ **Above:** *Make sure you have your dog vaccinated at the correct age and thereafter have a booster injection anually.*

Urinary system

Common symptoms

■ Difficulty in passing urine
■ Frequent urination
■ Blood in urine
■ Perhaps increased thirst

What you can do

Although kidney disease is a major area of canine medicine, it is outside the scope of normal owner treatment. Wherever and whenever you notice that there is something wrong with the dog's waterworks, you must see the vet. Inflammation of the bladder (cystitis), stones in the bladder or associated tubes and kidney disease are common and need immediate professional advice. Whatever you do, don't withhold drinking water from an animal with urinary problems.

Leptospira

The commonest and most important disease of the dog's kidneys is infection by Leptospira canicola, a bacterium. As with the liver form of Leptospirosis, the infection of human beings by contact with dogs suffering from the disease is possible.

Dogs contract Leptospiral nephritis mainly through contact with some infected urine. The incubation period is four to twelve days. Symptoms can be acute with loss of appetite, depression, pain in the 'kidney' (lumbar) area of the back, vomiting, thirst, foul breath and mouth ulcers, or more chronic with thirst, loss of weight, frequent urination and, sometimes, hind leg weakness.

The vet will confirm a diagnosis by means of blood and urine tests. The treatment involves specific antibiotics and supportive measures. Protect against this disease by vaccination from six weeks with annual booster shots.

Kidney disease needs careful management and supervision of diet. Chronic kidney disease patients can live to a ripe old age if the water, protein and mineral content of the diet are regulated, bacterial infection controlled, protein loss minimized and stress of any sort avoided. Prescription diets for chronic kidney cases are available from the veterinary surgeon and good pet shops.

Cystitis

This inflammation of the bladder generally responds well to treatment with antibiotics, such as ampicillin, perhaps together with medicines that alter the acidity of the urine and urinary sedatives.

Calculi

A diagnosis of stones (calculi) in the urinary system can be confirmed by X-ray or by ultrasound and, in most cases, the stones are easily removed surgically under general anaesthetic.

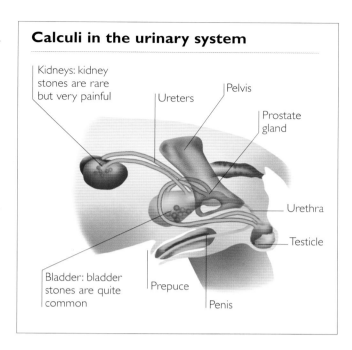

Calculi in the urinary system

Kidneys: kidney stones are rare but very painful

Ureters

Pelvis

Prostate gland

Urethra

Testicle

Bladder: bladder stones are quite common

Prepuce

Penis

Brain and nervous system

Via the intricate network of nerves that extends throughout the body the brain monitors and controls the myriad functions that make up life. But this amazing communications system no less than the infinitely cruder man-made internet, can go on the blink. As with humans, canine neurological disorders form a complex and frustratingly difficult field of medicine.

Inflammation of the brain (encephalitis)

Common symptoms

■ Seizures
■ Changes in personality
■ Depression/dementia
■ A range of nervous signs or failures of nervous function
■ Head pressing and pawing (usually indicating pain)

What you can do

Seek professional attention at the earliest opportunity. Give older dogs a diet of high-quality protein which contains plenty of vitamins and minerals, and have a medical check on them annually. The possible causes of encephalitis are numerous. They include virus infections, such as distemper or rabies, bacterial infection, tumours and so-called 'old dog encephalitis' which may be the distemper virus raising its ugly head in later life.

Other things that don't actually inflame the brain but can produce similar symptoms by affecting the nervous system in general are poisons, such as lead, strychnine and car anti-freeze, and advanced liver disease which produces high levels of toxic ammonia in the affected animal's blood.

The vet will make a diagnosis which is based on a careful

clinical examination together, as required, with X-rays, electro-encephalography and analysis of cerebro-spinal fluid. Treatment depends on cause and will usually mean a combination of specific drugs, such as antibiotics, and symptomatic drugs, such as corticosteroids and diuretics to reduce brain swelling. Special methods and antidotes can be employed where the poisons are producing encephalitis-like symptoms in the dog.

Epilepsy

Epileptic 'fits' are caused by electrical discharges, which could be described as 'shortings' in the 'wiring' of the brain's cells (nerves) and connections.

Symptoms include convulsions, loss of consciousness and collapse occurring usually when the dog is asleep or at least relaxed. They can last a few seconds or several minutes. Animals very rarely die while they are 'in a fit'. Before and after an epileptic episode the dog may be depressed, badly behaved or confused.

Causes are canine distemper (late stage), encephalitis, brain tumour, tetanus, severe kidney or liver failure or, in post-parturient bitches, eclampsia (see page 150). Some epileptic cases are of totally unknown origin.

What you can do
When an epileptic episode begins remove all stimuli from the dog's surroundings. Dim the lights, turn off the radio or TV and do not touch, stroke or generally fiddle with the patient. It is not in pain although it may be upsetting to watch. Do not try to administer tots of whisky or aspirins. When the animal comes out of the 'fit' contact your vet to arrange an appointment.

Veterinary treatment will be targeted at the cause of the epilepsy if this can be determined. In most cases anti-epileptic drugs such as primidone (Mysoline), barbiturates, certain hormones etc. will be prescribed. These may have to be

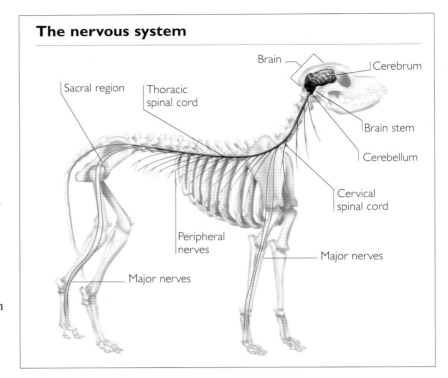

The nervous system

- Brain
- Cerebrum
- Sacral region
- Thoracic spinal cord
- Brain stem
- Cerebellum
- Cervical spinal cord
- Peripheral nerves
- Major nerves
- Major nerves

administered for a long period, perhaps for life, but they are very effective and, often, quite cheap.

Paralysis

Dogs can lose the use of parts of their body suddenly or gradually. The reasons are many and varied. Hind leg or hind end paralysis is one of the commoner and most alarming forms of paralysis. The

dog literally 'goes off its back legs'. This may be associated with pain in the back (lumbar) region or absence of sensation anywhere in that part of the body.

The causes include prolapsed intervertebral disc ('slipped disc'), particularly in long-backed breeds such as Dachshunds, spinal injury or inflammation, poisoning, distemper, eclampsia (see page 150) and pyometra (see page 119).

Medical treatment or surgical intervention will be indicated depending on diagnosis. In my opinion paralytic conditions which do not definitely begin to improve within three weeks of onset generally have a poor prognosis. If they do begin to improve many months may pass before total or maximum possible recovery.

What you can do
Paralysed limbs are liable to be damaged by trauma, abrasion or, in bilateral hind-leg paralysis, scalding

---

OVER-EXCITABILITY

Some dogs of certain breeds, blood-line, up-bringing or personal character show a tendency to marked excitability, to being a bit 'over the top'. Careful selection when acquiring a dog and the services of a training class or animal behaviourist may help to avoid or correct such individuals.

But over-excitability, hyper-excitability, nervousness, call it what you will, can be abnormally excessive. Causes include psychological aberration (a behaviourist's help is essential), hypersexuality and poisoning (e.g. snake bite, strychnine, lead and certain insecticides). The vet will endeavour to pinpoint the precise cause and give specific treatment. In general, sedatives and tranquillisers will also be prescribed.

by urine. 'Bed-sore' type ulcers may arise. Protective dressings, silicone-based barrier creams and extra-soft bedding can be useful during the healing phase. Severely paralysed animals can get into all sorts of trouble and be an embarrassment to themselves. Sometimes owners will go to great lengths to construct devices such as wheeled trolleys to enable their paralysed pets to live contented lives, but in many cases where more than one limb is out of action for many weeks, euthanasia is the kindest solution.

Skeletal problems

Arthritis and associated conditions

Common symptoms

- Lameness
- Difficulty in rising
- Stiff, slow or unusual gait
- Painful spots on bones or joints

What you can do

Most importantly slim down an overweight dog by modifying his diet (reducing the carbohydrates and fats), feeding special canned slimming rations, desisting from giving sweets, chocolates and other titbits and increasing his exercise gradually.

If you are too soft-hearted, ask about joining your vet's pet slimming programme. Expert guidance will be provided and your dog's progress monitored by regular weighing. Avoid taking the dog out in very cold or wet weather and consider giving him a snug coat for outdoor use. Make sure that he receives his daily multivitamins and minerals and give elderly dogs, in particular, 1–4 capsules or teaspoonsful (depending on size) of halibut liver oil daily.

Arthritis arises as a result of nutritional faults, congenital weakness of certain joints, over-use/excessive wear, injury and, in some cases, infections. Obviously it is commoner in senior citizen canines. Similar symptoms can, on occasion, be caused by fractures, abscesses, tumours or poisons, such as Warfarin.

Your vet can investigate by clinical examination, X-rays and, if appropriate, drawing off a little joint fluid for laboratory analysis including bacteriology.

Treatment

Treatment by medication is similar to that in humans: corticosteroids, non-steroidal anti-inflammatory drugs and various analgesic, such as aspirin, flunixin, ibuprofen and phenylbutazone, and, if indicated, sedatives.

Massages, perhaps using certain anti-inflammatory gels or creams under the supervision of your vet, homoeopathic remedies and acupuncture have also afforded relief and improved mobility in some cases. Whenever you are considering trying out alternative medical treatments for pets, consult your vet first.

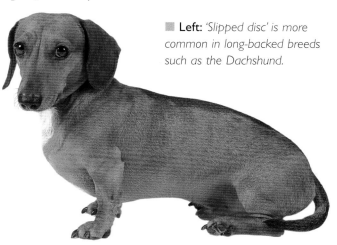

■ **Left:** *'Slipped disc' is more common in long-backed breeds such as the Dachshund.*

Prolapsed intervertebral disc

This condition is also known as disc protrusion or 'slipped disc'. The adjacent spinal vertebrae are separated by discs shaped rather like draughts pieces, which act as shock absorbers when functioning correctly. With the passing of time, as dogs, grow older, the discs lose their elasticity and become more brittle, less compressible and degenerated. Then, a sudden movement or trauma can cause a disc to 'burst' with the discharge of crunchy material that piles up against the spinal cord or a nerve root with consequent rapid onset of symptoms. The disc itself does

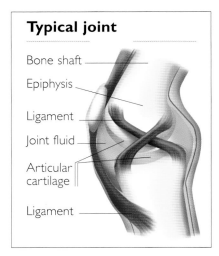

Typical joint

Bone shaft

Epiphysis

Ligament

Joint fluid

Articular cartilage

Ligament

The skeleton

The skeleton is the framework for the body. All the dog's ligaments, muscles and tendons are attached to the bones – 319 in total. By a process called ossification, cartilage template is calcified to produce bone. Bones are living tissue and respond to the stresses and strains placed upon them. To build and maintain healthy bones, dogs need a nutritionally balanced diet which contains adequate calcium, vitamin D and phosphorus.

Typical long bone

Epiphysis

Shaft, consisting of:
◆ Outer layer: cortex, hard calcified tissue
◆ Centre: bone marrow

Periosteum

Epiphysis

Orbit

Maxilla

Nasal bone

Mandible

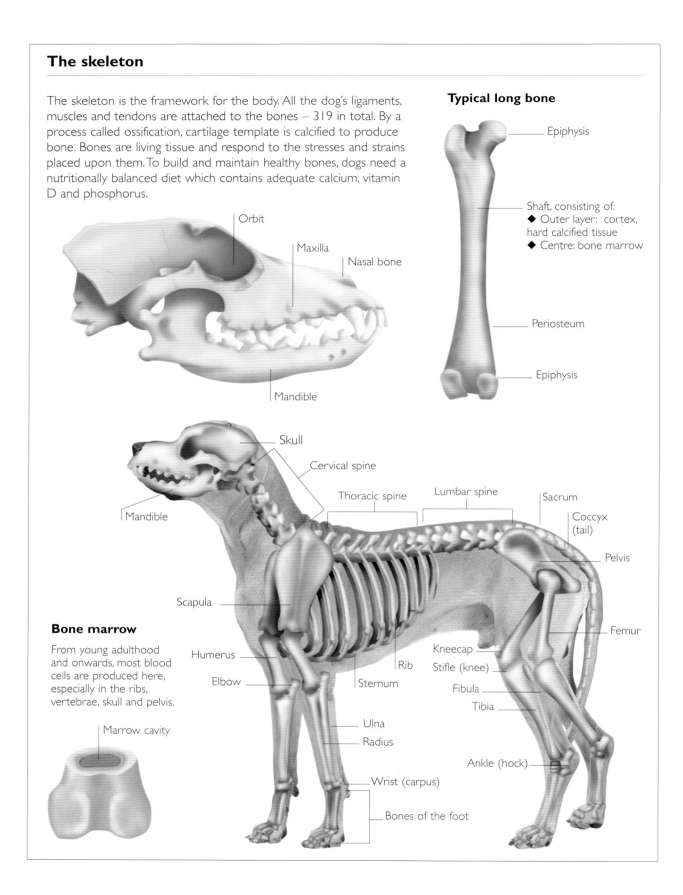

Skull

Cervical spine

Thoracic spine

Lumbar spine

Sacrum

Coccyx (tail)

Pelvis

Mandible

Femur

Scapula

Kneecap

Stifle (knee)

Humerus

Fibula

Elbow

Rib

Tibia

Sternum

Bone marrow

From young adulthood and onwards, most blood cells are produced here, especially in the ribs, vertebrae, skull and pelvis.

Ulna

Radius

Ankle (hock)

Marrow cavity

Wrist (carpus)

Bones of the foot

not actually 'slip' out of line with the spine. Certain dog breeds, particularly ones with relatively long backs for their size and short legs, such as Dachshunds, Basset hounds and Pekingeses, are more likely to suffer from disc prolapse.

Symptoms include sudden onset of neck or back pain, paralysis or weakness of the limbs, loss of sensation, limb spasms and loss of control of the bladder.

Accurate diagnosis is aided by X-rays, sometimes with contrast myelography. Treatment is by means of medication (analgesics, sedatives, anti-inflammatory drugs, anabolic hormones) and, in some instances, surgery to relieve the pressure on nervous tissues.

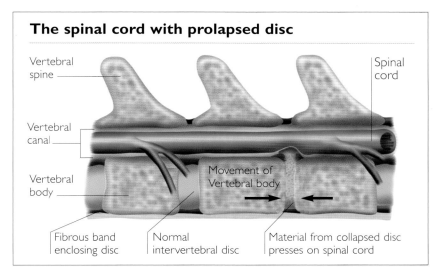

The spinal cord with prolapsed disc

Vertebral spine

Spinal cord

Vertebral canal

Vertebral body

Movement of Vertebral body

Fibrous band enclosing disc

Normal intervertebral disc

Material from collapsed disc presses on spinal cord

Good nursing by the owner of the dog under veterinary advice is essential for the animal's recovery. However, some dogs with severe spinal cord damage do not, unfortunately, improve significantly and may require euthanasia, which may be the kindest thing to do.

Sexual problems

Misalliance

This is when a bitch on heat is accidentally 'caught' by an opportunist dog. Acting rather like the 'morning after' pill in humans, some drugs can block an unwanted pregnancy. The vet can inject oestradiol benzoate within four days of the mating. Other prostaglandin hormones can cause a termination from the twenty-fifth day of pregnancy.

All these preparations can have side effects, however, and should only be used if really necessary and certainly not repeatedly.

Postponement of oestrus and contraception

Heat (oestrus) can be suppressed when symptoms of it first appear, postponed temporarily to a more convenient time or permanently postponed. You should discuss your requirements with the vet who will have a range of hormonal medications which may be administered by injection or as tablets by mouth. Some of these drugs can be employed to return a nymphomaniacal bitch to normal cycling. Side-effects to this kind of treatment are uncommon.

Pyometra

Common symptoms

- Loss of appetite
- Thirst
- Swelling of abdomen
- Vomiting
- Dullness
- In 'open cases' discharge of white, yellow or pinkish pus form the vulva

Literally meaning 'pus in the womb', pyometra is not an infection but a uterine disease which is caused by upset in the sex hormone balance in the body. It is commonest in bitches who have never had a litter of pups.

What you can do
If you do not intend your bitch to have puppies, then you should arrange for her to have an ovaro-hysterectomy (spaying, neutering) while she is still young.

Treatment
Although the vet may treat secondarily infected pyometra cases with antibiotics and give supportive medication, surgery – ovaro-hysterectomy – is usually the treatment of choice. It is a serious operation which carries more risk than normal spaying but it may be life-saving in some cases.

The reproductive system

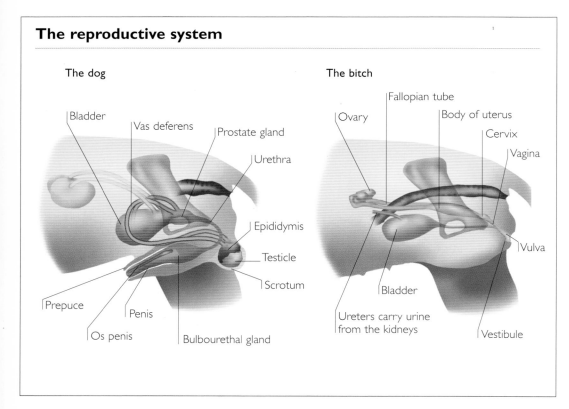

The dog

Bladder
Vas deferens
Prostate gland
Urethra
Epididymis
Testicle
Scrotum
Prepuce
Penis
Os penis
Bulbourethal gland

The bitch

Fallopian tube
Body of uterus
Ovary
Cervix
Vagina
Vulva
Bladder
Ureters carry urine from the kidneys
Vestibule

False pregnancy (pseudopregnancy)

This curious phenomenon where a bitch, frequently one who has not been anywhere near a dog, shows all the pregnancy signs, including an increased appetite, distended abdomen, making a bed for the expected litter, producing milk and, trying to 'suckle' objects such as slippers or childrens' toys. It is actually quite common.

Signs like these occur three to nine weeks after the bitch was on heat (in oestrus), but they do not indicate that she 'craves' puppies. The cause is still a bit of a mystery, but it is probably hormonal.

Treatment by the vet involves the use of hormones and, possibly, diuretics to increase expulsion of water from the body.

Prostate troubles

Only male animals possess prostate glands. They are situated in the pelvic cavity close to the urethra (the pipe carrying urine from the bladder to the outside), and also to the rectum (the terminal stretch of the bowel).

The dog prostate can be the seat of important disease conditions. There are three kinds of possible prostate disease:
◆ Inflammation (prostatitis)
◆ Prostate cancer
◆ Prostate hyperplasia (a non-cancerous enlargement).

Enlarged prostate

Compressed rectum
Anus
Bladder
Enlarged prostate

Common symptoms

The symptoms of prostate enlargement/cancer can include:
■ Constipation
■ Straining to pass motions/urine
■ Blood in the urine.

Prostatis may involve similar symptoms plus fever, dullness, lack of appetite, arching of the back and vomiting. Pain in passing urine may be noted in chronic cases.

What you can do

Seek veterinary attention quickly. The vet will make a clinical examination, probably including rectal palpation. X-ray, ultrasound, blood tests and urine tests.

Treatment
Treatment of prostate cancer and hyperplasia is by means of female sex hormones and, in some patients, castration. Pain killers may also be prescribed. Prostatitis requires antibiotic and corticosteroid anti-inflammatory medication.

Where a dog is constipated due to prostatic enlargement, a high-fibre, bulky diet can assist the passing of motions.

Skin disease

There are many kinds of skin disease in dogs. Diagnosis needs examination and often sample analysis by the vet.

Common symptoms

- Thin or bald patches in the coat
- Scratching; wet, dry or crusty sores

Mange, caused by an invisible mite, can cause crusty, hairless sores.
Fleas, lice and ticks, can cause damage to the coat.
Dietary faults, e.g. a shortage of certain fats can cause a poor coat.

Lumps and bumps on the skin may be abscesses, cysts or tumours which may need surgical attention if they persist and grow larger. The earlier a growing lump is attended to (certainly consult your vet by the time it reaches cherry size), the simpler it is to eradicate.

What you can do

If you see or suspect the presence of any of the skin parasites –

HEALTHY TIPS

- ◆ Careful attention to providing a balanced diet will avoid most dietary skin disease.
- ◆ Never apply creams, powders or ointments to skin disease without trimming back the hair. Don't encourage matting. Let oxygen get to the inflamed area.
- ◆ Groom your pet regularly; it keeps the skin and coat healthy as well as tidy.

mange mites, fleas, ticks or lice – obtain one of the antiparasitic aerosols, powders or baths from the pet shop, chemist or veterinary surgeon. Powders, however, are of little use against mange; drugs in bath or aerosol form are more appropriate. Tough, deep forms of mange such as demodectic mange may be treated by the vet using a combination of baths and drugs given by mouth. As there are several types of mange, let the vet advise on the best method of treating your particular case.

Ringworm, a subtle ailment, may need diagnosis by ultra-violet light examination or fungus culture from a hair specimen. Special drugs given by mouth or applied to the skin are used for ringworm; care must be taken to see that human contacts don't pick up the disease from pets.

With all anti-parasite treatment of skin diseases, follow the instructions on the label of the preparation being used.

Sudden, sore, wet 'hot spots' that develop in summer or autumn may be caused by an allergy to plant pollen and other substances. Use scissors to clip the hair over and round the affected area to a level with the skin, and apply liquid paraffin liberally. Such cases will need veterinary attention, perhaps involving anti-histamine or corticosteroid creams, injections or tablets. Through dramatic, they are quickly settled by treatment.

■ **Left:** *West Highland White Terriers suffer from their fair share of skin problems. Ask your vet if your dog has any particular problem relating to its breed.*

■ **Below:** *Certain flea preparations have to be applied directly to the skin, but they should be used in conjunction with flea insecticides to treat the carpets, upholstery and the dog's sleeping area.*

PARASITES

Dogs can play host to two different sorts of very unwelcome parasite, and these are as follows: external parasites (ecto-parasites) which live on the surface of the dog's body (lice, fleas, mites, ticks and ringworm); and internal parasites (endo-parasites) which exist inside the dog's body (roundworms, hookworms, whipworms and tapeworms).

External parasites

External parasites

(Not to scale)

Flea

Louse

Sarcoptic mange mite

Tick

Fleas

Dogs are usually infested by their own, and the cat's, species of flea but sometimes carry the rabbit, human or hedgehog fleas. The infestations are more likely to be worse in warm weather in the summer, but fleas thrive all the year round, particularly where there is central heating. Sometimes it is very difficult to find any fleas on the dog. Merely

Common symptoms

- Scratching
- Tiny reddish scabs or papules on the skin, particularly on the dog's back
- Flea droppings which look like coal dust in the coat

one flea can cause an allergic reaction when piercing a dog's skin and injecting its saliva.

Such a reaction can result in widespread irritation, skin sores and rashes. Flea eggs are not stuck to the dog's hair like those of lice, but, being dry, drop off onto carpets and furniture.

What you can do
Use insecticidal sprays, shampoos or powders, obtainable from the vet, chemist or a pet shop, at regular intervals throughout the summer. Also treat the floors and furniture, especially your pet's favourite sleeping places, basket and kennel with a specially formulated aerosol product every seven months. This procedure very effectively stops re-infestation of dogs by larvae emerging from eggs in the environment.

Lice

Common symptoms

- Scratching
- Lice and nits visible to the naked eye when the dog's coat is carefully searched

There are two kinds of louse:
- Biting lice which feed on skin scales

■ **Above:** *When using flea spray, remove and spray the dog's collar, and then spray the dog, making sure you protect his eyes and mouth*

■ Sucking lice which draw tissue fluids from the skin.
The latter cause more irritation to the dog than the former.

Lice are greyish-white in colour and about 2 mm (1/8 in) in length. Their eggs (nits) are white and are cemented to the dog's hairs. The dog louse does not fancy humans or cats and will not infest them.

What you can do

Sprays, powders or baths are available from the vet, chemist or pet shop. Apply on at least three occasions at five- to seven-day intervals to kill adults and the larvae that hatch from the nits.

Mites

See later under Mange (page 121).

Ticks

More often seen on country dogs rather than town dogs, ticks suck blood, their abdomen swelling up as they do so. The commonest tick of dogs is the sheep tick. It clings to the dog's hair, generally on the legs, head or under-belly, and pierces the skin with its mouth parts. In doing so it can transmit an organism called Borrelia, cause of the important condition called Lyme Disease. This is characterized by lameness and heart disease and requires veterinary diagnosis by means of blood tests, and then treatment using specific antibiotics and anti-inflammatory drugs.

What you can do

Remove a tick by dabbing it with some alcohol, such as gin or methylated spirits, waiting a few minutes for its head to relax, and then grasping it near to the mouthparts with fine tweezers and dislodging it with a little jerk. Do *not* ever pull it off without applying the alcohol first as the mouthparts left in the skin may cause abscess formation.

Another method is to spray the tick with flea spray and then to remove it the following day.

I would recommend regular application of a flea spray or fitting an insecticidal collar during the summer months in order to control tick infestation.

Ringworm

Another occasional skin parasite of dogs is the ringworm fungus (see page 121).

Tick tweezers

Specialist tick tweezers are useful in removing these nasty little beasts. Avoid squashing the tick and releasing its fluids or leaving any part of the head in the skin as both may cause infection. Afterwards use disinfectant on the affected area.

Internal parasites (endo-parasites)

Several kinds of parasitic worm can infest dogs and, in very rare cases, these parasites can spread to human beings.

Roundworms

These live, when adult, in the dog's intestines but their immature forms migrate through their host's body damaging such organs as the liver and lungs, particularly those of puppies.

Hookworms and whipworms

These blood-sucking parasites can cause severe anaemia.

Tapeworms

The commonest dog tapeworm, Dipylidium, is spread by fleas, in which its larvae develop. You can see segments of this tapeworm like wriggling white grains of rice in droppings or stuck to the hair around the dog's bottom.

Roundworms cause the most trouble for dogs, particularly puppies. Symptoms can include bowel upsets, emaciation, fits, chest and liver malfunction. Tapeworms may cause dogs to drag their rear ends ('scoot') along the floor.

What you can do

Against roundworms you should give 'worming' medication which will be available from your vet. Puppies usually should receive their first dose at three weeks of age. Repeat the worming every three weeks until sixteen weeks of age. Then again at six months and twice a year thereafter.

Give anti-tapeworm medication once a year or when any worm segments are seen in the dog's droppings or on the hair near and around the anus. Flea control will also help to combat tapeworms.

Some worm treatments are effective against all types of endo-parasite (consult your vet about suitable products and dosage).

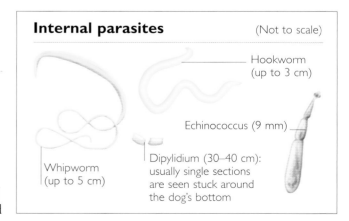

Internal parasites (Not to scale)

Hookworm (up to 3 cm)

Echinococcus (9 mm)

Whipworm (up to 5 cm)

Dipylidium (30–40 cm): usually single sections are seen stuck around the dog's bottom

MISCELLANEOUS AILMENTS

Diabetes

There are two quite separate types of diabetes. These are diabetes mellitus ('sugar diabetes') which is common, and diabetes insipidus ('water diabetes').

■ **Below:** *Always monitor your dog's eating and drinking habits. Increased thirst is sometimes a symptom of diabetes.*

Diabetes mellitus

Diabetes mellitus is a disease of, or damage to, parts of the dog's pancreas, but there are other less well understood factors, too. Basically there is a fall in the body production of the hormone insulin, which controls the blood sugar levels. However, some patients are not insulin dependent. The vet will confirm a diagnosis of diabetes mellitus through urine and blood tests.

Common symptoms

■ Excessive drinking, eating and urination
■ Weight loss
■ Rapid development of cataracts in the lenses of the eyes
■ Sometimes vomiting and dullness

Treatment

Treatment is by daily injection of a long-acting form of insulin – the vet will show you how to do this and advise on the proper dosage. It is very easy and your pet quickly gets accustomed to his 'shots'. Unfortunately, the oral anti-diabetic drugs sometimes used in humans instead of insulin injections seldom work in dogs. Spaying a diabetic bitch can assist matters.

What you can do

Discuss a 'diabetic diet' for your pet with the vet. It is important to time feeding correctly and to give a steady, consistent diet without changes. High-fibre, high-quality protein, low-carbohydrate diets often reduce or even eliminate the need for insulin injections.

Diabetes insipidus

This complex disease is associated with faults in the pituitary gland and/or the kidneys.

Common symptoms

■ Excessive drinking and urination
■ Blood and urine tests will differentiate this condition from diabetes mellitus

Treatment

This is by the use of pituitary hormone injections and, in some cases, paradoxically, certain diuretic drugs.

Eclampsia (lactation tetany)

Common symptoms

■ Panting
■ Stiffness
■ Muscle spasms
■ Excitability
■ Fast breathing
■ Collapse

This condition can occur in some bitches just before or, more often, just after giving birth. The cause is a fall in blood calcium levels.

The vet will rule out other possible causes of these symptoms and give an injection of a calcium compound. Recovery is swift – within minutes.

What you can do

Do not delay getting professional help – eclampsia can kill. Feed a calcium-supplemented diet during pregnancy and lactation. Seek veterinary advice as to the amount of calcium given – too much during pregnancy can be dangerous.

Lymphosarcoma

Common symptoms

- Enlarged lymph nodes
- Enlarged tonsils and some abdominal organs
- Poor appetite and weight loss
- Digestive and bowel upsets

Your vet will use clinical examination, blood tests and, perhaps, biopsies to confirm diagnosis. This serious form of cancer of the lymphatic system is not uncommon in dogs. However, it has not yet been proven that it is caused, as in cats, by a virus.

Treatment

Treating lymphosarcoma is very difficult and often not advisable. However, some dogs have had their lives prolonged by means of specialized corticosteroid and chemotherapeutic treatment.

Toxoplasmosis

Common symptoms

- Loss of condition and weight
- Fever
- Diarrhoea
- Pneumonia
- Eye and nose discharge
- Nervous signs

Toxoplasmosis symptoms can resemble those of distemper or infectious canine hepatitis. It can lead to abortion or the death of new-born puppies. Infection by Toxoplasma gondii, a micro-organism, can produce a range of vague symptoms in a dog or even nothing at all.

Treatment

Diagnosis can be confirmed by blood tests. Treatment is by means of sulphonomides or antibiotics. **Note:** Toxoplasmosis can spread to humans, and pregnant women should avoid contact with dogs known to have symptoms, or be carrying the micro-organism.

Mastitis (inflammation of the breasts)

Common symptoms

- Inflamed, hard breasts when producing milk may indicate the onset of mastitis

Once a month), roll your bitch over and run your hands along her undercarriage. If you feel any hard lumps in the substance of the breast tissue, within the teats or just under the skin, see the vet at once. Breast tumours spread quickly to other parts of the body once established. Caught early on, they can be removed surgically.

This condition is commoner in breeds such as the Boxer, especially where there is a small litter or if the bitch loses her pups.

Treatment

Treat with antiflammatory and antibacterial drugs. Sometimes the milk is sent back by prescribing tablets of oestrogen.

RABIES

This dread virus disease does not at present exist in the United Kingdom.

Symptoms and diagnosis

After an incubation period of 10–120 days, the signs can include change of temperature, restlessness, high excitability, salivation, abnormal appetite, difficulty in swallowing, paralysis and coma. Treatment is never indicated. Confirmation of diagnosis is by microscopical examination of the brain post-mortem.

Protecting your dog

Dogs can be protected from rabies by vaccination. The British government is currently changing its anti-rabies policy from strict quarantine to one of vaccination, micro-chipping and 'pet passports' for animals entering Britain from a limited number of other countries. As the situation is still fluid, seek veterinary advice before planning to export or import dogs for whatever reason.

NURSING A SICK DOG

In all your pet's ailments, mild or serious, you will normally have to be prepared to do something, usually acting in the capacity of nurse. There are some essential nursing techniques to be learned. You should also know how to handle and restrain your dog during visits to the vet.

Taking your dog's temperature

You can't rely on the state of a dog's nose as aa effective indicator of temperature, good health or sickness. As with children, being able to take your pet's temperature with a thermometer can help you to decide whether to call the vet and can help him in diagnosing and treating what is wrong with the animal.

You should use an ordinary glass thermometer bought from the chemist but preferably with a stubby rather than a slim bulb, or, better still, you can invest in an unbreakable thermometer, though these are more expensive.

Lubricate it with a little olive oil or petroeum jelly and insert it for about 2.5 cm (1 in) into the rectum. Once it is in place, hold the thermometer with the bulb angled against the rectal wall for good contact. After half a minute, remove and read the thermometer.

A dog's normal temperature is 38–38.6°C (101–101.6°F). Taking into account a slight rise for nervousness or excitement in some dogs, expect under such conditions to read up to 38.7°C (101.8°F) or even 38.8°C (102°F). Higher than that is abnormal. Shake down the mercury in the thermometer before use, and clean and disinfect the instrument afterwards.

Administering medicine

Pill gun

An alternative method of giving pills is using a water-filled pill gun that 'shoots' the pill from a syringe with a dose of water to aid swallowing.

Try to avoid putting medicines into food or drink; it can be a very imprecise method. Tablets, pills or capsules should always be dropped into the 'V'-groove at the back of the dog's mouth while holding it open as illustrated, with one thumb pressed firmly against the hard roof of the dog's mouth.

Liquids should be given slowly, a little at a time, by the same method or direct into the lip pouch with the mouth held closed. If wished, they can be squirted through a syringe.

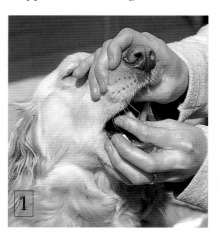

1 When giving a tablet, hold the dog's mouth open and drop into 'V'-groove at the back of his mouth.

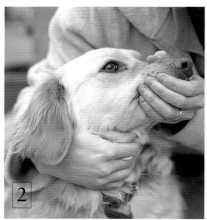

2 After giving a tablet whether by hand or applicator, massage the throat to help the tablet on its way.

■ **Above:** *Liquids can be poured into the mouth or syringed direct into the lip pouch, thereby ensuring that all of the medication is administered.*

Handling and restraining a dog

Making a makeshift muzzle

This is essential where nervous, possessive, aggressive or sensitive (in pain) animals have to be handled or examined. Use a length of bandage, string, nylon stocking or even a tie. By carefully positioning the muzzle not too far back, liquid medicine can be administered to such a disarmed dog by pouring it into the gap between the lips behind the encircling band.

1 Tie a knot in the bandage and wrap it around the dog's muzzle.

2 Cross the ends of the bandage at the bottom under the jaw.

3 Bring the ends round to the back of the dog's head and tie firmly.

Restraining a large dog

It is important to make sure you know how to adequately restrain your dog, especially at the vets where many dogs can be nervous and panic. Very large dogs will usually be looked at on the floor whereas the vet will examine small to medium-sized dogs on the examination table.

■ **Above:** *To restrain a large dog, place one arm firmly around his neck and the other around his body. Hold him tightly and speak reassuringly to him.*

Lifting a dog

To avoid injury to not only your dog but also your back, always bend your knees when picking up a large dog. Make sure that you support the dog's body properly.

1 If lifting a medium-sized dog, place one hand under his rear and the other around his chest.

2 Hold the dog securely while you rise to your feet, bringing him up to chest height.

■ **Above:** *To lift a small dog, support him under the rear and at the front with one hand on his chest between the front legs and the other taking most of his weight at the rear.*

FIRST AID

First aid is the emergency care given to a dog suffering injury or illness of sudden onset.

AIMS OF FIRST AID
1 Keep the dog alive. 2 Prevent unnecessary suffering. 3 Prevent further injury.

RULES OF FIRST AID

| 1 | Always keep calm. If you panic, you will be unable to help the dog effectively. |

| 2 | Contact a vet as soon as possible. Advice given over the telephone may be life-saving. |

| 3 | Avoid injury to yourself. A distressed or injured animal may bite so use a muzzle if necessary (see page 127 on how to make one). |

| 4 | Control any haemorrhage. Excessive blood loss can lead to severe shock and death (see stopping bleeding on page 132). |

| 5 | Maintain an airway. Failure to breathe or obtain adequate oxygen can lead to brain damage or loss of life within five minutes (see opposite). |

COMMON ACCIDENTS AND EMERGENCIES
Common accidents and emergencies will all require first aid. In an emergency, your priorities are to keep the dog alive and comfortable until he can be examined by a vet. However, in many cases, there is important action that you can do yourself immediately to help preserve your dog's health and life.

Burns

Burns can be caused by very hot liquids or by contact with an electrical current or various types of caustic, acid or irritant liquid.

Chemical burns

■ *Below: To treat chemical burns, wash the affected area of the coat with copious warm soapy water.*

Recommended action
Wash the affected area of the coat with copious warm soapy water and then seek veterinary advice.

Scalding with a liquid

Hot water or oil spillage most commonly occurs in the kitchen. Although the dog's coat affords him some insulating protection, the skin beneath may well be damaged with visible signs only emerging after several hours have passed in many cases.

Recommended action
Apply cold water immediately to the affected area and follow this by an icepack – a bag of frozen peas from the refrigerator is ideal. Then gently dry the burnt zone with mineral oil (liquid paraffin) and seek veterinary advice.

Electrical burns

Most electrical burns are the result of a dog chewing a live flex or cable. Prevention being better than cure, such wires should be

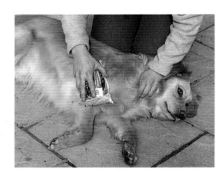

■ *Above: Apply lots of cold water and follow this by an icepack.*

hidden, particularly from puppies, and electrical devices should be unplugged after use. Biting live wires can cause burns to the inside of the lips and the gums but may, in the worst cases, result in shock, collapse and death.

Recommended action
First, switch off the electricity before you handle the patient. Examine the insides of the mouth and apply cold water to any burnt areas. If the gums are whiter than normal or blue-tinged, shock may be present. Seek veterinary advice.

RESUSCITATING A DOG

Checking the heart rate

If the dog is unconscious check the breathing and heart action with one or more of the following techniques:

Feel for its pulse on the inside of a hind leg.

Press the flat of your hand against the chest just behind the elbow.

Place your ear on the chest to listen for heart beats. Normal respiration rate is 20–30 breaths per minute. Normal heart rate ranges from about 50 beats per minute in large breeds to 150 beats per minute in very small breeds.

No heart beat: cardiac massage

If the dog's heart is not beating you should try cardiac massage by:
◆ Placing the animal on his right side and then placing the heel of your left hand on the left side of his chest just behind the elbow.
◆ Put your other hand on top and then press down and forwards very firmly and sharply.
◆ Do this about 10 times at regular one-second intervals.

No breathing: mouth-to-nose resuscitation

Assuming that the dog is also not breathing, you should now give mouth-to-nose resuscitation.
◆ Maintain an airway. Clear any saliva or obstruction from the mouth and pull the tongue forwards, allowing it to flop out to one side.
◆ Keep the head and neck straight and then, cupping the nose with your hands, exhale strongly into the nostrils for 2–3 seconds. The chest should expand as the lungs fill with air.
◆ **If the heart is still not beating, return to cardiac massage another 10 times** and then go back again to artificial respiration.
◆ Continue alternating the massage and the mouth-to-nose until you get a response. It is worth you trying for up to a quarter of an hour to re-start the heart, and artificial respiration should continue indefinitely where a faint heart beat can be detected. While all this is going on, make sure that veterinary assistance is urgently being sought.

■ **Left:** *Put one hand on top of the other and then press down and forwards very firmly and sharply. Remember that you are pushing down on the rib cage so be careful not to exert too much force!*

■ **Left:** *Keep the head and neck straight and then, cupping the dog's nose with your hands, exhale strongly.*

Poisoning

The house, the garden and the world outside contain a multitude of substances, both natural and artificial, that can poison a dog. Wherever poisoning is suspected, contact your vet without delay. Frequently some symptoms, such as vomiting, blood in the dog's stools or collapse, which owners may imagine to be the result of poisoning, are caused by other kinds of illness.

Poisonous chemicals may come in contact with a dog through ingestion or by the animal licking its coat when contaminated by a noxious substance. Canine inquisitiveness and the tendency to scavenge can lead dogs to eat or drink some strange materials and sometimes owners negligently give dangerous substances to their pets. Occasionally poisonous gases or vapours are inhaled by animals.

■ **Right:** *Flush out the mouth carefully with warm water. Let the dog drink some water or milk if he will take it.*

> **POISONOUS PLANTS**
>
> Dangerous plants include the bulbs of many spring flowers, holly and mistletoe berries, leaves and flowers of rhododendrons and hydrangeas, leaves of yew, box and laurels, sweetpea, wisteria and bluebell seeds and all parts of the columbine, hemlock, lily of the valley and ivy. Some mushrooms are as poisonous to dogs as they are to humans as are the blue-green algae that sometimes bloom on ponds in hot weather.

Among the thousands of highly poisonous compounds to be found in everyday life are weedkillers, pesticides (rat, slug and insect killers), fungicides, disinfectants, car antifreeze, lead compounds, caustic cleaning fluids, paint thinners, creosote and excessive amounts of patent medicines, such as paracetamol and aspirin.

Poisoning can also be caused by certain plants, insect stings and the venom of snakes and toads.

Common symptoms

■ Digestive upsets (vomiting and diarrhoea)
■ Difficulty in breathing
■ Convulsions
■ Uncoordinated movements
■ Coma

Recommended action
Determining which chemical is involved can be difficult if you don't know what the dog's come into contact with. Professional diagnostic methods at the earliest opportunity are vital.

First aid in poisoning cases

Corrosive poisons
Look for evidence of burning or

POISONS

Here are some poisons and their common sources:

◆ **Alphachloralose:** Mouse and rat killer
◆ **Barbiturates:** Sleeping tablets
◆ **Carbon monoxide gas:** Faulty heater, car exhausts
◆ **Chlorates:** Weedkiller
◆ **Corrosive chemicals:** Acids, alkalis bleach, carbolic acid and phenols, creosote, petroleum products
◆ **Ethylene glycol:** Antifreeze
◆ **Lead:** Paint, solders, putty, fishing weights
◆ **Metaldehyde:** Slug pellets
◆ **Organochlorines, Organophosphates and carbamates:** Insecticides, rodenticides, herbicides
◆ **Paraquat:** Weedkillers
◆ **Strychrine:** Mole killers, illegal bird baits
◆ **Warfarin:** Rodenticides
◆ **Zinc phosphide:** Rodenticides

blistering in the mouth. Flush out the mouth carefully with warm water. Let the animal drink water or milk if he will.

Other poisons

If the poison has been swallowed recently (within one hour) try to make the dog vomit by giving him a hazelnut-sized chunk of washing soda (sodium carbonate) or some English mustard powder (a level teaspoon in half a cup of water for a medium-sized dog and pro rata).

Corrosive substances

Wipe clean the contaminated area with rags or paper tissues and cut off congealed masses of hair with scissors. Cooking oil or petroleum jelly will help soften paint and tar.

Wash thoroughly with dog or baby shampoo and rinse well. Don't use solvents, paint thinners concentrated washing detergents or turpentine on a dog's coat.

Snake bites

Britain's only venomous snake, the common adder (*Vipera berus*) may sometimes bite a dog who disturbs it. Moors in south-west England and North Yorkshire are the most frequent venues for such accidents. The snake's bite will produce two tiny slit-like punctures in the dog's skin which rapidly become surrounded by a zone of swollen reaction.

Common symptoms

■ Trembling and excitement Salivation
■ Vomiting and staggering Followed later by:
■ Shock
■ Depression
■ Collapse and even death

Recommended action

Urgent veterinary attention is necessary. Some holiday-makers taking their dogs to parts of the country where adders are quite common carry a vial of adder anti-venom with them as a precaution to give to the vet just in case he has none in his surgery.

Bee and wasp stings

Painful, but usually single and with no serious general effects, insect stings require little more than removal of the sting itself in the case of bee stings (wasps and hornets do not leave their stings

behind) by means of tweezers and the application of antihistamine cream. Rarely, death can ensue if a dog is subject to a large number, perhaps hundreds, of stings. Stings can also be serious if the tongue or mouth are involved.

Common symptoms

■ Swelling blocking the throat or, if the dog is allergic to the insect venom, he will go into severe shock

Recommended action

Such cases need medical anti-shock therapy, such as intravenous fluids, adrenalin and antihistamine injections. Keep shocked animals warm and make sure that their breathing is unimpeded while veterinary attention is obtained.

Toad venom poisoning

Toads secrete a venom from their skin, particularly when upset. Dogs who lick this secretion when investigating a toad they may come across in their own garden or when out on a country walk quickly develop symptoms.

Common symptoms

■ Irritation of the mouth with copious amounts of saliva

Recommended action

Fortunately, toad bites are rarely serious, and such occurrences can be simply treated by washing out the dog's mouth with some warm water, preferably containing a little baking soda powder (sodium bicarbonate).

Bleeding

The appearance of blood anywhere on the dog's body necessitates immediate close inspection. A variety of accidents and some diseases may produce blood from the nostrils, eyes or ears or in the droppings or in vomited material. None of the above types of haemorrhage are usually suitable for first-aid by the owner. All need veterinary attention although the causes may often be trivial and ephemeral.

Bleeding from the body surface through wounds inflicted during fights, traffic accidents or other traumatic incidents can be copious and this does require prompt first-aid.

Recommended action
The most important thing is to apply pressure to the wound. Hand or finger pressure is always invaluable until a pad of gauze or cotton wool can be found. This should be soaked in cold water, placed on the wound and kept in place by constant firm pressure or, better, a bandage. Take the dog to a veterinary surgery as quickly as possible. Do not waste any time applying antiseptic ointments or powders to a significantly bleeding wound.

■ **Right:** *Soak the bandage in cold water before you applying it to the wound, then seek veterinary treatment as soon as possible if the bleeding does not stop.*

Heat stroke

Every summer one reads in the newspapers of cases of dogs dying from heat stroke as a result of the gross thoughtlessness of their owners. Animals that are left in hot, poorly ventilated spaces, particularly cars, and sometimes without water, overheat. They lose the ability to control their internal body temperature. As the latter rises, the dog will become distressed, pant rapidly and will quickly weaken. The mouth will appear much redder than normal. Collapse, coma and even death can follow in a reasonably short space of time.

Recommended action
Cooling the body, particularly the head, by means of cold water baths, hosing and ice-packs is essential. If the temperature-regulating mechanism in the brain has already been seriously damaged a fatal outcome may still ensue. Veterinary attention must be obtained at once. Of course, prevention of such emergencies by owner forethought is imperative.

■ **Below:** *A dog with suspected heat stroke should be hosed down with plenty of cold water immediately. You may also need to use ice-packs.*

Foreign bodies

In the eye

Foreign bodies in the eye cause the dog to rub his head on the ground and paw at his eye.

Recommended action
Flood the eye with human-type eye drops or olive oil to float out the foreign body. Do not use tweezers close to the eyeball.

In the ear

Plant seeds and grass awns are particularly likely to get into a dog's ears during summer walks. Their presence causes itching and irritation. The dog shakes his head and paws at his ears.

Recommended action
Pour some warm olive oil or other vegetable oil into the ear, filling it. The object may well float to the surface where it can be picked up by tweezers. Deeper, embedded foreign bodies will always require veterinary attention.

In the mouth

Sometimes pieces of bone or splinters of wood can become lodged in a dog's mouth. Often the offending object is jammed between the left and right upper molar teeth at the back of the mouth or in the space between two adjacent teeth. Less commonly, an object, such as a small ball, will become stuck in the dog's throat. In all cases the animal will show symptoms of distress, including pawing at the mouth, gagging, trying to retch or shaking its head.

Recommended action
While someone holds the dog firmly, you should open the mouth and try to dislodge the foreign body with a spoon or kitchen tongs. Where the dog is having difficulty breathing and literally choking, try holding him upside down by the hind legs, massaging the throat and slapping his back. If you cannot remove the object, seek veterinary help at once.

In the paws

Splinters of glass, thorns, particles of metal and fragments of stone can penetrate the pads on a dog's paws or lodge in the skin between the toes. As a result the dog limps and usually licks the affected paw.

Recommended action
Remove the object with tweezers, if visible. If not, because of being embedded, bathe the foot two to three times daily in warm water and salt (a teaspoon to a cupful) until the foreign body emerges from the softened skin. If lameness persists for more than a day or two, seek veterinary attention; infection may have set in.

■ **Left:** *A grass seed between the pads can be very painful. Use some tweezers to pull it out. Check that the seed is still complete.*

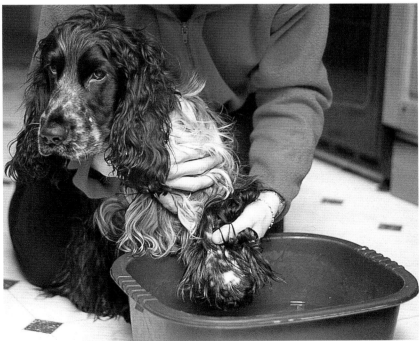

■ **Left:** *After removing a foreign object from a paw, bathe it in warm salty water. Do likewise if you can't remove it straight away as this may help the object to appear.*

Advanced dog care

Many pet dog owners will want to get involved in advanced activities with their dogs, including showing, obedience competitions, agility and flyball, and working trials. These are enjoyable occasions for both you and your dog. You will make new friends and broaden your social life as you discover the joy and sense of achievement that can come from participating in dog shows. Many dogs enjoy the experience of the show ring and like to perform. They are stimulated physically and mentally by trials and competitions. You may even consider breeding from your dog and want to start a strain of your own. Showing and breeding are both enjoyable hobbies but they carry certain responsibilities.

Chapter Eight

SHOWING YOUR DOG

Showing your dog can be an absorbing and even addictive hobby. Competitive people who like a difficult challenge find the ever-present possibility of breeding, exhibiting and winning with a really great dog is both exciting and stimulating to the extent of changing their lifestyle. From simple beginnings, with one pet dog, many people have gone on to make their living from dogs, to become famous judges of dogs and even world authorities.

■ **Below:** *Showing dogs successfully is a skilful pastime. A dog must learn to stand properly to show him at his best.*

Registering your dog

When you first contemplate showing your dog or indulging in any of the recognised activities with dogs, your priority must be to ensure that the dog is properly registered with The Kennel Club and has been transferred into the owner's name. Most dog shows in Britain are held under The Kennel Club's rules and regulations and if the dog is not registered, entries to the show will not be accepted. Although it is the usual practice for dog breeders to register their puppies, there are occasions when they do not do so, in which case negotiations have to be carried out with the breeder and The Kennel Club. It is the responsibility of the new owner to transfer the dog into their name.

Finding out about showing

You are walking with your dog along the High Street when somebody stops you to admire your dog. You are told that he is a very good-looking dog and well worth showing. What do you do? You know nothing about dog showing. Well, go to your local newsagent and buy one of the specialist weekly newspapers that

specialize in the pedigree dog, its exhibition and breeding. Within their pages, over a few weeks, you will find practically everything that you need to know, especially where the shows are being held, the type of show and the address of the secretary who will send you the show schedule. This is the first key document, which contains all the information pertaining to that show. It will also contain the entry form, and it is essential to complete this with the utmost care as even the smallest mistakes can lead to disqualification.

Learning about ringcraft

The next step is probably the most essential; you must find the nearest canine club or society teaching the required showing skills. The Kennel Club recognises literally hundreds of training clubs involved in different aspects of dog training, ringcraft, obedience, agility, flyball, working dog tests and Gundog trials. In the latter two, there are special clubs that deal with the needs of specific breeds. A quick telephone call will

■ **Opposite:** *Labradors love taking part in Gundog Trials. They are tested on their finding and retrieving abilities.*

Show leads

For showing certain breeds you will need to invest in the correct show lead. Usually it is a thin, long slip lead which is designed to hold the dog's head up as you walk him.

elicit the secretary's details of any club or society.

To exhibit a dog successfully you must realise that there are rules, both written and unwritten, with which you must familiarize yourself as a competitor; the ringcraft club is the ideal place at which to learn them. There will be instructors and experienced exhibitors who will be delighted to share their expertise, and if you have a relatively common breed the likelihood is that there will be skilled competitors in the breed who will undoubtedly help in the presentation of your dog.

Grooming and show presentation

In some breeds trimming is of the essence: it would be pointless to take a scruffy, unclipped Poodle into a show ring as he would not get a place; and

■ **Above:** *A Poodle in puppy trim. It takes a lot of time and care to show some breeds successfully. Poodles, in particular, have to be trimmed and groomed with great precision and skill.*

an over-grown Welsh Terrier, looking like a doormat, would also be ignored. However, when novices observe the perfection of the grooming of their chosen breed, inevitably they will wonder how it is achieved.

All the hairy breeds have their own style of trimming; some are scissored and clipped whereas others are hand-stripped into the traditional shape. The tools with which to do this are many and varied and the job is made easier with the use of the correct tools. They can be bought from specialist traders who will not only sell you the grooming equipment but also will give you some invaluable advice.

However, there are professional groomers who, for a price, will prepare a dog for the show ring, but this is likely to be expensive and will not reflect the owner's natural pride in their dog. Most exhibitors find that one of the pleasures of their hobby is in the preparation and they develop the arts of trimming, grooming and presentation to perfection themselves. All it takes is application, study and, above all, practice.

■ **Right:** *Even Springer Spaniels may need some specialist grooming techniques. This dog is receiving some last-minute attention.*

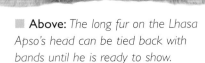

■ **Above:** *The long fur on the Lhasa Apso's head can be tied back with bands until he is ready to show.*

There are professional dog handlers who combine the skills of grooming and presentation of the dog and who will sell their expertise to owners who either cannot do it themselves or are too busy. Cases in point are some elderly owners of German Shepherd Dogs – the breed is customarily shown trotting fairly fast round the ring several times which may require a younger and more energetic handler. The formally trimmed terriers, such as Airedales, Wire-haired Fox Terriers

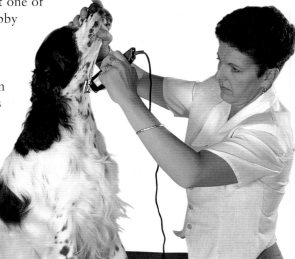

■ **Above:** *To prepare Yorkies for show, special paper 'crackers' are used.*

■ **Above:** *The crackers keep the show coat straight and in first-class condition.*

and Lakeland Terriers, are often prepared and then handled by professionals because of the difficulty of trimming their coat and the time involved. The cost has to be negotiated with each individual handler. Most of these handlers prefer to keep the dog on their premises so the cost of feeding as well as trimming has to be considered. On the other hand travel costs are likely to be less because the handler may be taking several dogs to a show.

Presenting your dog

Every breed is shown differently. For instance, a Fox Terrier can be shown 'stacked', which means placing the dog in a certain

position and holding him there, whereas a German Shepherd Dog is always posed in a particularly formal fashion. An English Setter is held in a natural standing position except his tail which is stretched out horizontally. There are as many ways of presenting a dog to the judge as there are dog breeds, and if, in a competition, you don't show your dog in the traditional manner, you lessen your chances of winning.

At the same time as learning yourself, your dog has to learn his role. He will learn to be handled by strangers – the judge may pass his hands over the dog's entire body and, most difficult, he will have to tolerate having his mouth opened and his teeth looked at. With practice, he will succeed in walking or trotting at the correct speed and style and will be at ease with all the bustle and noise of a big show.

Some dogs learn quickly, others take time. Terriers learn quickly but because of their independent characters will often deliberately do something surprising, such as shaking your trouser leg in front of the judge. To persuade a dog to behave correctly the club training should be reinforced at home – five to ten minutes a day will suffice. Dogs get bored very quickly so do not pressurize a puppy too much. Just let him settle in his own time; his spirit must not be broken. Firmness with kindness is the best way forward. A loss of patience resulting in shouting or even smacking will be counter-productive, and a puppy trained

CLUB MATCHES

To give you the feel of actual competition, most clubs hold monthly matches: an elimination contest between the members of the club and sometimes against their neighbouring clubs. Both owners and their dogs benefit greatly from these contests, the owner repeatedly going through the same routine as he would at the big championship shows and the dog getting used to being handled and mixing with other dogs.

like this will never give of his best.

Set up a little show ring in your garden and go through the same motions as you did at the training class. Use neighbours, friends or your family to play the part of the judge. Some trainers advocate getting the puppy accustomed to applause by asking the onlookers to clap their hands; they will also bang dustbin lids to accustom the puppy to unusual noises.

Small dogs are known as 'table dogs', and this means that they will be placed on a table for the judge to examine. The act of placing a dog on a table should be practised as he must be lifted gently and calmly and should not be handled by his tail. Take care not to hurt or drop him, otherwise he will lose confidence and this will reflect in his performance.

■ **Below:** *Some breeds, such as this Curly-coated Retriever, can be shown either stacked or free-standing. This dog is prepared by wetting the coat and combing gently through the curls.*

Dog shows

There are several different types of dog show and although the novice exhibitor is fully entitled to compete at any of them (with the exception of Crufts and specific breed shows) it is wise not to rush into things and is therefore best to start at the bottom.

The committee of the ringcraft club will be pleased to guide you through the labyrinth of class definitions for dogs at the various types of dog show. Entries to the appropriate shows must be posted with the correct fee before the appointed date. Any failure to pay will result in your disqualification. Puppies under six months of age cannot be shown.

Exemption shows

These are the simplest of shows, and anyone can enter regardless of whether their dog is registered or not, be it a mongrel or a pedigree. No champion or any dog that has awards towards its championship can be entered.

These shows are usually charity fund raisers staged by small agricultural shows, garden fêtes and similar events. They have cheap entry fees and entries can be made on the day. They are an ideal training ground for novice dogs and their owners. The dog becomes familiarized with crowds of people, dogs he has never seen before and surfaces on which he has never walked. The shows will be advertised locally but the canine newspapers will also carry advertisements. Exhibitors should satisfy themselves that the show is properly licensed by the Kennel Club.

Limited shows

These are small local shows which are limited to the members of the staging club although membership can be acquired with the entry. No dog that has won any awards towards his championship can enter. As with the following shows, Kennel Club rules apply

AGE-LINKED DEFINITIONS

◆ **Puppy:** Six to twelve months old
◆ **Minor Puppy:** Six to nine months old
◆ **Junior:** Six to eighteen months old

and entries are made and paid for in advance. Application for the schedules should be made to the secretary whose address and phone number will be advertised in the canine press or is available from the Kennel Club. A careful study of the schedule of this and other shows will reveal if your breed is scheduled or you may have to enter a variety class.

Open shows

As the name implies, these shows are open to all regardless of any previous awards. Kennel Club rules apply, and schedules and catalogues must be published and

■ **Right:** *Many people get hooked on showing when they first attend a local exemption show. These shows are great fun for owners and dogs.*

■ **Left:** *Everyone's dream is to win Best in Show at Crufts. The 2000 winner, the Kerry Blue Terrier, Champion Torum's Scarf, is shown here with the most coveted trophy of them all.*

entries made prior to the show. Again, the full details and class definitions will be published in the schedule. There are all-breed open shows and breed open shows.

Championship shows

Any show that gives Challenge Certificates can call itself a championship show. All the breeds are entitled to enter if they are scheduled. A dog will become a champion when he has won three certificates under three different judges, or in the case of a puppy he must win three certificates, at least one of them after he has reached one year of age. Not all breeds are eligible for Challenge Certificates, and the breeds that are must be declared in the schedule together with the class definitions and full details of the show.

Crufts

This is the most famous of all Championship Dog Shows, and dog lovers from around the world

flock to attend every year. More than 100,000 spectators make the annual journey to the National Exhibition Centre, Birmingham, to see approximately 20,000 dogs! It is the only dog show for which the exhibitors have to be qualified. The qualifications are wins in selected classes at other championship shows during the

previous year. To check on the qualifications, which can change, phone the Kennel Club which will send the schedule at an appropriate time. The same exhibition rules apply as for other shows.

Group shows (championship)

The same rules apply as for all other championship shows with the exception that these shows are restricted to breeds of the same Group. The Groups are defined as follows:
◆ Hounds
◆ Gundogs
◆ Terriers
◆ Utility dogs
◆ Working dogs
◆ Pastoral dogs
◆ Toy dogs

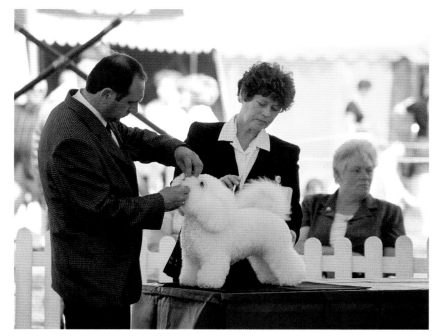

■ **Left:** *The judge will want to examine your dog. Small dogs, such as this Bichon Frise, are usually lifted on to a table.*

OTHER ADVANCED ACTIVITIES

There are many other equally interesting canine activities which can be enjoyed by enthusiasts. A network of clubs and societies specializes in teaching both dogs and owners. Details will be provided by the Kennel Club. Dogs must be registered in the Working Trials and Obedience Register to compete in Obedience, Agility, Flyball and Working Trials, and cross-bred dogs are admitted. The events are advertised and schedules are available from the host society. All disciplines are designed around teamwork and rapport between the owner and dog. Anyone can join in.

Obedience

In Obedience Competitions, the dogs are taught a series of simple formal exercises based on walking to heel on the lead, without the lead, recall, sit/stay and down/stay. Starting with the Pre-Beginners Class the work is structured so that there is a natural progression through the classes building up to Champion Class 'C' which is the most advanced. Top experts can be seen working their dogs which are trained to the highest level at Crufts and at the Kennel Club's 'Discover Dogs', which is a pure exhibition of all the Kennel Club recognised dog breeds without the competition.

Agility and flyball

These are the fastest growing canine sports; the action is very fast and is exciting for both the participants and audiences.
◆ In Agility the idea is for the dog to negotiate up to sixteen obstacles built to a strict criteria against the clock; smaller obstacles are erected for small dogs. There are three types of Agility Tests, and matches are restricted to members of a society. Limited matches are limited to members of the show society or competitors from a specified area, or are limited to certain breeds or sizes. Open tests are open to all. The seven classes (see the list below) are structured so that the competitor can compete against other dogs which are at approximately the same level of expertise.

Agility classes
◆ Elementary
◆ Starters
◆ Novice
◆ Intermediate
◆ Seniors
◆ Advanced
◆ Open

■ **Above:** *Most dogs enjoy competing in Agility Tests. They derive mental stimulation as well as physical exercise and a better rapport with their owner.*

■ **Above:** *This dog has learnt to scale a 2-metre (6-foot) jump from a standstill.*

◆ Flyball is furious, fast and fun for all. Teams of dogs compete against each other in relay. The object is to run a straight course of 30 cm (12 in) high hurdles, activate a pedal on a box which flings a ball into the air, catch the ball and return to base, the next dog being released on the return of the previous dog.

Working Trials

Many breeds were evolved to work alongside man in his many endeavours, such as guarding, herding, hunting and retrieving. Many of these attributes have been adapted to suit today's situations and there are working dogs in the armed services, the police force, customs and excise, and in the hunting field. Working trials have been devised to develop the potential of all suitable dogs. The objective is to have complete control over the dog. The Working Trial consists of some elements of Obedience and Agility but is extended to include speaking, searching, tracking and manwork.

The five levels of competition are known as 'Stakes' and these are as follows:
◆ Companion Dog (CD) Stake
◆ Utility Dog (UD) Stake
◆ Working Dog (WD) Stake
◆ Tracking Dog (TD) Stake
◆ Patrol Dog (PD) Stake

Field Trials

There are four Gundog categories:
◆ Retrievers and Irish Water Spaniels
◆ Sporting Spaniels other than Irish Water Spaniels
◆ Pointers and Setters
◆ Breeds that hunt, point and retrieve

Any dog that competes should be a pedigree and properly registered with the Kennel Club. The Field Trial Societies will send schedules to members together with the entry form which must be accurately completed. Because of the great demand, not all competitors can be accepted and a draw is conducted.

TYPES OF WORKING TRIALS

◆ **Matches and Rallies**
Competition between club members or two or more clubs, this is the ideal competition for working trial beginners.
◆ **Members' Working Trials**
These are limited to members of the organising club.
◆ **Open Working Trials**
Open to everyone; very fierce competition attracting entries from all over the country.
◆ **Championship Working Trials**
Open to all; the best dogs in the country take part because competitors can compete for the Working Trials Certificate which, when won, will entitle the dog to be known as a Working Trials Champion.

The successful applicants will be notified by the secretary.

Hunting has been man's preoccupation for thousands of years and breeds of dogs have been developed to help him in his quest for food. Field Trials exist to test the ability of Gundogs to do their specific work in situations resembling, as far as possible, a day's shooting in the field.

Anyone wishing to compete should become a member of an appropriate club which will help in the training of your dog and advise on the regulations and traditional behaviour. Because of the use of shotguns, safety is of the essence and full instructions are given at the morning's briefing at the venue. There are several eliminating faults, such as whining or running out, and it is considered bad form to leave the Trial early even if a dog is eliminated on his first run. Most people take food and drink to enjoy fully a day out in the country.

Gundog Working Trials

The same rules and procedure apply as with Field Trials. They are restricted to the members of the organising society only so all the training and competition are among friends. This type of work is the most suitable for beginners as it does not involve shooting live game and teaches the dog control. Many can become over-excited if introduced to live game too young. It can be described as a natural extension of simple Obedience but with dummies or cold game used as objects for search and retrieve.

There are three types of tests:
◆ **Retrievers:** These are tested on finding ability, quick pick-ups, quickness and directness of retrieve, natural nose, marking ability, quietness, drive and style.
◆ **Spaniels:** As above but also the ability to quarter the ground, finding and flushing game within range of the handler.
◆ **Hunt, point and retrieve breeds:** The tests are roughly the same as for both Retrievers and Spaniels.

Please note: Every endeavour should be made to arrive on time because if the competitor is late he may lose his place to the reserve. Care should always be taken of the dog.

Chapter Nine

BREEDING

It is no longer considered socially acceptable to have a litter of puppies without an understanding of the implications. It is too easy to fall in love with an entrancing puppy, not realising that without careful training he will be chewing the carpets, being dirty in the house and annoying the neighbours by barking. If it's a bitch, she is also likely to have unwanted puppies unless she is carefully controlled. Many male dogs are still thrown out of homes to become one of the thousands of stray healthy dogs that walk the streets and need rehoming or are even put down but not before he impregnates another stray bitch and adds to the problem.

Government legislation, such as the Dangerous Dogs Act 1991, and local authorities' by-laws, supported by certain sections of the media, are gradually creating a hostile attitude towards dogs and it behoves both dog owners and dog breeders to be aware of the law regarding ownership and breeding. Basically, to avoid any trouble, all dogs must be kept under control in a public place, any faeces should always be picked up and dogs must not cause a nuisance. If it is the intention to breed on a regular basis the breeder should contact the local authorities to check the regulations regarding licences. The Breeding and Welfare of Dogs Act, which came into force in January 2000, allows a hobby breeder to have up to five litters a year as long as they are not making it a business, but should the licensing authorities deem it a business they can demand licensing for less than five litters.

Spaying and castration

Unless it is an owner's intention to breed from their bitch the right thing to do is to have her spayed when she is around six months old. Ask your vet for advice. The operation consists of surgically removing the bitch's reproductive organs – by today's standards, a routine surgical procedure. The cost of the operation varies considerably depending on where you live, but there are charities that offer financial assistance. Apart from negating the risk of cross-bred puppies, spaying will stop neighbourhood male dogs haunting your street and garden when your bitch is in season.

It would be an act of real social responsibility to have a male dog castrated if there is no intention of using him as a stud dog. The surgical removal of the testicles will usually stop him from wandering in search of a bitch and adding to the stray problem. The dog will recover remarkably quickly and there will be no change to his basic character.

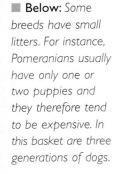

Below: *Some breeds have small litters. For instance, Pomeranians usually have only one or two puppies and they therefore tend to be expensive. In this basket are three generations of dogs.*

Back-street breeding is one of the major causes of canine over-population. In recent years, the price of pedigree puppies has shot up and this accounts for the main motivation for casual breeding – to earn extra undeclared income to purchase a holiday, a video or to pay off the car. However, there are traps for the unwary and unless a person knows what they are doing they are likely to have a litter of ten puppies of a popular breed, such as a Golden Retriever, reaching twelve weeks of age and not a buyer in sight; and that is very heavy on the pocket. After this age the worth of a puppy becomes progressively less, and the end result will probably mean a financial loss.

Be well informed

If your motivation for breeding from your dog is based on a love of dogs and the desire to breed excellent animals in optimum circumstances, go ahead. If you are a novice, you must seek detailed information and obviously an excellent source will be breed books, the best of which will contain detailed information of different lines which will be invaluable when selecting the dog.

Next, consult the breeder of your bitch. If he or she is a well-known breeder/exhibitor they will be interested in improving their own strain and will offer all the help necessary. If you adopted the proper procedure when buying your puppy, the breeder selected will be someone who has all the breeding stock tested for whatever genetic anomalies may exist in the breed. The bitch should be of a calm temperament, not given to nervousness, and she should be subjected to all available and applicable BVA/KC genetic tests. If she's within normal parameters, a stud dog can then be selected.

■ **Right:** *The stud dog should be healthy with no family history of hereditary diseases. He should have a good temperament and be a fine example of the chosen breed.*

The stud dog

The choice of a stud dog is of ultimate importance and cannot be left to chance. The bitch must be studied objectively and her faults and strengths assessed; the dog you select should be strong in the areas in which your bitch is weak. For instance, if the bitch's head is not correctly shaped as demanded by the Breed Standard, the dog selected should have the correct head shape. The aim is that the influence of the dog on the puppies will correct this type of fault but, at the same time, maintain the good qualities of the bitch.

It is a good idea for the bitch's owner to visit the stud dog – be sure to telephone in advance to arrange a mutually convenient time. Take a good look at the dog. He should be fit, healthy and muscular with a good, friendly disposition. The fee, which will vary according to the breed, will be agreed, and as the bitch's owner you must satisfy yourself

that the stud dog is properly registered with The Kennel Club and the terms of the mating have been discussed and agreed upon.

It should be noted that the stud fee is for the service of the dog and not dependent on whether puppies are conceived.

ONE OR TWO MATINGS?

Traditionally, a breeder will allow two matings with twenty-four hours separating them, but this is not mandatory and is entirely up to the stud dog's owner. Opinions vary; some hold that only one mating is necessary but the author is of the opinion that because the timing of conception can be critical it is possible to miss the moment and therefore he has always advocated two matings. The main reason for bitches missing is because the mating is tried too early.

The bitch

If you intend to breed from your bitch, you must ensure that she is healthy and has no hereditary conditions. It is considered best to mate her in her third season when she is about two years old.

The season (oestrus)

It is popularly thought that a bitch comes into season (oestrus) every six months from the age of six months, but there is no hard and fast rule about this and it does vary. It is not considered correct practice to take a litter from a bitch under the age of one year or from her first season. There is no need to worry if the first season is delayed; after the first time the likelihood is that she will come into season roughly three times every two years.

Watch carefully for the onset of the season; the first physical indication is a blood-coloured discharge from the vulva. When the first signs are seen, contact the owners of the selected stud dog, explain what is happening and then be guided by their experience.

The colour of the discharge will gradually change to a light straw colour and by the eleventh day will be virtually colourless – normally this is the time to mate the bitch. Again, the timing is flexible, and twenty-four hours either way is not unusual. A good test is to stand the bitch on her four legs squarely and press your hand firmly on her back by the tail root. If the tail switches from left to right exaggeratedly over the back, she is ready for mating.

■ **Right:** *Some breeds need more specialist knowledge to breed them successfully. Pugs are notoriously difficult and may have either an easy pregnancy or serious problems.*

Litter restrictions

The value of puppies is enhanced by Kennel Club registration but by paying for and accepting a registration a breeder accepts the Rules and Regulations regarding that litter. Puppies born of a dam under the age of one year will not be accepted for registration, and neither will puppies born of a dam over the age of eight years. No more than six litters will be accepted from a bitch during her productive life. This is an attempt to minimize the exploitation of poor bitches from whom some unscrupulous breeders will take a litter every time they come into season until they are too old or incapable and then dispose of them in unpleasant circumstances.

■ **Left:** *Some breeds, such as Retrievers and Wolfhounds, have very large litters.*

Mating

It is traditional for the bitch to be taken to the dog. On arrival at the stud dog's home, she should be allowed time by herself to get over the journey and to relieve herself. From now on it is better that the bitch is not fussed over – what will happen is natural and therefore too much interference from well-meaning owners may be counter-productive. It is better that an experienced dog is used for a first-time bitch and novice owners would be well advised to be guided by the stud dog's owner. During the mating there may be snarling which the novice may think is aggression but it is extremely

■ **Right:** *The happy couple should be allowed to get to know each other before mating.*

unusual for dogs to bite bitches and vice versa during foreplay or the mating.

The two animals are introduced and may play together a little. The dog should be interested if the bitch is ready and he will try to mount her. At this point the stud dog owner will probably ask you to hold the bitch's head. The stud will probably enter the bitch now and if not will be assisted by the owner. The amount of assistance varies from a great deal to none, dependent on the breed. The seminal fluid is passed in the first few seconds of the mating.

The 'tie'

A 'tie' usually takes place and this is when the dog's penis is grasped by the bitch's vaginal muscles and the two dogs are tied together. This varies in time and can last for anything between five minutes and an hour. The reason for this tie has never been satisfactorily explained scientifically, and the canine is the only mammal to exhibit this trait.

However, conception does not rely upon a tie as sometimes there is no tie at all and yet puppies are still conceived, but breeders are happier when it has been achieved.

■ **Above:** *Dogs may play fight before mating but it is rare for them to bite each other. Give them time to play together and don't hurry them.*

Post mating

After the mating the bitch should be given a drink of water and be allowed to rest, either in the travel box or in the car.

WHAT NEXT?

Now is the time for business and a cup of tea. The agreed fee should be handed over to the stud dog's owner who must give you a receipt together with the Kennel Club Form (Form 1) confirming the mating and noting the date and the registered names of both the dog and bitch. This form must be signed by the stud dog's owner and it is very important that, as the owner of the bitch, you do not leave without this document.

PREGNANCY AND BIRTH

As soon as possible, you should notify your vet of the probable date of birth. The period of gestation averages sixty-three days, but a few days either way is not unusual. For the first six weeks there is nothing much for you to do except feed the bitch normally with high-quality food, exercise her to ensure that she stays in good condition but gradually phasing it down until the day of the birth.

Signs of pregnancy

There are indications that the bitch is pregnant:
◆ Her demeanour will change
◆ Her teats will slowly enlarge and get pinker.
It is not easy to determine the number of puppies she will have so it is probably best to leave her in peace and then be pleasantly surprised. Some bitches will have a colourless discharge after three weeks but there is no need to worry; this is just a normal sign of her pregnancy.

Preparing for the litter

Decide now where to put the bitch for the birth and for the first eight weeks of the puppies' lives. She will need a small, quiet room in which the temperature can be maintained at about 20°C (70°F). Ideally she should have a whelping box which should be big enough for her to stand up in and to lie down at full length. There should also be sufficient room for her to lie away from her puppies.

Around the inside of the box will be rails high enough for a puppy to get under to avoid being accidentally squashed by his mother. Train the bitch gently to go into the box, so there'll be no surprises.

Pre-natal feeding

Your bitch should be fed high-quality dog food – sweets, cakes and biscuits should be avoided. At about six weeks into the pregnancy, begin to increase the amount of food by about ten per cent and feed her three times a day. As the puppies grow inside her, the stomach capacity will be less and she will need smaller, more frequent meals. Gradually increase the overall amount of food per day but serve it four times daily. Always leave down

THINGS YOU WILL NEED

Be prepared for the birth and make sure that you have the following items:
◆ Whelping box
◆ Book on puppy birth
◆ Several pieces of man-made fur fabric bedding (available from pet shops)
◆ Several pieces of clean towel, 45 cm (18 inch) square
◆ Surgical scissors
◆ Gentle baby antiseptic
◆ Veterinary milk substitute
◆ Glucose and plain water drinks
◆ Underfloor heating pad
◆ Supply of newspapers
◆ Rubbish bin.

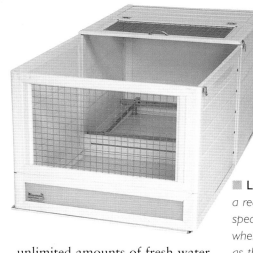

■ **Left:** *You can buy a ready-made, specially designed whelping box, such as this one, or you can construct your own if you are good at DIY projects.*

unlimited amounts of fresh water which is easily available for her. After the puppies are born, the bitch will probably eat up to three times her normal quantity of food as she will have become a milk-producing machine.

Getting ready for the birth

About a week before she is due, introduce the bitch to her new quarters and watch her carefully. Cut away any excess hair from the vulva area and from around the teats. Twenty-four hours before the birth she is liable to be restless, her temperature will drop, she'll scratch up her bedding and pant. At this point, put in several layers of newspapers and phone the vet to warn him that his services might be needed.

The birth

Here is a brief description of the birth process; the trick really is to allow the bitch to give birth naturally but to be there to assist and comfort her if necessary. Some breeds experience difficulties and may need Caesarean sections. Before you start, do scrub your hands and cut and smooth the nails. Watch carefully for the first contraction and make sure that the bitch is in her whelping box. A first-time bitch may be confused so you should comfort her with some soft, reassuring words.

The birth process

◆ The first sign is usually a grey membrane protruding from the vulva like a bubble; it may be withdrawn and emerge several times. Be patient and watch the contractions; they'll get quicker.
◆ When the puppy's head appears, she should expel it. If it seems not to be moving, you may have to step in and help. Grasp the head lightly with a towel piece and pull gently with the contractions. A green liquid will come out and stain your fingers, but don't worry as this is quite normal.
◆ Cut the umbilical cord about 5 cm (2 in) from the body, being

■ **Below:** *This tiny Cavalier King Charles Spaniel puppy is just emerging into the outside world.*

careful not to pull it. Open the mouth and clear out any mucus. Clear away the membrane which may be around the pup's body.
◆ Briskly rub all over the body with the towel. When the puppy is squeaking loudly, open its mouth and place it on a back teat. If it rejects the nipple, keep trying.
◆ The bitch will turn and lick the new arrival which she must be allowed to do. She may expel the placenta (afterbirth) with the puppy and then may eat it (it looks like a piece of liver). It is said to stimulate milk production but it is wise only to allow her to eat one or two, otherwise her motions will be loose. Try to count the number of placentas – there should be the same number as there are puppies; if not, the vet should be told.

Birth problems

If a pup presents itself backwards it is a breech birth and every effort should be made to get it out quickly because of the possibility of suffocation. However, any attempt by you to help the puppy out must always be in time

■ **Above:** *After the birth, the bitch will suckle her puppies. If any are reluctant to suck, place them on a teat.*

with the mother's contractions.

If the bitch stops contracting during the whelping, contact the vet immediately; she may be suffering from primary inertia. Always have some tepid glucose water available to refresh her. When the bitch is apparently contentedly suckling her new family, take her outside to relieve herself; meanwhile, get someone to remove the soiled newspaper and put in the clean fur fabric. This should be changed on a daily basis for the next eight weeks.

IMPORTANT

Should the bitch show signs of acute distress, such as violent trembling, whining or staggering, after the whelping and up to three weeks after the birth, it's an emergency! She may be suffering from eclampsia and will need urgent veterinary treatment immediately; without treatment she may die.

POSTNATAL CARE

Apart from removing the dew claws and docking, according to the Breed Standard, by a vet on the second day there is little for you to do until the pups are ready to wean at three weeks. It is a good idea for the vet to visit them and check them over to make sure that they and their mother are healthy and the puppies' nails aren't too long.

Don't allow strangers or young children near the bitch; she may be defensive. Children should not handle the pups for a week or so as they can be delicate. Examine and handle the puppies every day; it's important to socialize them even when their eyes aren't open. They open at around fourteen days and what they see and hear will have a profound effect on their lives. Take the bitch out to relieve herself several times a day and start giving her a little exercise.

Weaning

When the puppies are three weeks old, scrape a piece of stewing steak with a sharp knife to make a paste. Let the puppies suck it off your fingers, and after two days put it in a dish for them. The next day, add a little scrambled egg and mash up some baby's rusk in puppy milk substitute (available from your vet). Offer this once a day for two or three days, and then add some cooked minced meat – this should always be good-quality meat, not pet grade, because of the possibility of tiny slivers of bone. After about a week, offer meat meals twice a day plus two milk and egg meals but only in small amounts because of the puppies' small stomachs. Gradually increase the amounts and always provide fresh water in a shallow bowl.

During this time the pups will still take milk from their mother but in smaller amounts so gradually reduce the amount of food she is getting. By the time the pups are five to six weeks old, her milk supply will dry up and any suckling is for comfort only. If she wants to leave her pups she can, but let her sleep with them at night. Vaccination against Parvovirus is advisable at six or seven weeks where there is history of Parvovirus in the house but it can be given with other vaccines at ten weeks. If given at six to seven weeks, you will be advised to repeat it at ten weeks because antibodies in the mother's blood may make the first injection ineffective. In any case, seek veterinary advice.

Left: *Do not wean the puppies until they are three weeks old. While they are very young, they will get all the nourishment they need from their mother's milk.*

Above: *Always be gentle when handling very young puppies. This Yorkshire Terrier puppy is particularly tiny and fragile and no force can be used.*

SELLING THE PUPPIES

Make preparations for the sale of the puppies a week after birth and sell them after eight weeks of age. Try the bitch's breeder, stud dog's owner, breed club, advertisements in the canine press and The Kennel Club which, for a small fee, will put potential buyers in touch with you. The best breeders include the following in the price of a puppy:
◆ One month's insurance
◆ A week's free supply of the puppy's usual food
◆ A diet sheet
◆ Unlimited advice
◆ A buy-back agreement if the puppy is unsuitable

◆ A receipt for all monies you have received and any special terms agreed in writing.

Finding good homes
Ask some searching questions of any potential buyers:
◆ Will someone be at home during the day with the puppy?
◆ Do they have young children?
◆ Are they prepared to exercise the puppy?
◆ Do they have other pets?
◆ Do they have a secure garden?
If you aren't satisfied with their answers or feel that something's amiss, don't sell them the puppy.

The most popular dog breeds

Some of the world's best-loved and most popular breeds of dog are featured in the following pages with detailed information and expert advice on their history and origins, their temperament, working ability, appearance and suitability as family pets. If you are considering owning one of these dogs, you can check on how much exercise they need and also their grooming requirements.

Chapter Ten

DOG BREED GUIDE

In the following pages you will find detailed information on the thirty most popular dog breeds plus brief descriptions of some other well-loved breeds that make good family pets. The way in which dogs are classified varies, and different countries and their canine governing bodies still use different systems. However, they are usually classified according to the type of work they perform.

Gundog group

These gundogs were specifically bred to work at finding, flushing out and retrieving gamebirds.

Hound group

These speedy dogs were developed to hunt, chase and kill prey. They are divided into scenthounds and sighthounds for locating prey.

Working group

These dogs have been bred over the centuries to perform specific tasks, including guarding, rescue work and police work.

Terrier group

These dogs were bred to hunt and dig out vermin and small game. Most terriers evolved in the British Isles and they all adore digging.

Toy group

These miniature dogs were first developed and bred to become companions and pets. Their size makes them suitable for city life.

Pastoral group

These ancient dogs have been used to protect livestock for centuries. They tend to be highly intelligent but need a lot of exercise.

Utility group

This group of popular pet dogs contains all the breeds that do not fit easily into the other categories. Dogs in this group make good pets.

HOW TO USE THE BREED GUIDE

Guarding instinct

Longer bars mean a stronger guarding instinct and denote a good watchdog which will warn of approaching strangers and deter any unwanted intruders.

Temperament

Longer bars mean a good temperament and indicate a breed that is noted for its friendly nature, making it more suitable as an affectionate family pet.

Exercise

Longer bars mean that a breed needs a lot of daily exercise, including free running and playing stimulating games in addition to regular walks on the lead.

Grooming

Longer bars mean that you must be prepared to spend more time grooming and tend to apply to long-haired breeds and those that need clipping or stripping.

Other dogs

Longer bars mean that a breed is friendly and non-aggressive to other dogs, and will socialize well with dogs of most breeds in a range of surroundings.

Summary and height

This sums up the specific breed's main attributes, temperament and suitability as a family pet, followed by a box related to the height ranges for the breed.

Gundog group

Cocker Spaniel

Guarding instinct

Will warn of any approaching intruders

Temperament

Sweet natured and co-operative

Exercise

As much as possible

Grooming

Daily attention to ears and feathering

Other dogs

Friendly and sociable

Summary

Happy-go-lucky, makes a lovely family pet

H

Males:
39–41 cm (15½–16 in)

Bitches:
38–39 cm (15–15½ in)

■ *Right: The friendly Cocker Spaniel loves to join in all family activities and makes the perfect pet.*

This charming spaniel is believed to have originated in pre-fourteenth-century Spain. It evolved through selective breeding from several Gundog breeds, depending on the terrain worked and the prey. Originally Cockers assisted in falconry and were later used to drive birds into nets. When game bird shooting reached its zenith during the nineteenth century, the Cocker was found to be particularly effective in putting up woodcock.

Temperament

Today there are more pets than there are workers because Cockers are gentle, intelligent, biddable and easily trained. A classic companion, mainly because Cockers love the fellowship of their human family. Their greatest pleasure is to join in family activities, lying by the fire, horse-play with the children, shopping with mother and shooting with father.

Work

A hallmark of this breed is its happiness when working. Indeed, the Cocker's enthusiasm knows no bounds, underlined by the incessant tail wagging. It hurriedly quarters the ground, freezing as it bolts a bird or rabbit waiting for the shot and then goes after the next. Remembering where the game lies, the Cocker can easily find and retrieve it unmarked because it has an extraordinarily soft mouth.

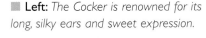

■ *Left: The Cocker is renowned for its long, silky ears and sweet expression.*

General care

To stay happy, the Cocker Spaniel needs all the exercise possible, particularly free running in woods and fields. It is important to comb the ears daily, and a good idea to feed your dog from a tall narrow dish which keeps the ears out of the food. Comb out any debris after exercise and groom the dog at least once a week.

Appearance

A square dog with a merry nature and a soft expression. It is well-muscled with good bone and an easy mover. It has a silky, flat coat, well-feathered forelegs and underparts and above the hocks.

Health problems

Some hip dysplasia (page 102) and kidney problems (page 114). Only buy puppies from eye-tested parents.

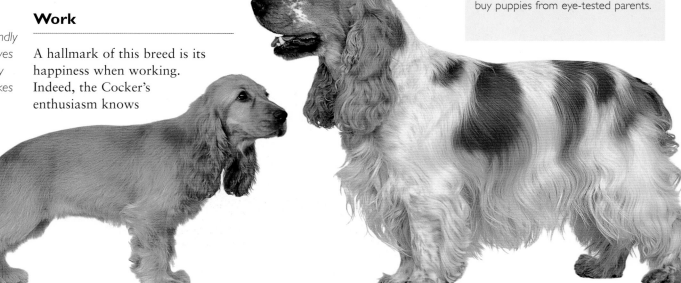

English Springer Spaniel

O ne of the oldest recorded sporting dogs, the lively Springer Spaniel was first mentioned in literature by the poet Chaucer. The word 'Spaniel' may be derived from the Spanish word 'Espangnol'. The Springer was developed to become one of the great working Gundogs during the nineteenth century.

Temperament

This is a gentle, loving dog whose natural desire is to please. The Springer is highly intelligent and reacts well to kind training. Being so energetic, these dogs become a nuisance without early training. They need things to do, especially retrieving games and play, and take to Agility and Flyball with enthusiasm. They crave and give affection, hating to be alone, and are very good with children.

Work

Springers are working gundogs with boundless energy. Their prime object is to 'spring' game from their hiding place for the shooters but they can also point and retrieve. They will enter the thickest cover fearlessly and leap into freezing water to retrieve a bird. Their extraordinary sense

Health problems

Some hip dysplasia (page 102). Eye problems include Progressive retinal atrophy (page 103). Buy only from tested parents.

of smell has recently been exploited by police and customs who train Springers to sniff out drugs and explosives.

General care

Springers need plenty of free running and play daily. They should be brushed and combed once a week. Trim the feathering with scissors and make sure you keep the ears dry and clean.

■ **Above:** *Springers like nothing better than to be outside in the open air.*

Appearance

The Springer is taller than the Cocker Spaniel with a weather-resistant coat and feathering on the ears, forelegs and hindquarters. The coat may be black and white, liver and white or one of these with tan markings.

■ **Below:** *This show Springer has a weather-resistant coat.*

Guarding instinct

Will warn but friendly

Temperament

Gentle and kind

Exercise

A great deal daily

Grooming

Weekly brushing, ears daily

Other dogs

No problems

Summary
A loving family pet

H

Males:
Approx 50 cm (20 in)

Bitches:
Approx 50 cm (20 in)

Gundog group # Labrador Retriever

Guarding instinct

Will warn but friendly

Temperament

Cool and laid back

Exercise

As much as possible

Grooming

Negligible

Other dogs

No problems

Summary

A wonderful companion dog

H

Males:
56–57 cm (22–23 in)

Bitches:
54–56 cm (21–22 in)

■ **Below:** *Labrador puppies may look small and cute but they grow up into large, powerful dogs. Their natural desire to play makes them good family pets.*

The seventeenth century saw trade between Britain and Newfoundland – slates out and salt fish back. An all-purpose water dog helped the fishermen to retrieve dropped articles, haul carts and retrieve game. Called St John's Dogs, they were originally brought to Poole, England, by sailors. The Earl of Malmesbury, recognising their skills, developed them as gundogs. Worldwide, this is the most popular Retriever of all. Almost the perfect gundog, the Labrador Retriever has a natural inclination to retrieve on land and water, a desire to please and the ability to learn easily.

Temperament

An affable breed, the Labrador Retriever is tolerant and easy-going with dogs and human beings, enjoys the company of children and will allow them to take liberties. However, it is easily upset by shouting or harsh treatment of any kind.

General care

Puppies are very ebullient but with early and kind domestic training they fit into the family quickly. Labradors have a voracious appetite and a tendency to over-weight, so monitor your dog's diet carefully. Stimulating their brains prevents destructive habits forming; owners should invent search and retrieve games and involve them in all family activities.

■ **Above:** *This line-up of working dogs shows the range of colours, from black through yellow to liver and cream.*

Health problems

Hip dysplasia (page 102). Some eye conditions: Multi-focal retinal dysplasia (MRD), Progressive retinal atrophy (PRA), hereditary cataracts and entropion (see page 103). The best breeders test their breeding dogs.

They have a need for love and understanding. The Labrador is an active, country dog needing plenty of exercise, free running and play. Grooming is minimal; all you need to do is just clean the ears and brush the coat weekly to rid it of dead hairs.

Appearance

A strongly built dog, the Labrador has a broad, deep chest and a distinctive short, dense coat which can withstand the cold and wet. Coat colours are chocolate or liver, yellow or black.

Golden Retriever

In 1825 Lord Tweedmouth mated his 'Yellow' Retriever to a Tweed Water Spaniel (now extinct). One of the resulting progeny was mated to another Tweed Water Spaniel, the progeny of which was mated back again. It is rumoured that a Bloodhound was added together with a Sheepdog from a troupe of performing Russian circus dogs with which his Lordship became enamoured and bought. And thus today's Golden Retriever evolved.

Temperament

A gentle, biddable dog which is highly intelligent and capable of combining the best working qualities with those of a near perfect pet dog. Delightful family pets, Golden Retrievers are happy to be the gundog for the father, an elegant companion for the mother, and a playmate for the children.

■ **Right:** *The handsome Golden Retriever makes a wonderful family pet and working dog.*

■ **Left:** *The eyes are gentle and loving.*

Work

These excellent retrievers have a soft mouth and a good nose for finding lost game. They are easily trained to be all-purpose gundogs and work with great enthusiasm, braving the thickest cover and the coldest water. Their versatility and intelligence have led them to becoming great guide dogs for the blind and assistance dogs for the disabled.

General care

Being mainly a country hunting dog, the Golden Retriever needs frequent exercise and plenty of mental stimulation. It excels at Obedience and Flyball. These dogs should always be brushed and combed twice a week to rid the coat of dead hairs and tangles from the feathering.

Appearance

This medium-sized dog is strongly built and muscular with a gentle, loving expression in the eyes. The coat is dense with good feathering and a water-resistant undercoat. The colour varies from a cream to a rich, lustrous gold.

Health problems

Hip dysplasia (page 102), elbow dysplasia (page 103) and some eye problems. Buy from tested stock.

Guarding instinct

Will warn of approach but no aggression

Temperament

A gentle, kindly disposition

Exercise

Can never have enough

Grooming

Twice-weekly brush and comb

Other dogs

Friendly

Summary

A great companion

H

Males:
56–61 cm (22–24 in)

Bitches:
51–56 cm (20–22 in)

Hound group

Beagle

Guarding instinct

Will warn but no aggression

Temperament

Easy-going, friendly

Exercise

Plenty

Grooming

Weekly brush and polish

Other dogs

No problems

Summary

A happy, laid-back companion

Ideally: **H**
33–40 cm (13–16 in)

A small hound dating from Norman times, the Beagle evolved and was developed from the Talbot Hound and the Southern Hound. A further mix with small hounds produced the breed first recorded by name in the 'Privy Accounts' of Henry VIII. As the larger hunted animals became scarce, huntsmen developed the Beagle to hunt hares which they do with enthusiasm and skill.

Temperament

An intelligent dog with a peaceful nature, the Beagle can adjust well to town or country life. It readily accepts children as part of its family and likes to feel part of the human pack. Beagles are happy, easy-going and people-orientated, adapting well to most environments. However, they are not the easiest dogs to train and require a lot of kindness and patience.

Work

As a pack dog, the Beagle has few equals. It is not quarrelsome and is relatively easy to train to be behaved when hunting. Having short legs, it works slower than the Harrier or English Hound but hunts cheerfully with its flag (tail) held high and enters dense cover with equanimity. Packs are usually hunted with huntsmen on foot.

Health problems

Rare hip problems. An eye problem under investigation. Otherwise, a hardy, long-lived companion.

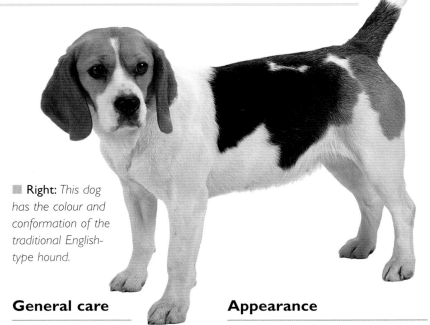

■ **Right:** *This dog has the colour and conformation of the traditional English-type hound.*

General care

Beagles need plenty of exercise which must be augmented with playing in the garden. They eat well and care should be taken to keep them in athletic form as they have a tendency to overweight. A weekly brush and a polish with a chamois leather keeps them looking good.

■ **Below:** *The build and markings of this Beagle are favoured in America.*

Appearance

Small to medium in size, two varieties of Beagle exist in the United States, one not exceeding 33 cm (13 in) in height whereas the other is taller but does not exceed 38 cm (15 in). However, in Britain, 33–40 cm (13–16 in) is acceptable. Tri-colours are most popular with a black back, tan sides and top of legs, and a white chest, stomach and lower legs.

Dachshund

Mystery veils the real origins of this breed. Its German name is *Teckel*, a word that is found at the base of an ancient Egyptian sculpture of familiarly long-bodied, short-legged dogs. 'Dachshund' means

'badger dog' and it is one of the oldest hunting breeds in Germany, mentioned in records since the fifteenth century. The different sizes and coats have evolved since around 1850 and today the most popular variety is the Miniature Long-haired Dachshund. Few, if

■ **Right:** *The Smooth-haired Dachshund makes a spirited companion and pet.*

any, Dachshunds hunt in Britain but they have not lost their instincts. A few are still used in Germany and in France, particularly the very small variety know in Germany as the Rabbit Dachshund. They will go underground but are in danger of being trapped. At one time, the Standards were general hunters of foxes, deer and even boar.

Temperament

The Dachshund is easy to live with and very affectionate within its human family. Playful and mischievous, it is sometimes stubborn as befits a hunting dog. A most adaptable breed, living with equal ease in town or country. Intelligent and easily trained, it is sometimes spirited,

■ **Below:** *The Dachshund is a game little dog who loves hunting.*

always humorous. The Long-haireds are more independent than the Wires and Smooths which are more demonstrative.

General care

All varieties adore activity and need free running and play daily. Each variety has its miniature equivalent. Whereas the Smooths need a soft brush and polish weekly, the Long-haireds need brushing and combing bi-weekly, and the Wire-haireds should be hand stripped every three months.

Appearance

A long, low dog known as the 'sausage dog', it is full of life and always alert. All colours are acceptable but only small white patches on the chest are permitted.

Health problems

All varieties can have back problems and they should not be allowed to run up and down steps or stairs. Only buy miniature Dachshunds from eye-tested parents.

Guarding instinct

Distrustful, all sizes will warn off strangers

Temperament

Easy-going, playful but can be stubborn

Exercise

Needs plenty plus play and hunting in woods

Grooming

Smooths: minimal

Long-haired: bi-weekly

Wires: weekly

Other dogs

No great problems

Summary
One of these varieties will suit any family

H

Miniatures and Standards:
13–25 cm (5–10 in)

Working group

Boxer

Guarding instinct

A serious guard

Temperament

Good natured but boisterous without aggression

Exercise

Must have plenty

Grooming

Weekly brushing

Other dogs

Easy going

Summary

The right dog for the right family

H

Males:
57–63 cm (22½–25 in)

Bitches:
slightly smaller

The Boxer is a German manufactured breed derived from the ancient Mastiff-style dog which accompanied the Roman legions across Europe. Like several other big breeds, Boxers have, in their lineage, the blood of the Bullenbeiser – dogs bred for the purpose of bull baiting. However, the Boxer did not come to the fore until around 1890, after bull baiting was outlawed.

Temperament

Bred to be a companion, guard and show dog, the Boxer's intelligence and brightness of spirit endear him to most nationalities. An alert house guard with a booming voice but never vicious. As a member of a family, the Boxer is truly a fun dog, very affectionate and loyal to the end.

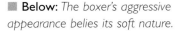 **Below:** *The boxer's aggressive appearance belies its soft nature.*

Work

Once over the puppy stages, Boxers are easily trained for all manner of security work. The breed is used in Europe as a police dog where its muscular, hard body can stop a criminal in his tracks. Armed forces make use of its determination and confident attitude. The Boxer's aggressive appearance often warns off wrong-doers, but this dog is not a biter and its formidable looks belie its soft nature.

Above: *Easily trained and strongly built, the Boxer is a good guard dog.*

General care

The Boxer can be boisterous and exuberant and should be trained kindly not to jump up on children whom it loves. Natural athletes, Boxers need plenty of activity, free running and play. Minimal grooming is required: a weekly brushing will remove dead hairs, then polish with a chamois leather or hound glove.

Appearance

A superb athletic body rippling with muscles, of medium size with a short, glossy coat in fawn shades from light to deep red, or distinct brindle stripes. White is allowed but not exceeding one-third of the base colour.

Schnauzer

This friendly, muscular dog was almost certainly derived from the ancient Wire-haired Pinscher to which it bears a startling resemblance, as can be seen in a picture by Albrecht Dürer (1492). A fourteenth-century statue of a hunter in Mechlinburg, Germany, has a similar-looking dog crouched at his feet. This old breed was once a general farm dog, keeping down rats, hunting and protecting its owners. It was used to accompany stagecoaches in order to defend them against robbers who worked the forests, and thus it became known as the 'Carriage Griffon'.

Temperament

Absolutely devoted to its family, the Schnauzer is a happy dog who can be trained fairly easily to be obedient. There is no need to worry about your property or children if this fellow lives with you – it is an outstanding

■ **Above:** *Although this dog may look fierce and is very protective of its family, it has a very friendly nature.*

watchdog. Courageous and assertive, it is a friendly dog and needs strong but kind handling.

Work

The original Pinscher was an all-round farm dog doing anything that was expected of him. The modern Schnauzer is usually a much-loved family pet and does not generally have

work to do but even so it still retains the will and the ability. In some European countries, these dogs are used as guard dogs – a role they relish.

General care

All Schnauzers require frequent running exercise and play to maintain their athleticism and mental health. They are also the natural friends of horses. The wire coat needs hand-stripping four times a year, and the leg and face furnishings should be combed out twice a week.

Appearance

A chunky, medium-sized muscular dog, the coat is black or pepper and salt (greyish) in colour. The outer coat is wiry, harsh to the touch and is distinguished by a beard and bushy eyebrows; the undercoat is dense.

Health problems

None. This is generally a very healthy, hardy breed.

Guarding instinct

Suspicious so prowlers beware

Temperament

Affectionate family dog; brave, loyal and cares deeply

Exercise

Enough to keep muscle tone

Grooming

Needs hand-stripping quarterly

Other dogs

Males can be dominant

Summary
A good all-round family pet

H

Males:
48 cm (19 in)

Bitches:
46 cm (18 in)

■ **Left:** *The dense, wiry coat will need combing through twice every week.*

Working group

Siberian Husky

Guarding instinct

Not a guard dog, too easy-going

Temperament

Kind, gentle and very affectionate

Exercise

A glutton for running; try cart training

Grooming

Twice-weekly deep grooming required

Other dogs

Generally friendly, good disposition

Summary

An excellent companion for energetic families

H

Males:
53–60 cm (21–23½ in)

Bitches:
slightly smaller

Husky sled dogs were the only means of transport in Alaska during the gold rush of 1900. Dog team drivers developed rivalries and started to stage races. In 1920, a team of

twenty Siberians pulled a sled for 340 miles carrying vaccines to the diphtheria-stricken city of Nome, saving the population. A statue of a sled dog in Central Park, New York, celebrates that achievement. Because the breed lived closely, probably for thousands of years, with the Chukchi nation, they are 'people orientated'.

■ **Right:** *Huskies are very energetic, friendly dogs.*

Temperament

The Siberian Husky is gentle, friendly and people-loving, intelligent and biddable. Easy-going, easy to train and anxious to please, the Siberian Husky is a pack dog who understands its family, particularly the children.

Work

In the land of their origin, the Husky is a much-cherished working dog and was used for hauling sleds laden with meat and fish. Their tremendous strength and stamina allows them to make some phenomenally long journeys. When necessary, they also helped with hunting. Today, in the West, they are usually companion dogs although the sport of sled dog racing is growing rapidly.

General care

Without their work, all Huskies will need frequent free running and exercise, and new owners should consider joining a specialist club which races with wheeled carts. These dogs moult freely and have a double coat which needs grooming with combing at least twice a week; the undercoat can knot.

Appearance

The medium-sized Husky looks very alert and is lithe with grace. It has an abundant weatherproof coat with a thick, soft undercoat. The breed comes in a variety of colours; the facial colours can be contrasting, unusual and striking.

■ **Below:** *Elegant and athletic, the Siberian Husky does not bark but howls and talks.*

Health problems

Hip dysplasia (page 102) with a low breed average. There are some eye problems so puppies should come only from eye-tested parents.

Rottweiler

The likely origin is from the Mastiff-style dogs which travelled with Roman armies driving livestock as they swept northwards conquering Europe. First used as boar hunters, then as cattle drovers in the German city of Rottweil (a cattle market town in mediaeval times), they doubled as custodians of traders' money. The Rottweiler is devoted to its family but must be taught its place kindly but persistently. Because of its intensely protective nature, it is not advisable to leave this dog with young children as, like all guarding breeds, it might misinterpret their signals.

Temperament

Highly intelligent, the Rottweiler's strong naturally protective instincts need socialization with firm but kind training. These dogs can be difficult in the wrong hands.

Work

Very few Rottweilers are used for their droving ability nowadays. Instead, their strong protective instincts are now put to use in security work. In Great Britain they are often used to patrol building sites and industrial installations as well as acting as security van guards. Because of their singular intelligence, other countries train them as customs and police dogs, mountain rescue dogs and even use them for sled hauling.

■ **Below:** *In spite of its powerful body and formidable appearance, this dog can make a good pet if properly trained.*

General care

Keep these big dogs' muscles hard with walking, free running and play. If you live in a town, you should take them out for a brisk walk at least twice a day. With their thick, smooth coat, they need only be brushed once a week with a stiff brush to remove dead hairs.

Appearance

A big, thick-set, muscled dog, the Rottweiler should show

Health problems

Occasional hip dysplasia (page 102); Osteochondrosis dessicans (OCD) largely under control (page 103); entropion (page 103).

boldness and confidence, never nervousness or aggressiveness. The Rottweiler has a calm look which indicates a good nature and needs no training as a house guard.

Guarding instinct

Great guard dog, malefactors beware

Temperament

Good-natured but can be dominant without training

Exercise

Frequent, thrives on plenty of activity

Grooming

Easy care; weekly brush and comb

Other dogs

Take care as they will not back down

Summary

The time spent training pays dividends

H

Males:
63–69 cm (25–27 in)

Bitches:
58–63 cm (23–25 in)

■ **Left:** *A young puppy will need kind but firm training and lots of socialization if it is to grow into a good-natured adult.*

Working group

Dobermann

Guarding instinct

A powerful guard dog

Temperament

A great family dog needing to be trained

Exercise

An hour a day walking plus free running

Grooming

A weekly brushing

Other dogs

Seldom picks a fight but never backs down

Summary

A family dog for experienced owners

H

Males:
69 cm (27 in)

Bitches:
65 cm (25½ in)

■ **Left:** *If it is well-socialized and trained, a Dobermann puppy can adapt really well to family life.*

'dog catcher', gave him the ideal opportunity to study various breeds. The Rottweiler, the old German Pinscher and also the Manchester Terrier were probably the foundation. Later the breed may have been refined even further with the addition of Pointer and Greyhound blood.

Temperament

A devoted, affectionate house dog, the Dobermann is very intelligent and is easily trained but its power must be kept under control. It is a devout family companion who loves to be part of daily activities. Its guardianship of the family's children is legendary but it must be trained firmly but kindly.

Work

Highly regarded as a guard and security dog, the Dobermann is much favoured by many security companies moving large sums of money. It was a watchdog soldier and messenger in battles during World War II, and it is now used by the police

This breed was designed in the 1880s by Herr Louis Dobermann, a German tax collector. At a time when taxes were collected personally, he wanted a fearless, alert dog with stamina to defend him as he travelled the country extensively on horseback. His secondary job, a

■ **Above:** *Powerful but elegant, this big dog makes an ideal guard dog and an affectionate pet.*

Health problems

Low to average hip dysplasia (page 102). Buy from eye-tested parents and test the puppy. Von Willebrand's disease (page 103) is also possible.

■ **Above:** *A well-trained Dobermann can be a formidable guard dog as well as a loving and loyal family pet.*

in many countries worldwide because of its bravery, intelligence and alertness, to say nothing of its athletic strength.

General care

An hour or so of walking every day with about ten minutes' free running will suffice. Add fifteen minutes' play in the garden and a Dobermann will be happy and fit. Very little grooming is required; a weekly brush and polish with a chamois leather will be enough.

Appearance

A big dog, the Dobermann is very graceful with a refined outline; a powerhouse athlete. The coat is a glossy black, brown, blue or fawn (Isabella) with rich tan which must be well defined.

Great Dane

■ Above: *The Great Dane is a majestic-looking dog with its powerful physique and appealing expression.*

There is no doubt that this dog's ancestors were giant war dogs from Asia Minor known as Allens. They probably originated from ancient Egypt. They were used as war dogs by Attila the Hun and fought wild animals in Rome's Colosseum. The modern dog was developed in the 1500s in Germany for hunting wild boar. A pack owned by Earl Philip of Hessen killed 2,572 boar in 1563, and another German aristocrat had a pack of 600 Great Danes. From about 1882, when the Breed Club was formed, the breed changed course and became a pet and guard dog. It

has been many years since Great Danes were worked in any form. Mediaeval pictures depict them in their fighting gear, consisting of an armoured coat with spikes.

Temperament

It is a courageous, devoted but sensitive breed which belies its bloodthirsty past. Very family oriented, Great Danes are easily trained and obedient. Although large, they are not clumsy and don't take up too much space. However, a big house and garden are best. Seriously fond of their family's children, they will defend them if any danger threatens.

Health problems

Hip dysplasia (see page 102), elbow dysplasia (see page 103), bloat and eye problems which are under investigation.

General care

These dogs need only some gentle exercise when young which can be built up gradually over time to develop their muscular, athletic body. A fully-grown adult Great Dane will demand plenty of walks and free running. Never play fight with this breed. A weekly good brushing will keep the dog's coat lustrous; the ears need cleaning at the same time.

Appearance

A majestic dog, the Great Dane has a soft expression and an athletic body with a look of 'dash and daring'. Colours range from brindle with stripes to fawn-light to dark, blue-light to dark slate, black or harlequin with black or blue patches which appear torn.

■ Below: *The Great Dane is a gentle giant in spite of its size.*

Working group

Guarding instinct

Suspicious nature, will guard owners

Temperament

Friendly, outgoing, favours children

Exercise

Puppies not too much; adults need plenty

Grooming

Minimal: just a weekly brush and polish with a hound glove

Other dogs

Gets on with others

Summary
A deeply affectionate big dog, loyal and caring for his family

H

Males:
Min. 76 cm (30 in)

Bitches:
Min. 71 cm (28 in)

Parson Jack Russell Terrier

Guarding instinct

A very watchful dog; intruders beware

Temperament

Happy-go-lucky fun dog, very intelligent and trainable

Exercise

Running and playing as much as possible

Grooming

Smooth-haired needs very little grooming; rough-haired needs brushing

Other dogs

Not aggressive but will stand his ground

Summary

Ideal for the dynamic country family

H

Males:
35 cm (14 in)

Bitches:
33 cm (13 in)

Parson Jack Russell was a cleric who was, rather unjustly, more famed for his hunting exploits than for his pastoral work. Born in Devon in 1795, he took a good degree at Oxford and was ordained in 1819. As a student he aggravated the college authorities by keeping an illicit small pack of hounds. It was whilst he was up at Oxford that he acquired the terrier bitch who was to be the foundation of the breed that was named after him. While strolling in Magdalen Meadow one day he met the local milkman and saw, for the first time, the terrier named Trump. He did not move until he had persuaded the milkman to part with her. The parson died at eighty-four, still in the saddle, his breed of dogs a fitting memorial.

Temperament

Highly intelligent, the busy Jack Russell is always doing things and is very affectionate as well as being a good guard – ever alert and watchful. Their wonderful friendly nature blossoms within a happy family and they are very patient with children. This is an easily-trained, fun dog which is into everything.

Health problems

A generally healthy breed but buy from eye-tested parents.

■ **Above:** *The long-legged Parson Jack Russell loves to be outside hunting.*

Work

This is a working terrier which is reflected in the Breed Standard. The Jack Russell must have the conformation to go to earth and to run with hounds. Its job is to either mark the fox underground or

■ **Left:** *Ever vigilant, the Jack Russell's keen senses will flush out small prey, such as rats and mice.*

bolt it. This dog has courage without recklessness coupled with stamina. It is also one of the great ratters with razor-sharp reactions.

General care

There are two coats: the smooth variety requires only a weekly brush whereas the rough coat needs hand stripping or trimming every four to five months as well as weekly brushing. Basically, this is a country dog needing plenty of exercise and mental stimulation.

Appearance

A small athletic dog, it is full of vitality, slightly longer than height at the shoulders. The wiry or smooth coat is mostly white with black and/or tan patches. Note that the long-legged Parson Jack Russell should not be confused with the smaller-legged Jack Russell terrier.

West Highland White Terrier

U p to the mid-1800s the terriers of Scotland were a rough, hard, ill-disciplined and nondescript mixed lot which kept down the rats and foxes on the small crofts. As foxhunting became fashionable, gentlemen began taking notice of terriers but white dogs were not liked. Some people thought they were not as game as coloured dogs. However, a Colonel Edward Malcolm, thinking one of his own brown terriers was a fox as it emerged from an earth, accidentally shot it, and from then on he developed this unmistakable white terrier and was the club's first chairman in 1906. The Westie was used as an all-purpose worker and was kept as a 'vermin' killer and was taken out to hunt foxes, otters and wild cats. It had stamina and courage and was agile enough to clamber over rocks and penetrate the smallest holes where its prey could hide.

Left: *Westie puppies are spirited and extremely energetic.*

Temperament

Feisty, stubborn, friendly, playful and affectionate, the Westie is a bright pet for town or country. Very few pet dogs can replicate this bundle of paradoxes – a fun dog who one minute will be digging up your flower beds while hunting non-existent moles and the next minute will be lying on your lap with all the love of a spaniel. A clean and biddable terrier.

General care

Twice-daily walks are essential and the Westie needs the freedom to run and play-hunt in a garden with the family. It needs stripping and shaping every three months and combing daily.

Right: *The Westie is a fun-loving little dog with a feisty character.*

Above: *The head should be slightly domed with very dark eyes.*

Appearance

A short-legged, square dog with a profuse wiry white coat which needs careful attention in order to maintain the typical shape.

Guarding instinct

A good, alert guard

Temperament

Playful, mischievous, happy

Exercise

Plenty of play and running

Grooming

Frequent combing to stop tangling; stripping every three months

Other dogs

Seldom picks a quarrel but will defend itself

Summary
A family dog full of zest

H

Males:
28 cm (11 in)

Bitches:
slightly less

Health problems

Some eye problems are under investigation; a type of eczema and fairly rare Perthe's disease.

Staffordshire Bull Terrier

Guarding instinct

A forceful deterrent

Temperament

Easy-going, happy clown

Exercise

Walking, running and play essential

Grooming

Very little; use a hound glove to polish

Other dogs

Not confrontational but beware, he will never back down

Summary
A wonderful family dog but not for the novice owner

H

Ideally:
35.5–40.5 cm
(14–16 in)
Note: Height is related to weight

As a breed the 'Staffie' is a comparative newcomer. However, its antecedents probably go back 6000 years as it belongs to an exclusive club of Mastiff-style dogs bred game enough to fight against all odds on the bidding of their masters. They fought in battles shoulder to shoulder with the soldiers; they fought wild animals in Roman times; and they fought bulls, bears, rats and, finally, each other. The Duke of Hamilton, a sporting rake of around 1770, developed a lighter fighter, the big Bulldogs not being fast enough, which is claimed to be the forerunner of the breed today. At the end of the eighteenth century, they were the best fighting dogs. Later on, they also proved themselves in rat-pits where a dog, Billy, killed 100 rats in seven minutes thirty seconds. However, it was not until the

■ **Right:** *Even though it is very muscular, the Staffie is an agile dog.*

1930s that a Breed Standard was created and the Staffie became a showdog and companion.

Temperament

The loyal Staffie is fearless, people-friendly and intelligent but must be disciplined and trained. This dog is relatively easy to train providing patience is asserted. Despite its bloody history it is, today, one of the most faithful and affectionate, family-loving pets. A Staffie will fiercely guard babies and is good with older children when they show respect. An outstanding house guard.

General care

Grooming is minimal; all that is needed is a brush and polish weekly to get rid of dead hairs. Staffies need both physical and mental stimulation, with plenty of exercise including free running and play.

■ **Right:** *The Staffie has a wide, deep chest and straight forelegs.*

Appearance

A chunky, well-muscled, medium-small dog, the Staffordshire Bull Terrier has a wide head, a pump handle tail and walks with a jaunty air. The smooth coat is red, fawn, white, black or blue.

Health problems

Generally a healthy breed but buy from eye-tested parents and have your puppy tested.

■ **Right:** *Affectionate and loyal, these dogs make good pets.*

Cavalier King Charles Spaniel

The modern Cavalier King Charles was almost certainly developed from the land spaniels of the fourteenth century which may have come from Spain. The Stuarts were besotted with them and named them 'King Charles'. Indeed, Charles II shared his bed with several. They went out of fashion when William of Orange reigned but staged a comeback in the nineteenth century when a toy red and white spaniel was bred at Blenheim in Oxfordshire by the Duke of Marlborough. Although the breed started as a gundog and companion, it became a showdog and pet when dog shows started in the mid 1800s. A fashion developed for short-nosed dogs and the original breed began to decline again. An American, Roswell Eldridge, then offered handsome prizes to anyone who could reverse the trend and, gradually, by selective breeding, today's type of longer-nosed Cavalier King Charles evolved, and it has become the most popular of the Toy Spaniels.

Temperament

Docile, gentle and intelligent, the Cavalier King Charles quickly learns the ways of its human family. With its friendly character, this dog is a joy to own. Confident and gently assertive, it loves to play with children but doesn't like roughness.

Health problems

Some hip dysplasia (page 102); both sexes should be heart tested; and puppies and their parents should undergo eye testing.

General care

Being small, the Cavalier King Charles needs less exercise than the bigger spaniels. However, it's keen on activity of all kinds, particularly play. The silky coat needs weekly combing; look for any tangles in the feathering and ears after walks.

Appearance

An elegant, refined small dog with a kind expression and out-going, perky character displaying a free action when moving. A silky coat with colours that are vivid and clearly delineated.

■ **Left:** *These perky little dogs come in a range of colours, including ruby, the traditional Blenheim and tricolour, as well as black and tan.*

Guarding instinct

Will warn but with no aggression

Temperament

Kind and gentle

Exercise

Loves frequent free running and play

Grooming

Pay strict weekly attention to ears and feathering

Other dogs

Not aggressive

Summary
An ideal family companion

H

Ideally:
30–33 cm (12–13 in)

■ **Left:** *A five-month-old King Charles looking eager to please.*

Toy group	# Pug

Guarding instinct

Not a guard dog but will warn

Temperament

Even-tempered, lively and humorous

Exercise

Regular exercise, not excessive

Grooming

A light brushing daily

Other dogs

No problems

Summary

A great companion if you don't mind a little snoring

Ideally: **H**
25–28 cm (10–11 in)

■ Left: *The Pug is always an amusing companion.*

The great canine authority Clifford Hubbard believes that the Pug and Pekingese were originally related because of the striking similarity of their muzzles and their body shape. However, they were separate by the 1600s, as shown in Chinese art. Dutch mariners brought them to Holland whereupon they became favourites of royalty after a pet Pug warned William, Prince of Orange, that Spanish soldiers were approaching to capture him at the battle of Hermingny and he escaped. William and Mary introduced the Pug to Britain where it was often decorated with orange ribbons as an honoured member of the Royal Household of Orange. There is no evidence that this breed ever worked although, from an evolutionary point of view, they are Mastiffs. Their 'work' has always been to bring solace to human beings for whom they have an uncanny understanding.

Temperament

Tolerant, easy-going with children, Pugs are very intelligent with an independent comical character. They are guaranteed to bring laughter into any house with their strange facial expressions. They like sitting up high to watch the world go by. They can easily be trained to be clean.

■ Above: *The Pug has a distinctive flat face and prominent eyes.*

General care

Pugs do not require excessive walking but enjoy a walk twice a day as they like seeing the world. Grooming is easy; a light brushing daily gives a glow to a Pug's coat. In addition, you should keep the eyes and ears clean.

Appearance

A sturdy, thick-set small dog with flat features and a fine, smooth, short coat, which may be coloured silver, apricot, fawn or black with a facial mask.

■ Left: *Pugs have forceful characters and are very strong-willed. They make rewarding and entertaining pets.*

Health problems

The Pug enjoys good health generally but sometimes experiences a little difficulty in breathing so take care in hot weather.

Chihuahua

Experts are baffled as to the real origins of this tiny dog. Some Americans discovered the breed in Chihuahua State, Mexico, and they thought it was Mexican, but there is no evidence to support this. Some believe the ancient Toltecs bred them, others that they were sacred dogs of the Aztecs but, again, there is no evidence. Interestingly, some European breeds resemble them closely, especially the Portuguese Podengo and the Maltese Kelb Ta But (the pocket dog). In 1519, the Spanish Conquistador Cortes conquered the Aztecs. His forces took their war dogs so did little companion dogs go too? In 1530, the Knights of St John, including the Spanish and Portuguese, captured Malta, so did they take back tiny dogs for their ladies?

Health problems

Slipping patella and some heart murmurs. Check with your vet.

When the Spanish colonized Mexico would not the ladies have taken their companion dogs?

Temperament

Totally unaware of their truly diminutive size, these dogs believe themselves to be Mastiffs in heavy disguise. Intelligent and easy to live with, their only work is to be amusing companions and hairy hotwater bottles in the past! Most

■ **Left:** *The long-haired Chihuahua will need regular twice-weekly grooming.*

people keep more than one as they live together easily and will share their home with cats and other household pets. Care must be exercised when children handle them as their bones are very small. Most Chihuahuas adore being fussed over.

General care

The smooth-coated variety needs minimal grooming, but the long-haired variety should be brushed and combed lightly twice weekly. Active and athletic, this little dog loves a walk and to play in the garden. However, it does not need excessive exercise.

Appearance

Tiny, dainty, active and even feisty, the Chihuahua comes in smooth-coated and long-haired varieties in any colour or mixture.

Guarding instinct

Will warn of approach of strangers

Temperament

Very affectionate, active and a bit feisty

Exercise

A daily walk with plenty of play

Grooming

Brush and comb long coats twice weekly; minimal for short coats

Other dogs

No problems, quite sociable

Summary

Ideal for the elderly, easy to keep

Ideally:
15–23 cm (6–9 in)

■ **Left:** *The smooth-haired Chihuahua is a dainty little dog. Affectionate and bright, it makes the perfect companion.*

Toy group

Pomeranian

Guarding instinct

Will shout a warning

Temperament

A joyful, active and dynamic dog

Exercise

Running and playing in the garden

Grooming

Essential to brush deeply daily

Other dogs

Being self confident, big dogs are no worry

Summary

An ideal pet for a busy urban family

Ideally: **H**
22–28 cm (8½–11 in)

A type of tiny Spitz dog is depicted on some Roman artefacts and there is evidence of this dog's existence throughout Europe ever since. However, almost certainly the close relations of this miniscule dog are the much larger Nordic Spitz breeds, such as the Samoyed and Keeshond. It came to Great Britain from Pomerania, Germany, around 1870 in the form of the much bigger German Spitz weighing 13.6 kg (30 lb). The British bred them smaller and gave them their new name, and by 1896 they were down to 3.6 kg (8 lb). However, they did not become popular until Queen Victoria exhibited her own dog at the Kennel Club's show after which the breed's future was assured.

Temperament

A happy and amusing dog which is very fond of its family and given to being noisy unless trained otherwise. Full of vitality and fun, Pomeranians are always anxious to involve themselves in family activities. They are docile with children who must take care not to be rough as the Pomeranian's bones are very small.

General care

Running and playing in the garden is sufficient exercise for most Pomeranians but they do enjoy an outing. It is also essential to brush the coat deeply on a daily basis to prevent knotting and tangles which form due to the plush thickness.

■ **Left:** *Pomeranians have a large, distinctive Spitz-type ruff of fur.*

■ **Left:** *A wide range of colours is permissible for the Pomeranian, including cream, sable, white, brown, red and orange.*

Appearance

A Lilliputian dog, a tiny round ball of fluff. The adult coat is abundant, thick and plush. All colours are permissible, including whole colours – white, black, brown, pale blue or vivid orange – and parti-coloured.

■ **Below:** *Pomeranians look very cute but they are actually good watchdogs and will warn of approaching strangers.*

Health problems

Very healthy but can suffer slipping patella.

Yorkshire Terrier

In the early nineteenth century, coal mines were ridden with rats and some miners in northern England developed a terrier small enough to carry in their pockets when they went down the mines. Starving workers came south from Scotland seeking work and bringing their rough terriers, the Clydesdale and Skye Terriers, and these were inter-bred with the Old English Broken-haired and Manchester Terriers to produce the Yorkshire Terrier. When dog

showing began around 1850, the breeders realised that pretty little companion dogs were worth more money and therefore refined the terrier, producing today's dog.

Health problems

There are rare cases of slipping patella and Perthe's disease. Some eye problems are under investigation.

Temperament

This little dog will give you his unlimited affection, but because he is independent by nature his early training will need patience and kindness. Under the gentle looks and loving nature lurks some of the feisty nature inherited from his rough ancestry. He will still hunt mice and rats but at home he is full of fun and mischief. Children need to be careful as the Yorkie is very small.

General care

The Yorkshire Terrier makes a perfect house pet, particularly for the elderly as he eats only a tiny amount of food and takes up little space. His acute hearing picks up strangers in the vicinity and, although he's not a yappy dog, he will let you know they're there. He loves going out and will need a long walk or once round the block twice daily. Sniffing around the garden

and play hunting are an equal joy to him. Because of the length and texture of his coat, it does tangle and matt so a daily gentle combing session is essential. Otherwise, keep the coat cut short.

Appearance

The tiny Yorkshire Terrier is an extremely elegant dog with a spectacular coat, which is long and silky and of a steel blue colour with a rich golden tan on the head, chest and legs.

Below: *Whether a pet or a show dog, your dog will be a spirited companion.*

Guarding instinct

Suspicious; will bark warning

Temperament

Fun, mischievous, loving

Exercise

A little or a lot

Grooming

Very important: daily brushing and combing essential

Other dogs

No great problems

Summary
A great pet for old and young

H

Males:
25 cm (10 in) or less

Bitches:
slightly less

Toy group

Bichon Frise

Guarding instinct

Will warn but not a guard

Temperament

Happy, friendly, active

Exercise

Needs plenty to keep calm

Grooming

A deep brushing daily and a monthly bath

Other dogs

No worries

Summary

An ideal gentle dog but the coat is a priority

Ideally:
23–28 cm (9–11 in)

This is a breed of antiquity stemming from the Barbet of the Mediterranean region from which four breeds emerged: the Bichon Maltaise, Bichon Bolognese, Bichon Havanese and Bichon Teneriffe. The latter breed was adopted by fourteenth-century Italian and Spanish nobility and thence the French court. King Henri III (1547–1589) was so enamoured of them that he carried them in baskets attached to ribbons round his neck. However, the breed went out of favour in the late 1800s reverting to 'commoner' status and was extensively used by circus performers and street musicians owing to their lively intelligence. Eventually recognised by the French in 1934, it was given its name, Bichon à Poil Frise, or 'Bichon of the Curly Coat'.

■ **Below:** *The Bichon should have a black nose and really dark, round eyes.*

Health problems

There are some eye problems under investigation. Perthe's disease and slipping patella exist within the breed.

Temperament

This dog has a lively, kind nature and is very faithful, following its favourite person like a white shadow. It is an ideal canine companion with an undiminished ability to perform tricks. A happy, friendly breed without vices, the Bichon is boisterous with a sense of humour, quick to learn and inventive.

General care

Because of their enthusiasm these dogs need plenty of walks and things to do like inter-active play in the garden. Their

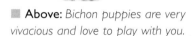

■ **Above:** *Bichon puppies are very vivacious and love to play with you.*

coat must have attention daily otherwise it tangles and knots easily and may smell. If wished, it can be kept short in a 'puppy cut'.

Appearance

A small dog with corkscrewing silky curls which are always white. When trimmed correctly, the Bichon has a rounded aspect with the black of the eyes and nose contrasting vividly.

Miniature Schnauzer

This is the most popular of the three Schnauzer breeds, particularly in America where its final development took place. A manufactured breed with its foundation in the Standard Schnauzer, it was first exhibited as a breed by itself in 1879 in Gerrmany. It has been suggested

Left: *The Miniature Schnauzer's expression is bright and alert.*

that as well as the Wire-haired Pinscher, the blood of the Affenpinscher runs in its veins. The combination of these two breeds may well be the reason that Mini Schnauzers are the only one of the three breeds to be described as ratters. Because of their working antecedents, Mini Schnauzers are very active dogs and just love doing things, particularly fun activities with their owners such as Agility, Obedience and Flyball.

Temperament

Immensely affable, sensitive and intelligent, the Mini Schnauzer learns its manners very quickly, suiting all homes, especially those with children. An excellent pet dog who learns quickly what is expected of it, it is small enough to be carried but is not a toy. These dogs are very playful and they will get on well with other animals and also with children.

General care

The breed tends to overweight so Mini Schnauzers must be exercised. They will take as much as their owner is prepared to give although smaller amounts are acceptable. Their coat requires particular attention and should be hand-stripped about four

Left: *The long beard and hair on the legs need frequent combing.*

Health problems

Generally a hardy little dog but puppies should be bought from eye-tested parents and tested themselves in the fullness of time.

times a year. The furnishings and beard must be combed out at least two or three times a week.

Appearance

A small square dog with a wire coat and profuse furnishing on the legs, a distinctive beard and lowering eyebrows. The coat colour is either pepper and salt (greyish), black or a very striking black and silver.

Below: *Intelligent and very sensitive, this game little dog makes a good companion for both adults and children.*

Guarding instinct

Slightly suspicious, good guard

Temperament

Loving, easy-going happy, playful pet

Exercise

Will run ten miles or take less

Grooming

Hand-stripping four times yearly; furnishings combed frequently

Other dogs

Not quarrelsome

Summary

Ideal for a young active family

H

Males:
35 cm (14 in)

Bitches:
33 cm (13 in)

Utility group

Boston Terrier

Guarding instinct

Very good guard; the 'bat ears' miss nothing

Temperament

A tractable dog, happy and friendly

Exercise

A couple of walks a day and a bit of play

Grooming

Just a brush weekly; take care of the eyes

Other dogs

A non-aggressive dog, never seeks trouble

Summary

An easy-going character bringing pleasure

Three sizes: **H**
38–43 cm (15–17 in)

Around 1865 in Cotter's tavern in Charles Street, Boston, USA, some coach drivers, stable men and ostlers used to gather together whilst their masters were attending functions. They wondered what the result would be if they were to mate some of the fine imported pedigree dogs belonging to the gentry. Thus Bulldogs were mated to Bull Terriers and then to Pit Bull Terriers, and the result was a handsome fighting dog weighing up to 27 kg (60 lb). However, the Boston Terrier's strange beauty was recognised and fanciers of the breed then selectively bred for a smaller dog (possibly they saw a commercial advantage). In 1891, the breeders formed their own club and they created a Breed Standard, and the Boston Terrier has now become deservedly one of America's favourite dogs.

■ **Below:** *Boston Terriers make good companions as they are easy-going and fun-loving.*

■ **Below:** *The large ears are held erect and the eyes are gentle.*

Temperament

An amiable, docile dog, the highly intelligent Boston Terrier is easily trained, full of character and a good guard dog. Although it is now just a well-behaved house pet, it was evolved as a fighting dog. A boisterous dog, it is full of fun with a penchant for playing with toys.

General care

Hardly any grooming is required: just a soft brush and polish once a week. Two or three good walks a day with playtime in the garden

Health problems

Buy from eye-tested parents. There is some slipping patella.

are all the exercise that a Boston Terrier needs. The eyes are easily damaged so you should try to keep the dog out of bushes.

Appearance

A muscular, small, square dog with a large head and a short muzzle, the Boston Terrier's trademark is the large 'bat ears'. It should be brindle with white markings for preference but black with white is acceptable.

Shih Tzu

This breed was developed in ancient China; its Chinese name, Shih Tzu Kou, means 'Lion dog'. Its absolute origin is in Tibet where it enjoyed the status of a 'holy dog' as far back as the seventh century. These dogs were often presented to visiting foreign dignitaries which is probably how they entered China. After the death of the empress Tzu-hsi in 1908, the breed deteriorated and the best stock was sold. Outside China there was confusion as Shih Tzus were mixed with Apsos and were given different names. The first three dogs came to Britain in 1930 and by 1934 Lhasa Apsos and Shih Tzus were recognised as different breeds. Shih Tzus are first and foremost a companion; they like to be out and about with their owners and to be fully integrated within family activities. However, they are extremely alert watchdogs and will not allow any strange noise to pass without marking it.

Temperament

An amusing and independent pet which fades away without human

Health problems

The Shih Tzu is generally very healthy. Some pinched noses cause breathing problems; check the puppy's parents.

companionship. Undoubtedly, the Shih Tzu is a fun dog – bouncy with an enthusiasm for life. An extremely intelligent and happy companion, the Shih Tzu presents no problems in the home but, craving human contact, it will dislike being left alone.

General care

Two walks a day and playing in the garden will suffice. The main attraction of the breed is the magnificent coat, but do not take on a Shih Tzu unless you are prepared for the work needed to maintain it. The hair knots and tangles easily and requires daily attention. It should be kept clean and conditioned.

Appearance

A short-legged dog with a well-muscled body under a profuse flowing coat, sometimes trailing to the floor. Shih Tzus come in

■ **Above:** *Shih Tzus must be groomed every day if their coats are to be kept free of tangles and in prime condition.*

any colour, but a white blaze on the forehead and the tail tip are admired in parti-colours. Some owners keep their dogs in a 'puppy clip' with the hair cut to about 5 cm (2 in).

■ **Below:** *Enthusiastic and intelligent, the Shih Tzu is a good family pet.*

Guarding instinct

Very wary, will warn vociferously

Temperament

Outgoing character, happy nature

Exercise

A walk twice a day and plenty of play

Grooming

Gentle combing every day plus conditioning

Other dogs

Non-confrontational

Summary

A fine family dog with a hint of the orient

H

Ideally:
No more than 26.7 cm (10½ in)

Lhasa Apso

Guarding instinct

Very suspicious; will warn of approach

Temperament

Affectionate but can be independent

Exercise

Three short walks a day or long walks

Grooming

Daily grooming and detangling.

Other dogs

Not aggressive

Summary

An unusual breed for a discerning family

Males:
25 cm (10 in)

Bitches:
Slightly smaller

H

Right: *These cute puppies will eventually have a heavy adult coat.*

High in the mountains of Tibet, monks bred this little dog as a watchdog and companion before the birth of Jesus Christ. The Lhasa Apso may have evolved from the Central European herding dogs, such as the Pumi or the Puli. The breed was regarded as a talisman and although the dogs were never sold, they were often gifted to Chinese nobility. They were held in very high esteem by Tibetans which made it difficult for any Westerners to acquire them. Officers who were serving in the 1904 Younghusband expedition brought a few of these dogs out, followed in the early 1920s by a Mrs Bailey, the wife of a political officer, and other ladies whose dogs formed the nucleus of the breed in Great Britain. Although in Western countries the dogs are bred as companions and show dogs, in their native land they are used as watchdogs, often sitting in a high place where they can keep an eye on the comings and goings of the monks and warning them of the approach of strangers.

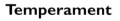

Temperament

Although wary of strangers, the Lhasa Apso is loving with its human family without being too effusive. As a sole dog, it will probably bond with one person very strongly but it has an independent streak and may not be so clingy as some people might like their pet dogs to be.

Left: *This magnificent champion dog is in superb show condition.*

General care

This tough little dog is full of energy and is able to walk long distances. However, several short walks are sufficient. The crowning glory of the breed is its glorious coat but it needs daily attention, otherwise it will tangle and matt. The coat can be kept short if you don't intend showing the dog.

Appearance

A short-legged, long dog with a profuse and heavy coat in several colours, including shades of gold, dark grizzle, smoke, parti-colour, black, white or brown.

Health problems

Generally tough as befits a dog that has evolved in the harsh, cold climate of the Tibetan mountains. Some eye conditions are currently under investigation so it is wise to buy only from tested parents.

Poodle

Like so many ancient breeds, the Poodle has its origins in hunting. The breed comes from Germany; the name *Pudel* is derived from *Puddeln*, meaning to 'splash in water'. The French name *Caniche* is derived from '*chien-canne*', literally meaning a 'duck dog', as the Poodle was originally a wildfowler. The development of today's three varieties as pet dogs began in the 1800s. The Belgians liked big white dogs which they bred for hauling their milk carts, whereas the French bred small whites, and the Russians liked black miniatures. Although it is doubtful if any Poodles are used

Right: *Looking at the modern fashionable dog, it's hard to believe it was originally a water breed.*

as Retrievers any more, they still betray their wildfowling antecedents by their joy in retrieving games. They are the most active of breeds and love work of all kinds, excelling in Agility, Obedience and Fly-ball.

Temperament

A loving sensitive breed possessed of superior intelligence, the lively Poodle becomes totally involved with family activities, particularly with children. It is a sheer delight for novices to experienced dog lovers. If the Poodle is trained with kindness it will become an obedient and much-loved member of any family.

General care

All varieties have an unbounded energy and they will take more exercise and play than you can give. Poodles do not moult but they must be combed every other day to prevent tangles. Unless the owner is a hairdresser, it is better to take the dog to the grooming parlour four or five times a year.

Appearance

Poodles have a springy movement and invariably look proud and happy. The Miniatures and Toys

Health problems

Standard Poodles have a low incidence of hip dysplasia (page 102). Puppies from all varieties should come from eye-tested parents.

look like small versions of the Standard. They come in all solid colours and the hairdressing styles vary according to taste, the lion lamb clips being most often seen.

Guarding instinct

All Poodles will bark warnings

Temperament

Gentle fun-loving breeds playful with children

Exercise

Should be played with and exercised frequently

Grooming

All varieties need combing every other day; should visit grooming salons 4–5 times annually.

Other dogs

They are happy with all non-dominant dogs

Summary

The almost perfect pet

H

Standard:
38 cm (15 in)

Miniature:
under 38 cm (15 in)

Toy:
28 cm (11 in)

Left: *The way in which a Poodle is clipped reflects its role as a water dog and is designed to protect the joints in cold water and help buoyancy.*

Utility group

Dalmatian

Guarding instinct

Will warn off intruders

Temperament

Devoted, anxious to please

Exercise

Cannot get enough

Grooming

A weekly brush up

Other dogs

Generally friendly

Summary

Ideal for an active country family

H

Males:
58–61 cm (23–24 in)

Bitches:
slightly smaller

No-one knows the exact origin of the breed name 'Dalmatian', but almost certainly it is not from Dalmatia on the coast of what used to be Yugoslavia. Spotted dogs have been present in Europe for many centuries as is proven by the numerous paintings and friezes of them. The breed was a farm dog and it has a strange affinity with horses. In fact, it was known as a 'carriage dog' and would, by nature, run for miles under a carriage between the wheels or beside the horses.

Nowadays Dalmatians are companion dogs and they are rarely used for work but this was not always the case. From the eighteenth century up until the mid-nineteenth century, they lived roughly in the gentry's stables keeping down rats and guarding the premises. The graceful shape and striking colour attracted the attention of the fashionable young bucks of the day who delighted in using these dogs to ornament their carriage turn-out.

Temperament

These dogs love the company of humans and are affectionate and anxious to please. Being essentially a farm dog, the Dalmatian came rather late to intimate living with humans and it still seems to be trying to make up for this. It is long-suffering with clean habits, devoted and loyal, and gets very attached to children.

General care

With their famous working past, Dalmatians obviously want and need as much exercise as their owner can give. Undoubtedly, it is preferable that they should live in

■ **Left:** *This striking good-looking dog with its distinctive spots makes a good companion and family pet.*

■ **Above:** *It's hard to believe that the puppies, such as this one, are born white. Their spots develop later on.*

the country although many are kept successfully as pets in towns. Little grooming of the short, fine coat is required. It does not need daily attention, and a weekly brushing will suffice.

Appearance

The Dalmatian is one of the most elegant of all the dog breeds. It is tall and slim with a smooth, shiny coat, which may have either striking black or liver-coloured spots on a white background. The distinctive coat is a talking point wherever a Dalmatian goes and never fails to attract attention.

Health problems

Some hip dysplasia (page 102). Deafness is also a worry but tests are available.

Shetland Sheepdog

■ **Left:** *Alert and tireless, the Sheltie is among the world's most popular breeds.*

Temperament

The Shetland Sheepdog has a sweet nature, always wanting to please and invariably willing. This is a one-man dog with a liking for outdoor activities. Even freezing cold, snow and appalling weather conditions do not worry this tough breed. A naturally clean dog, the Sheltie is very intelligent and thus easily trained, gentle and responsive caring deeply for its family.

Work

This dog's standard work was to assist the shepherd in all his duties. Shetland Sheepdogs would protect their charges by keeping them from the edge of cliffs and running back to warn their owners of approaching trouble in the form of humans or beasts.

General care

A tireless breed, this dog will take all the moorland walking that the owner can give. However, in urban situations they should have frequent walks, free running and play. The coat will need weekly attention: deep brushing with a radial nylon brush is recommended and knots behind the ears are a problem. The feet, hind legs and the hair under the tail should be trimmed with sharp scissors.

Appearance

A very pretty, perky little dog with an abundant double coat, which consists of a harsh-textured outer coat and a soft, dense undercoat. It comes in brilliant colours, ranging from gold to mahogany, tri-colours, blue merle and black and white.

■ **Below:** *The Shetland Sheepdog has an easily recognisable and abundant ruff of long hair around its neck.*

Shetland is a windswept island lying off the north coast of Scotland, and its cold, bleak aspect produces famous miniature livestock – Shetland ponies, cows and sheep – so it seems natural that the dog used to control them should be small. There always were Collie-type dogs present on Shetland but they must have been crossed with dogs from visiting whaling ships or fishermen from Scandinavia and Holland. A visit from Queen Victoria cruising the waters probably introduced crosses with the King Charles Spaniel, producing colours unknown in Collies.

Health problems

Some hip dysplasia (page 102) and eye anomalies. Puppies should be bought from tested parents and should themselves be tested.

Guarding instinct

Suspicious, will warn vociferously

Temperament

Responsive, amicable nature

Exercise

When adult, as much as possible

Grooming

Important to groom every week

Other dogs

A friendly non-stress dog

Summary
An affectionate dog suitable for a lively family

H

Males:
37 cm (14½ in)

Bitches:
slightly smaller

Border Collie

Guarding instinct

Suspicious; will defend family and territory

Temperament

Very affectionate but energetic family dog

Exercise

Must have a great deal; needs lots of mental stimulation

Grooming

Minimal with smooth coats; long coats need frequent brushing

Other dogs

Non-aggressive, but likes to herd little dogs

Summary

Ideal for the knowledgeable, active country owner

H

Males:
53 cm (21 in)

Bitches:
slightly less

Sheepdogs have been a vital part of the shepherd's equipment since man first domesticated farm animals; without them the vast flocks of millions of sheep just would not exist. Undoubtedly, there were sheepdogs working flocks in Scotland long before the Romans invaded England, bring with them their own breed of sheep and probably their own sheepdogs. They were interbred with the native dogs and the long process of evolution of the five Sheepdog breeds began. Shepherds are naturally secretive and nobody knows which breeds went into making today's Border Collie, although some pinpoint the Newfoundland and the Borzoi. Queen Victoria fell for the Collie on her visits to Balmoral and under her royal patronage the breed prospered.

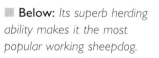

■ **Below:** *Its superb herding ability makes it the most popular working sheepdog.*

■ **Right:** *The Border Collie is always alert and responsive.*

Temperament

Always anxious to please, highly intelligent and easily trained, the Border Collie is a good, sensitive dog although it is inclined to be headstrong. It cares deeply for its family, especially the children, and is an excellent guard dog.

Work

The most enthusiastic working farm dog, the Border Collie is very popular in Australia where it has adapted to the heat and harsh environment. At home, it's a general farm dog working cows and sheep with equal facility. Some become good show dogs, and they excel in Obedience, Agility and Flyball.

General care

There is no escape: this dog does need a great amount of running exercise and things to occupy its mind; really, an Agility course in the garden would be ideal. The smooth-coated variety requires very little grooming – just a weekly brush. However, the longer coat will require combing every other day.

Appearance

The Border Collie is medium-sized, always watchful and very inquisitive. It has a fairly long body and comes in two different coats: smooth and moderately long. Any colour is permissible including blue but there should not be too much white.

■ **Above:** *The Border Collie's large eyes are set wide apart for better all-round vision when working.*

Health problems

Some low-level hip dysplasia (page 102). Genetic eye problems are being controlled but buy from tested parents and get the puppy tested. There is also some deafness.

German Shepherd Dog

This breed was produced from an amalgam of North European herding breeds. The prototype for the breed has existed in Germany for centuries. Tacitus, the Roman historian, mentioned the 'wolf-like dog of the Rhineland'. In the nineteenth century, a German army officer called Rittmeister von Stephanitz recognised the potential of this breed and created the *Verein für Deutsche Schäfehunde* to control its development.

Temperament

The German Shepherd Dog is highly intelligent, versatile and steady, whether as a pet in the home or as a working security dog. When properly socialized, no breed is more caring or loyal to its human family. It is easily trained to a high standard and needs firm but kind handling.

Work

Arguably the greatest all-round working dog of all time, it is an invaluable and fearless police dog worldwide, as well as a tracker dog, a guide dog for the blind, an assistance dog for the disabled and a patrol dog for security companies.

Health problems

Unfortunately, there are several genetic anomalies: hip dysplasia (page 102), haemophilia in males (page 103), elbow dysplasia (page 103) and digestive problems. Buy puppies from breeders who test their stock.

■ **Below:** *The highly intelligent German Shepherd is the most numerous breed.*

General care

This dog requires a lot of exercise and mental stimulation, especially games. It excels at Obedience and Agility training. Because it is so active, it needs high-quality food. A good combing followed by a brushing twice weekly will rid the coat of dead hairs and keep the German Shepherd in good condition, especially during the moulting season.

Appearance

A big dog whose coat consists of harsh outer guard hairs about 5 cm (2 in) long with a thick undercoat. There is also a long-coated variety which cannot be shown. The German Shepherd's conformation gives it a far-reaching, enduring movement and an elegant head carriage. The pricked ears and bright eyes create an alert and intelligent expression for this very popular dog.

Guarding instinct

One of the best security dogs

Temperament

Loyal and affectionate

Exercise

Must have plenty

Grooming

Twice-weekly brush and comb

Other dogs

Take care; males can be dominant

Summary
With socialization and sympathetic training, a great companion

H

Males:
63 cm (25 in)

Bitches:
58 cm (23 in)

■ **Left:** *The puppy's coat is fine and downy and will change colour as it grows.*

Other popular breeds

There are literally hundreds of dog breeds in the world and they have been bred selectively for their ability to perform a particular job (as in working dogs), for temperament (as in pet dogs) or to produce specific physical characteristics. Consequently, the canine world is infinitely varied and interesting, and there are many breeds from which you can choose when you consider owning a dog. Here are some brief descriptions of more popular breeds plus some less well-known ones, such as the Mastiff and the Italian Spinone.

Airedale Terrier

The largest terrier, the Airedale is intelligent, loyal and good with children. Like the other working dogs, it needs plenty of exercise. It needs regular brushing and hand-stripping twice yearly.

Bull Terrier

If properly trained and socialized, this powerful dog is gentle and good-natured. It needs plenty of exercise and is easy to groom. A natural fighter, care must be taken when mixing with other dogs as it has a strong bite and won't let go.

Border Terrier

This game little dog needs lots of exercise but the wiry, weather-resistant coat needs only minimal grooming. Friendly and highly intelligent, it is easy to train and makes an affectionate family pet.

Welsh Terrier

A good companion dog and ratter, this intelligent, jaunty terrier is quite easy to train but can be stubborn. It needs regular weekly grooming and will require stripping twice a year.

Cairn Terrier

This game little dog has a typical Terrier temperament. It is easy to train and makes a good watchdog. Lively and affectionate, it will take as much exercise as you can give but needs minimal grooming.

Labradoodle

This relatively new 'breed' is the result of crossing a Labrador with a Poodle. A gentle, fun-loving dog which is easily trained, like a Poodle it does not shed a lot of hair or require a lot of grooming.

Flat-coated Retriever

This intelligent dog is often used as a gundog, picking up game. It makes a devoted, affectionate pet but will need plenty of exercise. The dense coat will need brushing daily to keep it in good condition.

Weimaraner

This striking gundog is reliable and alert. It has speed and stamina in abundance and needs free running and lead walking every day. Easy to train, the more common short-coated variety is quick to groom.

Italian Spinone

This ancient gundog is loyal and affectionate. It is a good country dog, needing lots of vigorous exercise and enjoying swimming. The rough, thick coat needs daily grooming to tease out tangles.

Curly-coated Retriever

This handsome dog loves to swim and retrieve. A reliable working dog, it is also an ideal pet if you have the time to exercise it. The curly coat does not need grooming, just dampening and massaging.

German Short-haired Pointer

This popular dog is easy to train and makes a good pet as well as an excellent gundog. It doesn't need much grooming but it must be walked daily and allowed to run. A good companion dog, it is very responsive and enjoys Field Trials.

Irish Wolfhound

This is the tallest breed of dog. A gentle giant, the Wolfhound is very affectionate and only requires daily moderate exercise, no more than any other large dog. The wiry coat needs daily combing to remove tangles and loose hairs.

Irish Setter

A racy, extrovert dog with a silky, flowing red coat, the Irish Setter makes an affectionate pet as well as a gundog. With its boundless energy, it requires lots of exercise, and the coat needs daily brushing.

Deerhound

This ancient breed makes a loyal, gentle pet. The Deerhound needs an energetic owner who will give it lots of exercise and free running over open ground. The weather-resistant harsh and wiry coat is easy to groom every day.

Welsh Springer Spaniel

This distinctive red and white Spaniel is a hard-working gundog as well as a family pet. Loyal and obedient, it is easy to train. It loves swimming and requires lots of exercise, especially free running. The coat requires daily grooming.

Afghan Hound

This elegant sight hound is highly intelligent and affectionate but does need careful handling. Its long coat must be groomed daily to prevent it matting, and it will need plenty of walks and free running to keep it fit and healthy.

Whippet

This gentle, adaptable dog makes an affectionate family pet. As well as daily walks on the lead, it must have plenty of free running. Docile and easy to train, this dog's coat needs only minimal grooming.

Old English Sheepdog

This breed demands affection. It is very exuberant and must be trained and socialized from an early age. Not only does it need plenty of exercise but also you must be prepared to spend considerable time grooming the profuse coat.

Lurcher

This athletic dog is common in Great Britain and Ireland and was bred originally from Greyhounds and Collies or Terriers. It loves to run and will chase and kill small game. It needs lots of exercise.

Chow Chow

A good watchdog, the Spitz-type Chow Chow is very loyal. When provoked, it will not back off from a fight. It needs regular exercise, and the long outer coat and dense undercoat need daily brushing.

Mastiff

This large, powerful dog may look frightening but it is usually easy-going and affectionate. Because of its great strength, it needs sensible handling by an experienced owner. A good guard dog, the Mastiff must be walked regularly and will enjoy free running across country. Its short coat is easy to groom.

Bulldog

Originally bred for baiting bulls, the Bulldog can look aggressive but is actually very good natured and gentle. It needs regular but not too strenuous exercise and a quick daily brush and comb. It is very good with children.

Useful addresses

Association of Pet Behaviour Counsellors
PO Box 46
Worcester WR8 9YS
Tel: 01386 751151

Association of Pet Dog Trainers
Peacocks Farm
Northchapel
Petworth
West Sussex GU28 9JB

The Blue Cross
Shilton Road
Burford
Oxon OX18 4PF
Tel: 01993 822651

The Kennel Club
1–5 Clarges Street
London W1Y 8AB
Tel: 0171 493 6651

Royal Society for the Prevention of Cruelty to Animals
Causeway
Horsham
West Sussex RH12 1HG

People's Dispensary for Sick Animals
PDSA House
Whitechapel Way
Priorslee, Telford
Shropshire TF2 9PQ

British Veterinary Association
7 Mansfield Street
London W1M 0AT

Royal College of Veterinary Surgeons
62–64 Horseferry Road
London SW1P 2AF

Training a deaf puppy
A guide can be obtained from:
Barry Eaton,
Pine Cottage
Station Road
Chilbolton
Hants SO20 6AL

Acknowledgments

The publishers would like to thank the following people and their dogs who gave up their valuable time to assist with the special photography for this book:
Gail Alecock and her Staffordshire Bull Terriers
Mrs Allen and her Cavalier King Charles Spaniel
Mrs Allum and her Cairn Terrier, Holly
Caroline Barc and her English Springer Spaniel, Maisie
Mark Barker and his Bull Terrier, Maisey
Carola, Lady Beevor and her Pugs, Clemlee Spring Fern at Butthard, Butthard the Saltcote Belle, Butthard the Dannebrog and Butthard the Beatrice Maude
Carole Brame and her dog, Simba
Enid Burch and her Dobermanns, Harry and Gail
Sally Byrom and her Dachshund, Charlie Brown
Sally Cackett and her Pomeranians
Mr Chamberline and his Old English Sheepdog, Benson
Mr Collard and his Standard Schnauzer, Mollie
Beth Colmer and her Labradors, Bridie and Pup
Mr Cooke and his Shetland Sheepdog, Brandy
Jo Desmond and her Rottweiler
Ms Edwards and her Border Collie, Mij
Adrian Finbow and his Border Collie, Drake
Caroline Griffiths and her Irish Setters, Prudence and Florence
Mr Harrison and his Parson Jack Russell Terrier, Millie
Charlie Horrington and his Dalmatian, Amber
Mr Houchell and his Weimaraner, Sophie
Helen Hudson and her Jack Russells, Rosie Russell and Darcy, and her cat, Ben
Kevin Jarvis and his Standard Poodle
Judy Landvik and her Miniature Schnauzer, Scooby
Kayleigh Laws and her Staffordshire Bull Terrier, Millie
Mrs McKenzie and her Bichon Frises
Natalie Moye and her Dalmatian, Charlie
Mr and Mrs Noble and their Great Danes, Farrier and Jess
Simon Piers-Hall and his Labradoodle, Popeye
Mr Player and his Beagles, Harry and Emma
Tegan Potter and her Pug, Rocky
Mrs Reed and her Cavalier Kind Charles Spaniels, Baray Holly, Leelyn Red Dunster at Baray, Jirobander Juliette and Baray Crystal Lady
Thirza Rockall and her Parson Jack Russell Terrier, Gunner, and Border Terrier, Rudi
Brenda Sandford and her Lhasa Apso, Lizzie
Mark Sexton and his Siberian Huskies, Nikita, Natasha and Cadbury
Mr and Mrs Stones and their Bulldog, Louie
Mr and Mrs Stuart and their Lhasa Apsos, Chloe and Bridie
Lisa Taylor and her Rottweiler, Benson
Christine Ugolini and her Cocker Spaniels, Jasper and Sam
Angela Warren and her Miniature Poodle, Willow
Arron Wheatley and his West Highland White Terrier, Billy
Miss Williams and her Boston Terriers, Martha and Jessica
Mr Williams and his Mastiff, Toby
Ken Woosnam and his Lhasa Apsos, Champion and Irish Champion Saxonsprings Tradition, Saxonsprings Silent Memories, Saxonsprings Twist of Fate and Showa Quicksilver at Pantulf

INDEX

Abscesses, 100, 121
Acure abdomen, 112
Afghan Hounds, 82, 103, 188
Agility classes, 136, 142
Airedale Terriers, 137, 186
American Cocker Spaniels, 103
Anal glands, 113
Anal regions, 22, 100
Appetite, loss of, 100
Arthritis, 117
Bad breath, 100, 104
Ballooning of ear flap, 108
Barking, 59, 78
Basset Hounds, 86, 119
Bathing, 93
Battersea Dogs' Home, 15
Beagles, 103, 160
Beds, 26
Bee stings, 131
Bichon Frises, 176
Birth, 149–150
  problems, 150
Bladder stones, 115
Bleeding, 132
Bloated abdomen, 100
Blood in stools, 111
Blood in urine, 114, 120
Boarding kennels, 96, 97
Bone(s), 84
  marrow, 118
Border Collies, 103, 184
Border Terriers, 186
Bordetella, 110
Boston Terriers, 103, 178
Bowls, 26, 86
Boxers, 17, 103, 162
Brain, 115
  inflammation of, 115
Breeding, 144–151
Breeds,
  choosing a, 12
British Veterinary Association,
  21, 102
Broken tooth, 105
Bronchitis, 109
Bull Terriers, 186
Bulldogs, 92, 103, 189
Bullmastiffs, 89
Burns, 128
  chemical, 128
  electrical, 128
Cairn Terriers, 187
Calcium, 118
Calculi, 115
Car travel, 57
Cardiac massage, 129
Castration, 21, 144
Cataracts, 106, 158
Cats, 30

Cavalier King Charles Spaniels,
  17, 171
Cerebellar atrophy, 103
Challenge Certificates, 141
Championship Shows, 14, 26,
  141
Charities, 15
Chemical burns, 128
Cherry eye, 103
Chest, 109–110
Chews, 56
Chihuahuas, 95, 173
Children, 44
Chocolate, 87
Chow Chows, 90, 189
Circulatory system, 110
Cirrhosis, 113
Claws, 85, 100
Club matches, 139
Clumber Spaniels, 103
Coat, 101
  types, 89
Cocker Spaniels, 17, 86, 156
Collars, 26, 65
Collie(s), 89, 103
  eye, 103
Come when called command,
  72–73
Commands, 64
Conjunctivitis, 85
Constipation, 100, 111, 120
Contraception, 119
Convulsions, 115, 130
Corrosive poisons, 130
Coughs, 100, 109
Crates, 57–58, 67
Cross-breeds, 14, 22
Crufts, 26, 141, 142
Curly-coated Retrievers, 139,
  187
Cushing's Disease, 103
Cystitis, 115
Cysts, 121
Dachshunds, 116, 117, 119,
  160
Dalmatians, 17, 182
Danger zones, 64–65
Dangerous Dogs Act, 39, 82,
  144
Deafness, 47, 103, 182
Deerhounds, 188
Dementia, 115
Dental care, 84
Depression, 115
Destructive behaviour, 59
Diabetic cataract, 106
Diabetes, 112, 124
Diarrhoea, 100, 111, 112, 125
Diet, 27–28, 82, 86–87, 118

Distemper, 33, 106, 109, 112,
  116
Dobermanns, 17, 89, 103, 166
'Down' command, 74
Dull coat, 100
Ears, 22, 46, 47, 85, 101,
  107–108
  foreign bodies in, 133
  grooming, 92
Eclampsia, 116, 124, 150
Ectropion, 103
Eczema, 169
Elbow dysplasia, 159, 167, 185
Elderly dogs, 55, 87, 97
Electrical burns, 128
Encephalitis, 115
English Setters, 103
English Springer Spaniel, 157
Enlarged prostate, 120
Entropion, 103, 106, 158, 165
Enzyme deficiency, 112
Epilepsy, 103, 115
Equipment, 26
  for breeding, 149
  for grooming, 26, 88
Excessive drinking, 124
Exemption Shows, 140
Exercise, 39, 94–95
Extending leads, 73, 94
Eye(s), 22, 47, 48, 84–85, 101,
  106
  foreign bodies in, 133
  problems, 157, 159, 160,
    167, 184
False pregnancy, 120
Feeding, 82, 86–87
  elderly dogs, 87
  equipment, 86
  post-natal, 87
  pre-natal, 87
  puppies, 27–28
  supplements, 28
  travelling dogs, 96
Feet, 85
Field Trials, 143
Field of vision, 48
First aid, 128–133
Flat-coated Retrievers, 187
Flatulence, 112
Fleas, 121, 122
Flyball, 136, 142
Foreign bodies,
  in ears, 107, 133
  in eyes, 133
  in mouth, 133
  in paws, 133
Games, 35, 36, 61
  tug of war, 35
Genetic tests, 21, 102, 146

Gentle Leader, 70, 77
Gerbils, 30
German Shepherd Dogs, 17,
  89, 103, 137, 185
German Short-haired Pointers,
  103, 188
Gingivitis, 105
Glaucoma, 103
Golden Retrievers, 17, 103,
  146, 159
Gordon Setters, 103
Great Danes, 86, 103, 167
Greyhounds, 15
Grooming, 12, 82, 88–93
  for showing, 137
  tools, 26, 88
Group Shows, 141
Gums, 100
Gundog(s), 94, 141, 154
  trials, 136, 143
Haemorrhage, 132
Haemophilia, 185
Hamsters, 30
Hazards, 31
Head collars, 68
Healthcare, 84–85, 98–133
Heart , 110
  disease, 109
  murmurs, 173
  problems, 162
  rate, checking, 129
Heat stroke, 97, 132
Hepatitis, 113
Hereditary diseases, 102–103
Hip dysplasia, 21, 102, 156, 157,
  158, 159, 162, 165, 166, 167,
  171, 181, 182, 183, 184, 185
Home alone, 58
Hookworms, 123
Hormonal disease, 113
Hornet stings, 131
Hounds, 141, 154
House soiling, 54–55
House-training, 24, 66–67
Howling, 45, 59
Hydrocephalus, 103
Identity tags, 65
Indoor kennels, 32
Infectious canine hepatitis,
  112, 113
Insurance, 22, 33
Intestine, 111
Irish Setters, 103, 188
Irish Water Spaniels, 143
Irish Wolfhounds, 86, 188
Italian Spinones, 187
Jaundice, 113, 114
Joints, stiff, 117
Jumping up, 60

Kennel Club, 14, 15, 21, 23, 102, 136, 140, 142, 146, 147, 148, 151
 Good Citizens Scheme, 20, 82
Kennel cough, 110, 112
Keratitis, 106
Kerry Blue Terriers, 89, 103, 107
Kidney disease, 112, 114, 115
Kidney problems, 114, 156
Kidney stones, 115
Laboured breathing, 109, 110
Labradoodles, 187
Labrador Retrievers, 17, 103, 158
Lakeland Terriers, 139
Lameness, 117
Leads, 26, 34, 73, 77
Lead training, 34–35, 76–77
Leptospira, 114
Leptospirosis, 33, 114
Lhasa Apsos, 82, 180
Lice, 121, 122
Licking, obsessive, 100
Life expectancy, 29
Lifting a dog, 127
Limited Shows, 140
Litter restrictions, 147
Liver disease, 112, 113
Long-haired dogs, 89
Lurchers, 189
Lymphosarcoma, 125
Malabsorption, 112
Malteses, 89
Man/dog relationship, 42
Mange mites, 108, 121
Mastiffs, 189
Mastitis, 125
Mating, 146, 148
Medicine, administering, 126
Medium-haired dogs, 89
Middle-ear disease, 108
Miniature Schnauzers, 177
Misalliance, 119
Mites, 121
Mongrels, 14, 22
Mouth, 22, 49, 104–105
 -to-nose resuscitation, 129
 ulcers, 105
Multi-focal retinal dysplasia, 158
Muzzle, making a makeshift, 127
National Canine Defence League, 15
Nervous system, 115
Newfoundlands, 103
Nose, 101, 107
 bleeds, 107
Nursing a sick dog, 126
Obedience Competitions, 136, 142
Oestrus, 119, 147
Old English Sheepdogs, 22, 88, 90, 103, 189
Open Shows, 14, 140

Osteochondrosis dessicans, 103, 165
Outside runs, 55
Over-excitability, 116
Overweight, 87
Paralysis, 116
Parasites, 121, 122–123
Parson Jack Russell Terriers, 17, 168
Parvovirus, 33, 112
Pastoral group, 141, 154
Patent ductus arteriosus, 103
Paws, foreign bodies in, 133
Pedigree dogs, 14
Pekingeses, 95, 119
Perthe's disease, 169, 175, 176
Pet Passport Scheme, 97
Pet shops, 15
Pill guns, 126
Play, 35, 61
Play biting, 56
Playpens, 27
Pneumonia, 110, 125
Pointers, 143
Poisoning, 116, 130–131
Poisonous plants, 130
Poisons, 64, 131
Polydipsia, 112
Polyphagia, 112
Pomeranians, 95, 103, 174
Poodles, 17, 22, 88, 90, 103, 107, 181
Postnatal care, 151
 feeding, 87, 151
Pregnancy, 149
 false, 120
 feeding in, 87, 149
 signs of, 149
Pre-natal feeding, 87, 149
Presentation for shows, 139
Primary inertia, 150
Progressive retinal atrophy, 103, 157, 158
Prolapsed intervertebral disc, 117
Prostate cancer, 120
Prostate problems, 120
Prostatis, 120
Pseudopregnancy, 120
Pugs, 56, 172
Pulmonic stenosis, 103
Puppies, 20–23, 24–39, 51, 52, 56, 58–59, 64–65
 choosing, 21, 22
 collecting, 26
 feeding, 27–28
 house-training, 66–67
 selling, 151
 showing, 139
 training, 68–79
 weaning, 151
Puppy farms, 15
Pyometra, 116, 119
Rabies, 125

Registration, 23, 147
Reproductive system, 120
Rescue dogs, 15, 18
 choosing, 16, 18
Restraining a large dog, 127
Retrieve command, 75
Retrievers, 143
Retrieving dummies, 75
Rewards, 68
Rhinitis, 107
Ringcraft, 136, 138
Ringworm, 121, 123
Rottweilers, 17, 165
Rough Collies, 90, 103
Rough-haired dogs, 90
Roundworms, 123
Rubarth's Disease, 113
Safety, 29, 31, 61
Salivating, 104, 131
Salmonella infection, 112
Scalds, 129
Scent recognition, 49
Schnauzers, 163
 Miniature, 177
Scratching, persistent, 100, 122
Season, bitches in, 147
Seizures, 115
Setters, 143
Shar Peis, 89
Shetland Sheepdogs, 89, 103, 183
Shih Tzus, 179
Shock, 131
Short-haired dogs, 89
Short-nosed breeds, 56
Show leads, 137
Show presentation, 137
Showing, 136–141
 grooming for, 137
Siberian Huskies, 164
Sight, 47
Sinusitis, 107
'Sit' command, 70
Skeleton, 118
Skin, 121–122
 abscesses, 100
 inflammation, 100
Slickers, 93
Slipped disc, 117
Slipping patella, 173, 174, 175, 176, 178
Snake bites, 131
Sneezing, 107
Socialization, 24, 37, 68
Sound sensitivity, 46
Spaniels, 49, 143
Spaying, 21, 119, 144
Spinal injuries, 116
Spitz-type dogs, 90
Springer Spaniels, 17, 157, 188
Staffordshire Bull Terriers, 170
'Stay' command, 71
Stings, 131
Stomach, 111

Stripping, 90
 knives, 92
Stud dogs, 146
Subaortic stenosis, 103
Swimming, 94
Tail(s),
 grooming, 92
 signals, 50
Tapeworms, 123
Tartar, 105
Teeth, 22, 84, 100, 101, 104, 105
Teething, 56
Temperature, taking a dog's, 126
Terriers, 35, 49, 82, 90, 94, 141, 154
Thirst, 119
Ticks, 121, 123
Toad venom poisoning, 131
Toilet-training, 29
Tonsilitis, 105
Tooth abscesses, 107
Torsion, 11
Toxoplasmosis, 125
Toy group, 154
Toys, 26, 36
Training, 62–79
Training classes, 20, 82
Travel, 96–97
 boxes, 32, 57
Tumours, 105, 121
Ulcers, mouth, 105
Urinary system, 114
Utility group, 141, 154
Vaccination, 18, 22, 26, 33, 112, 114, 125
Ventricular septal 'hole in the heart' defect, 103
Vocalization, 45–46
Vomiting, 100, 111, 119, 131
Von Willebrand's disease, 103, 166
Warfarin, 131
Wasp stings, 131
Weaning, 151
Weight, 101
 loss, 100, 110, 113, 124
Weimaraners, 187
Welsh Springer Spaniels, 188
Welsh Terriers, 90, 137, 186
West Highland White Terriers, 17, 169
Wheezing, 109
Whippets, 189
Whipworms, 123
Wire-haired breeds, 90
Wire-haired Fox Terriers, 137
Wobbler syndrome, 103
Wolves, 42
Working dog(s), 44
 trials, 136, 142, 143
Working group, 141, 154
Worming, 85
Yorkshire Terriers, 17, 89, 139, 175